THE ORIGINS OF CHRISTIAN ANTI-INTERNATIONALISM

Religion and Politics Series

John C. Green, Ted G. Jelen, and Mark J. Rozell, series editors

The Origins of Christian Anti-Internationalism

Conservative Evangelicals and the League of Nations

MARKKU RUOTSILA

GEORGETOWN UNIVERSITY PRESS / Washington, D.C.

Georgetown University Press, Washington, D.C. www.press.georgetown.edu

Library of Congress Cataloging-in-Publication Data

Ruotsila, Markku.
    The origins of Christian anti-internationalism : conservative evangelicals and the League of Nations / Markku Ruotsila.
        p.   cm.—(Religion and politics series)
    Includes bibliographical references and index.
    ISBN-13: 978–1-58901–190–8 (hardcover : alk. paper)
    ISBN-13: 978–1-58901–191–5 (pbk. : alk. paper)
        1. Christianity and politics—United States.   2. League of Nations.   3. United States—Church history.   I. Title.
    BR516.R78   2008
    261.8'709730904—dc22

                                                                        2007016360

♾This book is printed on acid-free paper meeting the requirements of the American National Standard for Permanence in Paper for Printed Library Materials.

14   13   12   11   10   09   08   07   9   8   7   6   5   4   3   2
First printing

Printed in the United States of America

For my mother, Oili Elo-Ruotsila,
and the memory of my father, Otto Ruotsila

Contents

Acknowledgments

At the conclusion of a project that has lasted for five years, I am conscious of many debts to individuals without whose help this book would have been a much poorer production. At the top of the list are those historians who read various versions of the manuscript and gave freely of their advice, criticism, and encouragement. I feel the greatest debt to Lloyd Ambrosius, both for work that inspired this project and because he encouraged me to persist with it at a time when it appeared that few appreciated it. Likewise indispensable were the comments of Joel A. Carpenter, Frank Ninkovich, and the several anonymous readers who were commissioned by the publishing houses that reviewed the manuscript in its various incarnations. Richard Brown at Georgetown University Press was very helpful throughout, and I want to thank him and the series editors for believing in this book. Any mistakes and shortcomings that may remain in the following account are of course mine alone.

For their assistance, I wish to acknowledge the staff of several archival repositories. My thanks go to Mark Hail, Mary Lou Hovda, and Dave Solberg of the Berntsen Resource Center at Northwestern College; D. G. Hart and Grace Mullen of Westminster Theological Seminary; the Reverend Mark Loest of the Concordia Historical Institute; and Nancy Blostein and Scott Campbell of the American Baptist Historical Society. The research itself was made possible by financial assistance provided by the Finnish Academy and the Research Center of the Evangelical Lutheran Church of Finland. I am grateful to both.

Portions of this study have previously appeared in a slightly different form in "Conservative American Protestantism in the League of Nations Controversy," *Church History* 72 (2003); "'The Great Charter for the Liberty of the Workingman': Labor, Liberals and the Creation of the ILO," *Labor History Review* 67 (2002); and "American Baptists and the League of Nations,"

American Baptist Quarterly 25 (2006). I gratefully acknowledge the American Society for Church History, the Society for the Study of Labour History, and the American Baptist Historical Society for their permission to reprint portions of these articles.

I also acknowledge the permission to reproduce material to which they hold the copyright from the following organizations: American Baptist Historical Society (J. C. Massee Papers and John R. Straton Papers); Concordia Historical Institute (Theodore Graebner Papers and Walter A. Maier Papers); Filson Historical Society (Henry Watterson Papers); Abraham Lincoln Presidential Library, Springfield, Illinois (Lawrence Y. Sherman Papers); Department of Rare Books and Special Collections, University of Rochester Library (David Jayne Hill Papers); and Westminster Theological Seminary (J. Gresham Machen Papers). Materials from the William B. Riley Papers were made available in cooperation with Northwestern College, Saint Paul.

INTRODUCTION

Christian
Anti-Internationalism

The creation of the League of Nations in 1919 remains one of the pivotal turning points in American and world history. It marked the point of departure between a world system that had been structured around unfettered national sovereignties and merely ad hoc alliances and a new era of increasingly circumscribed sovereignty and institutionalized cooperation. By providing all nations with equal access to decision making, the League of Nations helped promote ethnic and religious egalitarianism. And by institutionalizing social reform in new multilateral agencies, it advanced purposive social renovation in ways that nation-states could never have done on their own. Its collective security apparatus failed in practice but did provide an abiding matrix for peacekeeping in the modern era. Although in the end the United States did not join this first world assembly of nation-states, no administration could ignore it in making foreign policy; nor could any politically aware American overlook the ascendancy of the new internationalism that it sustained. The age of internationalism that the League ushered in profoundly, if gradually, transformed American perceptions both of the world and of America's own role in it.

This multifaceted experiment interested many different constituencies, and perhaps none more so than the different groups of Christians who for decades had been at the forefront of those who called for international cooperation, peace, and solidarity. In the United States, the conventions of most

Protestant denominations enthusiastically endorsed the League, and their activists campaigned for the ratification of its Covenant. After ratification had failed, these denominations continued to demand that the United States join or cooperate with the new organization. As they argued their case, the clergy and laity of many denominations came to invest the League with definite religious meaning and even to associate it with the actual ushering in of the Kingdom of God on Earth.

Most historians who have treated the subject have suggested that the Christian community in the United States was practically unanimous in supporting such a League of Nations.[1] Some politicians who endorsed the League made the same claim in 1919, as did some ecclesiastical authorities.[2] This claim, however, is erroneous.

In fact, American Christians were profoundly divided on the League of Nations. In each denomination, a sizable theologically and culturally conservative section disapproved of the concepts of modern internationalism on which the League was based and that it proposed to follow in practice. These conservative evangelicals were especially critical of the religious arguments with which their liberal fellow Christians sacralized the League experiment. In 1919 and 1920, they launched a number of highly charged polemical forays against the churchly and secular proponents of the League, and a few of them even engaged in political lobbying against the ratification of the League Covenant. The League of Nations controversy of February 1919 to March 1920 thus became a religious as much as a political controversy.[3] During its course, conservative Christian clergy and laity came to build a considerable corpus of Christian anti-internationalist argument and biblical exegesis, a corpus that later generations of American evangelicals perpetuated as a key dimension of their religiopolitical public doctrine.

Christian anti-internationalism was distinguished from other critiques of modern internationalism by its four key presuppositions. First, its adherents refused to accept that cooperation between Christian and non-Christian states was legitimate. Second, they insisted that because such cooperation was not grounded in the absolute truth claims of traditional, orthodox Christianity and in them alone, it could yield neither world peace nor socioeconomic progress. This being the case, third, Christian anti-internationalists demanded that the United States should not join any international organizations that included non-Christians. Instead, it should remain a separate Christian example to others and, when needed, a unilateral enforcer of right dealing. Fourth, these anti-internationalists maintained that all who called themselves Christians yet supported secular international organizations were in a state of apostasy. Christian anti-internationalists still regarded the United States as at root a Christian nation, especially blessed and with a divinely given task of witnessing for the true faith, and they therefore believed that accepting the secular internationalists' proposals as the basis of national policy would lead God to curse and punish their nation.

These presuppositions did not equal either isolationism or a lack of interest in the affairs of the wider world. No missionary group could be uninterested in world affairs or wholly insular. On the contrary, those confessional conservatives whom this study calls the Christian anti-internationalists were just as active in the wider world as were their liberal denominational rivals, and in missionary and other activities they cooperated with the like-minded of other countries just as eagerly as did the liberal enthusiasts for the League of Nations. During the late-nineteenth-century wars of American imperialism, some of them had called upon their own government to assist in their endeavors in places like the Philippines and China, and most of them tried—before, during, and after the League controversy—to persuade political leaders of the need to recover America's supposedly Christian past and world mission.[4] But these people were also critics of modern international organization and its underlying ideologies; they were unilateralists and sometime Christian nationalists who could not accept any diminution in American freedom of action. As employed in this work, "Christian anti-internationalism" means, therefore, faith-based opposition to the international organizations that have existed since 1919—political organizations that were secular, invested with worldwide supranational authority, and predicated on multilateralism and the equality of all nations and religiocultural traditions.

Anti-internationalism of this kind still exists in various denominations. It is shown in the continuing evangelical opposition to UN peacekeeping, environmental, economic, and population policies that has been prominent in post–cold war discourse about "globalism" and the "New World Order," in evangelical campaigns against the International Criminal Court, and in the palpable demonization of international organizations that coheres such twenty-first-century evangelical publishing phenomena as the *Left Behind* series of dispensational novels. Through the diffuse processes that in America have kept much of the secular public conversation rooted in religious motifs and beliefs, the evangelical polemic also continues to exert a considerable influence in the background of the national public debates about American "empire," unilateralism, and exceptionalism in the age of a war on terrorism (for a detailed discussion, see chapter 8). By studying those who created the tradition, it is possible to shed more light on the persistent American aversion to institutionalized multilateral cooperation, and on its concomitant preference for nationalist unilateralism, which ever since the League of Nations was created has characterized the conversations and the political activities of large segments of the population.

In examining the origins of this Christian critique of modern international organizations, this study concentrates on three distinct traditions that were the source of significant doctrinal argument unreservedly opposed to the League of Nations. These were, first, the dispensational premillennialists, those bibliocentric prophecy investigators who expected the world to decline in all things until the any-moment Second Coming of Christ; second, the confessional Calvinists of various denominations, who were traditionalist believers in the church's right to cultural and political dominion and in worldwide Christianization; and third, the majority of American Lutherans, whose theological traditions disapproved of all mixing of secular and religious competencies.

In addition, the study gives attention to three other groups: to the Methodists, because they formed the largest Protestant denomination at the time of the League of Nations controversy and therefore cannot be ignored; to the Episcopalians, a much smaller but politically disproportionately powerful denomination; and to Christian Restorationism (Disciples of Christ and Churches of Christ), because its understanding of redemptive history is uniquely native to the United States and intimately intertwined with the notions of American exceptionalism that have fed American unilateralism. These three groups, though much less critical of the League of Nations than the Lutherans, Calvinists, and dispensationalists, did still produce some prominent Christian anti-internationalists whose unique theological input needs to be recognized.

The conservatives of each of these denominations might simply be called fundamentalists, were it not for the fact that that designation was unacceptable to the non-premillennialists of many confessions. The designation "fundamentalist" has therefore been reserved for the dispensational premillennialists of the World Christian Fundamentals Association and their closest conservative Calvinist allies. Though the designation "evangelical" can often be more confusing than instructive, it has been employed to denote the broader community of conservative American Protestants. In this study, it is used to mean those Protestants who regarded the Bible as their final authority and read it literally rather than analogously; who saw the historical Christ's redeeming work as the only way to eternal salvation; and who took traditional evangelism and personal spiritual change, rather than the transformation of material conditions, to be the principal, proper essence of Christian work.[5] The adjective "conservative" has been added both to underline the conservative cultural stances of those whose work is explored and to reject inferences that all liberal churchly enthusiasts for the League of Nations were theological nonmembers of the evangelical Protestant faith community.

Although other denominations could have been included, the limiting of the denominational terrain under review obviates the need for too much repetition yet covers the range of evangelical opinion on internationalism at the time of the League of Nations fight. The groups that will not receive detailed attention were either on the social and political fringes of American life and had little impact on politics at the time (e.g., the Holiness churches and the early Pentecostals) or then had no politically active, clearly conservative clergy left in their midst (e.g., the Congregationalists and the Society of Friends). The conversation of these groups, and such nonevangelical groups as the Roman Catholic Church and the Church of Jesus Christ of Latter-day Saints, will be referred to but will not be examined from primary sources in any great detail. Finally, African American churches are beyond the purview of this study, not because they did not address theological questions related to modern internationalism but because they, too, remained outside the main national conversation of the time. Their unique case deserves a study of its own.

In addition to examining these selected evangelical clergy and laity, the study reconstructs the role that religion played in the debates of the League of Nations' political opponents. Although there exists a highly sophisticated body of scholarship on most aspects of the political fight over the League, its religious dimension is still almost completely neglected.[6] Chapters 6 and 7 analyze this dimension in detail. They provide sketches on each of those senators who employed religious rhetoric in the course of the League debates, which included fourteen out of the sixteen so-called Irreconcilables who refused U.S. membership in the League on any and all arrangements. Religious aspects of the propaganda that was produced by the main extraparliamentary organization that opposed the League of Nations, the League for the Preservation of American Independence, will be reconstructed for the first time, as well. These campaigners' co-optation of Christian anti-internationalism should no more be ignored than the more strictly theological polemics of the conservative evangelicals themselves, for they yielded populist and secularized versions of Christian anti-internationalism that were, over time, at least as important as the confessional versions.

It is on such a basis that the examination in the following chapters aims to fill in a major gap in our knowledge of modern U.S. religious history. In recent decades, the study of American religion and politics has made great advances on a number of fronts, yet except for the late twentieth and early twenty-first centuries, we still know very little about clerical and lay Christian influence on the formation of U. S. foreign policy.[7] This needs urgent rectification. That foreign policy and religion have not been studied together results partly from the limiting "wall of separation" framework that directs attention to church/state issues and to clearly religious preoccupations with moral legislation and parochial education, freedom of expression, gay rights, and the unborn. In such a framework, foreign policy contention easily seems alien and unrelated to religious concerns. For the other part, the neglect results from the history of foreign policy having been the preserve of diplomatic historians, who have refused to acknowledge the foreign policy significance of anything as intangible as religious conviction. In the work of scholars like Lloyd Ambrosius, Michael Hunt, and Frank Ninkovich, secular ideology has, indeed, been put forth as a factor in foreign policy formulation more significant than traditional realist interpretations could ever allow. Yet even those who have dealt with ideology in this way have only rarely accepted religion as a connected, yet independent, key variable.[8]

The co-optation of religious themes in the twenty-first-century war on terrorism should finally have shown that religion remains an important factor in foreign policy. New approaches are needed that privilege religion as a category of influence that is just as important as race, class, and gender— approaches that cease to treat religion only as a tool of secular policy and start seeing it as a shaper of policy in its own right.[9]

In ways that are difficult to disentangle, secular prejudices undoubtedly contribute to a devout religious believer's worldview and politics. In some matters, they may even be determinative. But this reality should not be used to dismiss religious motivations or simply subsume them under class, race, or gender, for policymakers who happen to be devout religious believers do approach issues from vantage points that have been shaped by their religious values, motivations, and aspirations. For the devout, religious argument is not just a cover for secular interests; nor do the devout necessarily compartmentalize their faith in ways that allow them to be religious only part of the time and on some issues only. Rather, we should recognize that religious faith can provide the underlying world-and-life view, the set of presuppositions and categories of thought through which the devout examine all things. In the case of a professor of systematic theology, this is rather self-evident; but with qualifications, it also applies to devout laity, including those who make politics their profession.

Thus, when the evidence seems to suggest that opportunism rather than genuine religious belief was at issue in any given case that is examined in the pages that follow, this will be pointed out; and in all cases, the attempt will be made to relate class, race, and gender to religion. But the guiding principle of this study is that we should take seriously a person's faith and regard it as an important, independent determinant of opinion and of the action that results—in all areas of life, including foreign policy formation.

The religious League of Nations controversy serves as a particularly good entrance point for a study of this kind, because in the course of this controversy, the secular and the religious interacted and intertwined in many previously unexplored ways. By looking at the clergy and the laity—at the laymen who happened to be politicians and at the politicians who saw religious arguments as useful—all the different dimensions of modern American anti-internationalism can be canvassed and evaluated. Not only are the genesis and content of modern anti-internationalism illumined in new ways, but the continued political relevance of religion in an ostensibly secular age is also powerfully shown.

CHAPTER ONE

The Social Gospel and Modern Internationalism

In 1870, British prime minister William Ewart Gladstone wrote an anonymous article, "Germany, France, and England," for the *Edinburgh Review*. In this article, this devout Anglican addressed his hopes for the future of Christendom and sketched a coming new world order of morally enlightened, democratic nations preserving the peace of the world through voluntary cooperation. Later, the "Grand Old Man" of political liberalism elaborated on this vision by enunciating his celebrated six "right principles of foreign policy." The fifth of those principles was the inalienable equality of the nations of Christendom, which Gladstone saw as a spiritual family bound together in faith and divinely called to maintain peace and comity within its circle. At his most optimistic, he predicted that eventually "the general judgement of civilised mankind" would yield a new "ecumenical council" of nations where "Public Right" would reign as a disembodied "tribunal of paramount authority."[1]

In the founding of the League of Nations some fifty years later, Gladstone's dream had apparently come true. It had been brought about, moreover, by liberals who still revered Gladstone's memory and had never wavered in their belief no matter how unlikely success appeared. In the tortuous decades that followed the League's creation, these liberals were to remain the principal publicists and organizers for an internationalist consciousness and a moralized foreign policy. They kept their faith from the days of heady optimism and expectation in 1919 through the isolationism of the 1920s and the 1930s and through the dismal years of World War II, when all hope of international peace and understanding seemed to have escaped. Unperturbed though chastened, liberals carried their faith into the postwar world, and they reasserted it under the strengthened institutional auspices of the United Nations.

During the cold war that swiftly followed, dashing their initial hopes, liberals still kept the faith, defended it, and broadened its scope. Generally, they did everything that they could to strengthen the United Nations as the most promising instrument of peace and for rationally settling international disagreements. After the cold war, they once again tried to empower the UN's various specialized agencies and its conferences on women's rights, development policy, and environmental protection. They initiated the late-twentieth-century conversation on "the international community" and its supposedly universally shared code of moral values and responsibilities that became embodied in the International Criminal Court.

Throughout, the rise, institutionalization, and perpetuation of internationalism owed to the liberals' persistence and vision. Not least was the debt to churchly liberals. From Gladstone's time to the World War I campaign for an association of nations and through the League of Nations' troubled existence into the era of the United Nations, the leaders of most Christian denominations in the Western world were at the forefront of the internationalist project. They imparted their meanings to modern internationalism; they invested it with an aura of a high ethical endeavor, if not a certain sacredness; and they pushed their secular allies constantly forward, inspiring them with the high spiritual ideals of their own endeavor.

It is therefore impossible to properly appreciate the emergence, nature, and passion of churchly *anti*-internationalism without recognizing at the outset that anti-internationalism is but an aspect of a broader assault on modern theological and political liberalism. For as the Gladstonian vision matured at the end of the nineteenth and in the first decade of the twentieth centuries, it attracted ever more radical guises and ultimate goals, in the process inviting several equally radicalized forms of critique.

Internationalism and Modern Liberalism

The search for the roots of modern internationalism must begin with the transformation that took place in the latter part of the nineteenth century in that classical liberalism for which Gladstone stood. The Gladstonian internationalist vision arose out of classical liberalism, which was in several essential points very different from the later, or newer, liberalism that prevailed in the twentieth century. Without a profound transformation, the older liberalism could not have issued in the modern international organizations that have existed since 1919.

The classical liberal tradition revolved around the primacy of the Christian nation-state. It envisioned no blending of nationalities or state sovereignties, nor did it accept what later internationalists regarded as the crux of their pursuit, the institutional manufacture of a distinct supranational authority. Moreover, Gladstone's generation of liberals did not stand for those modern concepts of democracy that underlay the equality of peoples and nations in the twentieth-century concept of internationalism. Rather, they understood democracy in a distinctly limited sense that was informed by the pursuit of elite control over an unruly populace through law, yet hopeful that moral education might eventually yield more enlightened and trustworthy subjects. Finally, as the designation itself implies, Gladstone's concept of the "ecumenical council" was limited to the Christian states, for only those states were thought to possess the ability for meaningful international cooperation.[2]

These notions were rooted, above all, in the seventeenth-century writings of the Dutch Christian jurist Hugo Grotius, whom all classical liberals regarded as the ultimate authority in matters of international relations theory. Grotius had traced international law to "the law of nature and to the commandments of God" found in the Bible, and he had insisted that institutionalized cooperation for peace was possible only among those Christian nations whose rulers accepted both these sources of authority.[3] This remained the starting point for those Christian pacifist groups of Gladstone's own lifetime—the British Society for the Promotion of Permanent and Universal Peace, and the American Peace Society—which were among the first to call for an international congress of nations. These two groups and their more radical offshoots—the League of Universal Brotherhood, the Universal Peace Union, and the International Arbitration League—advocated nonresistance and conscientious objection as personal choices, but they also hoped for institutions that would codify international law and arbitrate international disagreements. On the whole, they shied clear of advocating any wholesale restructuring of international society or the creation of supranational, coercive institutions.[4]

Much of this had changed by the early twentieth century, when modern internationalism had become a reality both as a concept and as an organized movement. Celebrate Gladstone though they still might, the internationalists of the twentieth century were, in truth, as far removed from Gladstone's, Grotius's, and the Christian pacifists' mental framework as they were from the structures of international cooperation that these three had anticipated. The transmutation of classical liberalism into New Liberalism, of which this change was part, went to the very core of the Western experience of modernity, and it profoundly shaped concepts of internationalism. Those who were the twentieth century's most enthusiastic champions of internationalism were products of this transformation, which itself was a principal political offshoot of a much broader paradigm change. By the beginning of the twentieth century, this underlying paradigm change—meaning a profound transformation in the general, orientating ways of perceiving the world that were ascendant—had remodeled the conversation of all but the most conservative groups of people, and from it issued also modern, as opposed to the earlier, Gladstonian, internationalism.

At the core of liberalism's transformation, and hence also at the core of the internationalism that it brought in, was the transformation of the Christian religion. The liberals of the latter part of the nineteenth century strived for and those of the early twentieth century thought they had achieved the ascendancy of modernist theology, and it was this ascendancy that, more than anything else, produced modern internationalism.

Religious modernism could be understood either, as the historian William Hutchison put it, as the "conscious, intended adaptation of religious ideas to modern culture"[5] or, in the words of a major practitioner, Shailer Matthews, as the "use of the methods of modern science to find, state and use the permanent and central values of inherited orthodoxy in meeting the needs of a modern world."[6] In either rendition, modernist theology was a reaction by a section of Western Christianity to profound changes external to itself that had been taking place in the body of Western society ever since the start of the Industrial Revolution, an attempt so to recast the message of the churches as to retain the relevancy of their agency in a world increasingly naturalistic and materially oriented, unable to place its faith in traditional supernatural dogmas. The rise of evolutionary and other scientific types of thought had so shaken the foundations of popular allegiance to Christian creedal truths that these truths were to be restated in "modern" terms, and thus science was to be turned to the advantage of religion by co-optation.[7]

As it was sketched from the 1870s by its American theoreticians Walter Rauschenbusch, George D. Herron, George A. Coe, and others, the modernist "New Theology" was profoundly immanentist. This is to say that it saw divinity present in all aspects of human and material life and believed that the world itself could be treated as a revelatory, religious entity. There was no significant difference, after all, between Jew and Gentile, Christian and pagan, the spiritual and the material, the religiously faithful and the scientifically secular; rather, all these could attain but differently expressed insights into the divinity that was immanent everywhere.[8] Herron spoke of the "indwelling Divine Social Presence," of the "self-governing Divine Presence in man," which, he claimed, suffused the "one living and continuing organism, [the] one eternal mutual-membered family" that was humanity,[9] while George A. Coe insisted that "there is no separation between human society and the divine": God was "within human society in the democratic manner of working, helping, sacrificing, persuading, co-operating, achieving."[10]

As these quotations imply, the modernist new theologians made the doctrine of the Incarnation, God-become-human, central or exclusive, and hence they tended to see the unfolding of human culture as itself a divine process. The modernists suggested, in other words, that a process of ethical evolution and illumination was under way, that human ethical knowledge was constantly becoming more like divine knowledge, forever approaching a fuller understanding of God's laws and will for the world. On this basis, they proposed—as Lyman Abbott, the modernist Congregationalist pastor and editor of the *Outlook*, put it—to do away with the "conception of salvation as the rescue of the elect from a lost world." This notion was to be replaced with the "conception of the transformation of the world itself into a Human Brotherhood."[11] The transformation was said to be both inevitable and universal: All peoples were its agents, and it was irreversibly tending toward the divinely willed end state. Modernist American Christians were, however, believed to be its greatest spearheads, the people who were the most advanced in the incarnate divinity's "self-realization" and therefore supremely capable of speeding up the process.[12]

Immanentist and evolutionary suppositions reinforced each other and, from the perspective of internationalism, led to an important set of conclusions. The modernists believed that humanity was all one, constantly progressing, that every aspect of the world had divinity immanent in it, and that the task of the true believer was to encourage the process whereby ethical evolution was bringing humanity into ever-fuller unity and harmony with the divinity immanent in the world.

As its social arm, the new theology offered the Social Gospel. The proponents of the Social Gospel—who were organized in a range of denominational social service agencies and, after 1905, in the Federal Council of Churches of Christ (FCC)—were primarily concerned about the reform of social conditions at home. But given the Social Gospel's incarnational-immanentist terms of reference, it inevitably had global implications. Its practitioners believed, as Mathews put it, that "as civilization develops, sin grown corporate. We sin socially by violating social rather than individualistic personal relations."[13] It followed that sin was to be eradicated here and now, not by individual conversion but by tackling social structures. This required the purposive, collective removal of the material injustices that were, supposedly, structurally inherent in the capitalist system. The Social Gospelers, no longer content to circumscribe the church's preoccupations with doctrinal creeds and preaching about the hereafter, insisted on immediate, tangible results in the world at large.[14]

Practitioners of the Social Gospel like Rauschenbusch called this the "Kingdom Theology" as often as they called it the Social Gospel, and it was essentially a radically new version of the postmillennial pursuit of a perfected world, which humankind was to return to its Creator as the Kingdom of God on Earth. "No visible return of Christ to earth is to be expected," these people believed, "but rather the long and steady advance of the spiritual kingdom."[15] Seen logically, this vision could have no national boundaries. In fact, it led to much rhetoric about universalism and the brotherhood of all people, to an active ecumenical movement, and to a new departure in mission work that deemphasized the spreading of a salvific *evangelium* and accentuated the encouragement of ethical and reformist impulses in all peoples.[16]

A Social Gospel so conceived significantly eased the early-twentieth-century political liberals' embrace of collective, purposive means of effecting change. It helped them to argue that human evolution had reached a point where a sufficient number of people were sufficiently enlightened ethically to be able to use the powers of the state—which liberals had hitherto regarded as instruments of oppression—for the eradication of the supposed social causes of sin. Evoking the conceptions of the New Theology, one leading theorist of British New Liberalism, L. T. Hobhouse, called the process "orthogenic evolution,"[17] the gradual coming-about of a higher level of social consciousness and sense of responsibility—in effect, the human equivalents of the survival of the fittest, in this case the fittest of ethical ideas. By the early twentieth century, the New Liberals simply took it as granted that all well-meaning men and women regarded the use of collective means in the alleviation of social injustices and inequalities as a sign of the highest ethical consciousness thus far.[18]

This embrace of the collectivity was at the very core of the New Liberalism (or, as it tended to be called in the United States, "Progressivism"), and it led to the series of social reforms and strengthening of the state's powers that were legislated upon in the first two decades of the twentieth century by Presidents Theodore Roosevelt and Woodrow Wilson in the United States and by like-minded men elsewhere in the West. At the same time, the Social Gospel helped the New Liberals to affirm views of humanity as a single entity, cohered by shared ethical aspirations, however differently expressed in different cultures. It pointed them toward the necessity of cooperation and mutually sustaining reformist efforts throughout the world.

This was very much the case with the principal political protagonist for a League of Nations in the World War I period, President Wilson, a relatively modernist Presbyterian who had addressed the founding convention of the FCC. He stressed that the salvation of individual souls was "rather a petty business" and that "individual men can in conscience afford to be saved only as part of the process by which the world itself is regenerated."[19] He celebrated the Salvation Army, the YMCA, and the modernist mission workers whose principal interest was in the Social Gospel, not in "doctrinal teaching," and he insisted that "Christianity should be used to set things right here. It should be used to purify this world. We should rectify by social action backed by right motives." On this basis, he stressed at the FCC's founding convention, one needed first to make the "United States a mighty Christian nation," and then the Social Gospelers should proceed "to Christianize the world."[20]

Wilson's doctrinal investment may, as some historians have suggested, well have been much weaker than his emotional attachment to his church.[21] Nevertheless, when he told the archbishop of Canterbury in 1918 that he regarded "Christian principles" as the "solid foundation" of the coming League of Nations,[22] he *was* enunciating a worldwide social vision that was indeed rooted—as his critics then and later charged—in an evangelical school of politics. But it was a profoundly modernist sort of evangelicalism that was in question, grounded in those immanentist-incarnational theologies that saw humanity as a single entity ever progressing toward a fuller realization of its unity.

Like Wilson, most other late-nineteenth- and twentieth-century internationalists were religiously rooted. This applied even to those socialist sections of the internationalist community that had severed their ties with confessional faith and conversed in terms of their substitute ideologies.[23] John Spargo, a leading American socialist intellectual of the period, typified this when he wrote about the "new socialism of a quality and temper undreamed of by Marx and Engels" that had, according to him, been forged when the evolutionary insights of the Social Gospel had been grafted onto those of the political socialist movement. In both movements, Spargo claimed, "God is now conceived as working through evolution," as a spirit "immanent" in the "economic environment" that was constantly pushing humanity toward the "Kingdom of Human Brotherhood" by way of united ethical action.[24]

The specifically socialist internationalism of people such as Spargo maintained that the putative "Kingdom of Human Brotherhood" could be achieved only by destroying the profit motive, for they believed that as long as the profit motive remained at the back of policy, the temptation would persist to use state powers for class or national aggrandizement and exploitation. But this did not make them revolutionists; by the latter nineteenth century, most Anglophone socialists were in fact Revisionists of one type or another, or social democrats, who did not believe that socialism should be brought about by force or violence. Rather, they trusted the parliamentary system, public education, and not least Hobhouse's "orthogenic evolution."[25] To them, "the essentials of the Socialist State [were] being developed within the existing capitalist State"; there could be "no sharp, efficient division of the existing State from the future State of Socialism."[26] More often than not, this case continued to be made in a millennialist frame of reference that was at least as rooted in modernist theologies as it was in any secular theory.

The Anglophone socialists' pursuit of a new world order was not, then, essentially different from that of the New Liberals or of the clerical Social Gospelers. Theirs was a shared quest for a world made new—purified and perfected through collective action. Universalism instead of particularism; rationalism instead of supernaturalism; the power of purposive, collective human action instead of reliance on tradition and divine interventions; concentration on structural instead of personal sin; and, finally, internationalism instead of nationalism—these were the core ascendant themes in late-nineteenth-century and twentieth-century thought and rhetoric. Each theme was rooted in the major paradigm shift of the nineteenth century, which redefined democracy in social and industrial terms; the classical monotheistic faiths in immanentist ethical and universal, action-oriented terms; and Marxian socialism in more collaborative, gradualist, and nonrevolutionary terms.

Most of these internationalists did, nevertheless, retain a number of nationalist and racial prejudices that significantly shaped the expression of their beliefs. That is to say that the universal ethical community of nations that they envisioned was, in matter of fact, a community still defined by their own Western conceptions of ethics and not by truly polyvalent exchanges. The process of reasoning whereby American liberals had come to define all those who shared democratic egalitarian notions about progress as one artificial ethnicity—the "Americanism" into which immigrants were indoctrinated—also made them celebrate their own country as a "Redeemer Nation" or a "Crusader State." They were certain that this nation-state had a duty to export its supposedly perfected social ethics to the rest of the world. The long-established, Puritan-based tradition of seeing America as a redemptive force was thus appropriated by the Social Gospelers and reconfigured in terms of their own programs and aspirations.[27]

Seen in this context, a League of Nations itself made sense if it was under-stood as the spontaneous outgrowth of ethical evolution in other peoples' experience. And insofar as all ethical evolution pointed to what had already been achieved in America, American leadership of the League became a given. Thus on the level of guiding ideas and practical leadership, the liberal internationalists remained American nationalists and saw the putative League of Nations as America's tool, embodiment, and extension in the world.

Especially once thus linked to notions about a redeemer nation, the Christian, New Liberal, and social-democrat redefinitions of the nature of progress not only paralleled the rise of internationalism but also led to mod-ern internationalism. For every broad conception of modern liberalism, Christianity and social democracy included an international dimension, and every one of them insisted that modernity was inconceivable without such a dimension. On the political plane, this insistence may have issued in a multi-plicity of varied, apparently animadverted forms, but the incidental differ-ences were less important than the broader fellow feeling and shared anticipation. By World War I, the New Liberals, social democrats, and Social Gospelers in fact all essentially agreed on a core program of immediate mea-sures that should be implemented forthwith and on a broad international canvas.

The dynamism and drive of the liberal or progressive internationalism that the Social Gospelers, the New Liberals, and the social democrats together made up was in no small degree a result of the fact that these three constituencies, and they alone, had caught the optimistic and expectant spirit of their times. They alone had expansively associated their ideologies with an internationalism that was somehow synonymous with evolution, "progress" and "justice," "brotherhood" and universal peace, with human ability and potentiality, democracy, and the extension of democracy.

Liberal versus Conservative Internationalism

No inevitable trajectory existed, however, from New Liberalism's interna-tionalist worldview to a specific international organization. The term "league of nations" has since World War I been so closely identified with *the* League of Nations, a specific political institution, that it is easy to forget that it did not need to imply any corporate entity. That "league of nations" came to mean a specific institution and not, say, a collaborative arrangement or understanding between existing nation-states was entirely due to the liberal internationalists. Theirs was a rationalist faith, oriented toward organization and legislation, that led to the creation of *institutions*, and there was no reason why it should not lead to *global* institutions. In fact, the liberal faith naturally led to global institutions.

It was only in the course of World War I that liberal internationalists came to specify the institutional forms that their vision should assume. Once they did that, they had little difficulty in surpassing older, more limited conceptions of internationalism. These included what in a strict sense was a persuasion more loyal to Gladstone's original vision than that of their own—a persuasion made up of those whom the historian Thomas J. Knock has called the "conservative internationalists."[28] In truth, these individuals were classical liberals in a new guise. In their churches, these people stood for relatively traditional theologies, and in the economic sphere they affirmed laissez-faire and limited government. On the international plane, they were nevertheless conscious of the need for new mechanisms to control the anarchic competition of nation-states. The conservative internationalists were also sufficiently influenced by evolutionary thought to suppose that in the twentieth century some progress could now be made in this area.[29]

Gladstone and the American Peace Society had believed in a gradual evolution of the international system toward regularized but voluntary cooperation between nation-states. They had assumed that this was possible only in an "ecumenical" setting, that is, as the result of Christian concepts of equity becoming more generally accepted and translated into law. By the twentieth century, this vision was no longer radical but conservative, and it found its most avid supporters among those jurists engaged in the arbitration of international disagreements and in the codification of international law. These conservative internationalists were in search of stability and predictability. They tended not to desire any but the most minimal limiting of national sovereignty, and they certainly did not expect that any coming of a more internationally minded public opinion could obviate the need for traditional national organization. Nor did the conservative internationalists presume to offer a world without wars. At the most, they were offering mechanisms for limiting, regulating, and controlling wars, and for reducing their incidence.[30]

For the lack of a better word, these conservatives searched for "self-control." That was a code word much used in the World War I period, denoting a preference for such traditional means of control as inner restraints posed by religious and nationalist allegiances and by national and international law. When translated onto the international plane, such a search for control meant more often than not a rather pronounced elitism—the conviction that only a small group of properly sophisticated individuals was competent to guide the interaction of states. As such avid protagonists for this notion as the former U.S. president William Howard Taft and Senator

Elihu Root insisted, most peoples were but "children" who had to be educated into "self-restraint" and protected from the "bullying" of others.
Nation-states also had to be protected from the emotive passions and rapa-
ciousness of such "children," and this, maintained the conservative internationalists, was possible only if "liberty of action [was] regulated by law."[31]
Not the popular passions and the "expediency of the moment" that inevitably guided democratic, political assemblies, Root stressed, but only the
"development of law, and the enforcement of law, according to the judge-
ments of impartial tribunals," could promote international comity.[32]

This approach yielded the Hague arbitration movement of the late nineteenth century (and later the Permanent Court of International Justice).
Another of its results was the spate of bilateral arbitration and cooling-off
treaties at the turn of the century that were championed especially by William Jennings Bryan, the Democratic Party politician who became a key
participant in the fundamentalist/modernist controversy of the 1920s. Yet
even as this strand of internationalism developed, it did not embrace the
goal of a permanent international organization. As early as 1910, former
president Theodore Roosevelt had indeed suggested that the Hague experiment be developed further through a "League of Peace." However, Roosevelt's kind of league would not have been a political organization physically
located in a given place, nor would it have involved a permanent bureaucracy
or a constitution. His league would have been an "international posse comi-
tatus," a collaborative arrangement between certain like-minded (great)
powers, pledged not to resort to wars among themselves and also pledged
to use armed force, when necessary, to prevent others from breaking the
peace.[33]

By the time of World War I, this kind of conservative internationalist
effort had found important champions in the League to Enforce Peace (LEP),
an American association created in 1915, and in its approximate British
equivalent, the League of Nations Society. The LEP's platform embraced
compulsory arbitration of "justiciable" disputes (those relating to international treaties and laws) and called for the creation of special tribunals to
settle "non-justiciable" disputes (those involving vital national interests not
covered by existing international laws or treaties). Additionally, the LEP
envisioned putting collective economic and military pressure on any nation
that was set on war short of having submitted its points of grievance to
arbitration. Finally, the LEP was engaged in the kind of popular education
that Taft and Root thought was required if Western peoples were ever to
agree to elitists' control of international affairs, and to this end it began a
wide-ranging publicity campaign. Presided over by Taft, a conservative Unitarian, the LEP contained many conservatively inclined clergy and lay
activists.[34]

The limited scope and vision of LEP internationalism contrasted sharply with the suggestions that liberal redefinitions of theology, democracy, and community produced. "Progressive" or "liberal" internationalism, as it stood by the early twentieth century, sketched for itself a much more comprehensive agenda than that of the LEP.[35] Liberal internationalists wanted, first, to establish a specific political organization, supranational and distinct from noninstitutionalized forms of international cooperation—a fully fledged "provisional world government," as the *Independent*, a leading Progressive journal, put it.[36] Second, they wanted to have this new organization engage not only in the arbitration of international disputes and in the further codification of international law but also in novel, systematic, and organized efforts to enforce international peace through its own agency. Third, liberal internationalists insisted that a "scheme which merely provides for the prevention of war when conflicts of interests have arisen is inadequate."[37] They defined security most broadly, so that it came to refer not only to defense against the physical aggressions of nation-states but also to the removal of internal causes of strife and inequality. On this basis, the liberals stood for "organized economic government of the world"[38]—for an international organization that would be engaged in regulating commerce and industry worldwide and in creating "an internationally prescribed common minimum of social legislation."[39]

Whereas the conservative approach centered on voluntary collaboration between the leading great powers, the liberals countered with what came eventually to be known as the principle of "collective security." The new, proposed peace enforcement mechanisms that this principle implied were radical departures from previous practice, as well as from the proposals of groups like the LEP. Collective security was very much a Wilsonian concept, one that had formed part of each of President Wilson's various sketches of peacekeeping arrangements ever since his Draft Pan-American Treaty of 1914. By the end of World War I, its substance had become rather clearly defined in the core proposition that all nations would agree to guarantee each other's territorial integrity and independence and resort to economic or military sanctions against any nation that violated this general agreement. In this conception, the arbitration and conciliation of international disputes would still unfold under the auspices of a future League of Nations; but if these safeguards against war were ever to break down, the League itself would have its member states undertake the restoration of peace. The mere promise to do so was supposed in most conceivable circumstances to suffice in keeping the peace.[40]

Important as this innovation was, liberal internationalism was at its most radical when it maintained that conflict did not only arise from the competition for resources in which nation-states were engaged in present conditions of scarcity. They maintained that conflict was ultimately rooted in real and perceived social injustice *inside* nation-states. Collective security was therefore to be defined in the most inclusive terms, as covering not only the prevention of military conflict between nations but also the removal of social causes of strife *within* nations. This meant that liberals intended to "end all wars" not only through new international enforcement mechanisms but also by removing the supposedly deepest of all causes of conflict: the sense of grievance of all oppressed peoples and sections of peoples. From the late nineteenth century, liberals thus worked for an international organization that would have included a program of radical social, political, and economic rearrangement throughout the world.[41]

Liberal internationalists were no less interested in control than were their conservative counterparts; however, they did not aspire to the kind of "self-control" that animated the conservative worldview. As the historian Lloyd Ambrosius has suggested, the liberal concept of internationalism was predicated on the notion of "social control," that is, on the pursuit of a new socially generated set of consensually accepted values that would "control the person's will" and somehow automatically actuate "socially" oriented behavior.[42] Although it was originally used in the context of domestic social reform, "social control" worked just as well on the international arena. In that as well as in the domestic arena, liberals wanted to use the state's and other culture-transmitting institutions' powers to create new aspirations, perceptions, and institutional arrangements geared toward a more "social" and democratic policy. Nation-states were distinctly secondary in this search for control; and new institutions of international and supranational power, actuated by social control, were to be the principal loci of activities.

The World War I period witnessed the emergence of several liberal and socialist pressure groups that wanted to supersede the conservative "self-control" and work to forward their alternative "social control" on an international plane. The most important organizations of this type included, in the United States, the League of Free Nations Association; the Church Peace Union; the World Alliance for International Friendship through the Churches; and the FCC's two internationalist organizations, the Commission on International Justice and Goodwill, and the National Committee on the Churches and the Moral Aims of the War. Additionally, there were transatlantic radical liberal groups that campaigned actively for international organization, above all the Fellowship of Reconciliation, an originally British association of clerical pacifists that quickly spread to the United States and assumed a broader set of concerns. The international labor and socialist movement also had its own organizations, most notably the prewar Second

Socialist International and the postwar Labor and Socialist International, which worked for the goals of a specifically socialist internationalism.[43]

Whether they acted primarily in the joint organizations or within their own movements, the backbone of modern campaigns for international organization was with the political liberals, the labor and socialist activists, and the modernists of the main American churches and Jewish bodies. The first two groups played the leading role in constructing and then offering for acceptance the organizational specifics of the shared vision; the latter largely endorsed these specifics once they were sketched and then entered the contention themselves.

Conceptualizing the League of Nations

Of the collaborative threesome, organized labor and socialist activists were the first to sketch specific institutional structures for the internationalization of social control. When doing so, they blended the general New Liberal and Social Gospel precepts that permeated their immediate environs with specifically socialist versions of internationalism, and they issued a compound that was, generally speaking, quite acceptable also to the liberal and Christian internationalists.

The socialists disapproved of the Hague and LEP models of arbitration because, as John Spargo stressed, both were under elite capitalist control and therefore would not deal with the "uneven economic development" that was the chief cause of international friction. Also, they could easily be used to crush "social revolution."[44] At their wartime Inter-Allied Socialist and Labor Conferences, the socialists demanded instead the creation of a new "International Legislature" that would represent peoples, not governments or jurists. This legislature would be active above all in the economic, industrial, and social spheres, and it would use taxation and the planned control of resources to level distinctions between nations and classes. It would also further codify international law and impose a worldwide arbitral system. The socialists were interested in disarmament and decolonization as well, but they had little time for conceptions of collective security that included a readiness to use military force. Above all, throughout their wartime conferences (and especially at the 1919 Berne Conference), the crux of the socialists' internationalist vision remained social reform eventually leading to worldwide socialism.[45]

The socialists consistently stressed that their intention was to use the coming world legislature for the creation of a "new social order" and "common mind in the world" that would lead to the eventual "abolition of the capitalist system itself."[46] In the meantime, it should be made to compel all governments to "insure to the working class of all countries a minimum of

guarantees of a moral as well as material kind concerning the right of coalition, emigration, social insurance, hours of labor, hygiene, and protection of
labor." Free state-provided education and health services were demanded, as
well as state-imposed minimum wages, unemployment insurance, and social
insurance. It was also deemed essential that the decisions of the proposed
supranational labor authority be subject to the veto of the International
Federation of Trade Unions. All this socioeconomic rearrangement was supposed to take place through international legislation and coercion, not
through voluntary agreements, either national or international.[47]

Such demands for reform and legislation were a mean between the often
conflicting ambitions of those, mostly Americans, who preferred independent, cooperative labor union action, and those, mostly continental Europeans, who put the emphasis on legislation and coercion by class-directed
states. The American Federation of Labor stood for the former position, and
most of the organized socialist parties and labor unions of Europe stood for
the latter. However, by the time that the Paris peace conference created a
special labor commission and directed it to establish a permanent international legislative authority in the labor and industrial field (the future International Labor Organization), both camps came together and were ready to
use their collective powers to put their stamp on the League.[48]

Having been co-opted and modified by liberal politicians and intellectuals, the case for an international legislative agency had by that time come to
be one of the most important items of the liberal League of Nations concept.
Certainly by late 1918, most New Liberal and Progressive leaders in Britain
and in the United States had come to insist that the best way to advance
social reform was to assure its internationalization through the instrumentality of the League. They intended to use the international organization to
prescribe their preferred social policies on as universal a basis as possible.[49]
Thus did one leading Progressive publicist insist that "it is capitalism which
is on trial at the Peace Conference"; it was inevitable that the nations would
now become "less capitalistic and more socialist." Likewise, the *Independent*
celebrated the fact that the "United States is quietly absorbing the sounder
elements of the Social Democratic theory," and it endorsed labor's program
as the world's new "Magna Carta."[50]

President Wilson himself insisted that his charge "to make the world safe
for democracy" referred to a democracy that was to be understood "in a
larger sense than can be expressed in any political terms."[51] It meant the
lifting, and not merely the safeguarding, of existing labor standards and the
recognition that it was the laboring peoples of the world who had the highest
developed sense of moral values. In Wilson's view, it was time for the world
community to guarantee to the working class the increased power that it

deserved because of its high moral consciousness, time for others to learn from labor, and time to implement its unique ethical insights in global legislation.[52] He prefaced this line of argument with the incarnationalist-immanentist supposition that there existed a "common will of mankind" that the righteous nations now had to grasp and follow because it was "the hand of God" that had led them to it. If the nations would do this and join Wilson's League, each would become an "instrument of divine Providence."[53]

These kinds of statements led such leading American socialists as William English Walling and Upton Sinclair to declare that President Wilson's sketch for the postwar world order was "practically identical" to that of the socialist movement, a "moderately socialist program" that contained "no contradictions whatever" with their own demands.[54] Collective security was central to both groups' concept of the League. But part of collective security, as they saw it, was international social reform. It was essentially a spiritual vision—of humanity at peace and unified, together working for the attainment of important material outcomes, primary among which was the prevention of all future wars, the alleviation of want, and the translation into practice of the ethical vision of the laboring classes. International labor and social legislation was one natural embodiment of these new conceptions, and much of the liberal enthusiasm for the coming League was predicated on the confident expectation that it would undertake this kind of legislation.

Finally, modernist and liberal clergy entered the fight. They accepted practically all the propositions brought forward by socialist and liberal advocates of a League of Nations. In many cases, this acceptance was both enthusiastic and expansive, given that liberal clerics perceived in these propositions the practical fruit of their long-standing Social Gospel campaigns. In some ways, they had themselves been the initiators and inspirers, and the politicians they had influenced through their incarnationalist-immanentist preaching had been the ones to sketch the practical propositions; now the clergy could rejoin the political effort they had helped bring about, not only as inspirers but as activists in their own right.

In a path-breaking 1917 book, Walter Rauschenbusch, the most important American theologian of the Social Gospel, stressed that "before the war the social gospel dealt with social classes; to-day it is being translated into international terms. . . . All those whose Christianity was not ditched by the catastrophe are demanding a Christianizing of international relations." Redefining the Christian eschaton as the "hope of a Christian social order on earth," Rauschenbusch went on to specify that it meant the abolition not only of war but also of most forms of private property, "economic oligarchies," and all the "systematized oppression which the capitalist organization produces." All this, he insisted, could only be achieved through a combined organized, international effort by all enlightened individuals.[55] He stressed, too, America's special responsibility as the nation that, its many lingering inequalities aside, had embraced and put into practice the Social Gospel vision more nearly than any other nation.[56]

Charles Gore, the Church of England bishop who was known as the "Red Bishop," did not agree on the trope of American exceptionalism, but he, too, saw the coming League of Nations in radically socialist terms. He traveled around the United States in 1918, converting others to the view that "in international relations, . . . we need a socialism to subordinate nations to the good of the race." "It is the will of God," he maintained, for the nations to set up a system of collective security and international social reform, and he stressed how peace depended not only on justice between the nations but also, above all, on justice "between the warring elements within the several nations." The church would fail in its most fundamental duties if it did not cooperate in the ushering in of the "fellowship of humanity," "an idea that has mainly had its origins in Christian thought and imagination."[57]

Countless other modernist clergy and laity endorsed these sentiments and demanded the "Christianizing of international relations" through a postwar "World State" and "international government" with its own judicial, executive, and legislative branches and a far-reaching program for global social reform that should be based on the socialists' wartime proposals.[58] This, claimed the New York Congregationalist pastor Charles E. Jefferson, was the "direction which the God of history has unmistakeably indicated," while William H. P. Faunce of the Church Peace Union waxed eloquent about Christ having already returned—in the spirit of the League of Nations—and being in the process of sifting His aides and coworkers from among the nations.[59] Indeed, many of these modernists chose to depict the League of Nations as the "finest compliment to Christianity that has ever been paid or could be paid" and as "the application of the principles of Christianity on a cosmic scale," that is, as the principal international means for the full implementation of the Social Gospel.[60]

Furthermore, many a modernist argued that the "spiritual foundation of the League of Nations was [the] Christian Missions" and that the League itself was "a missionary organization." They claimed that "the world could not have been linked in laws and government, had it not been linked in conscience, in consciousness" first.[61] Thus the very existence of the League proved that the modernist redefinition of Christian missions had worked and had changed people's thinking. For some years, modernist mission workers had deemphasized the preaching of the saving Gospel and concentrated on vocational training, economic uplift, and social reform; now these methods apparently had yielded their expected fruit, and the nations were converted to the Social Gospel. In this framework, the League could be seen as a uniquely useful instrument for the further expansion of mission work redefined. Because it was a global organization, it could reach all peoples; and because it included a pronounced social reform program, it could be used to complete the Social Gospel.[62]

George Herron, the defrocked Social Gospel theologian who by this time resided in Europe but continued to wield a polemical influence in American Protestantism, summarized the whole project and frame of mind. He stressed in 1917 that the coming League of Nations would turn out to be the ultimate "organization of an inclusive kindliness," not least because it would thus incorporate the "indwelling Divine Social Presence." The League would create nothing less than an "expanded soul" and a new "beatific" state of human existence in which "another and different race of men, splendid alike in strength and gentleness will walk the earth and climb the sky." To Herron, President Wilson appeared to be a "colossal Christian apostle, shepherding the world into the kingdom of God," and his League seemed "a divine visitation," the "unfolding of the manful mind of God, of the omnipotent will to love in a mutual-membered humanity."[63] When told of this assessment, Wilson let it be known that Herron had reached a unique insight into his own thinking.[64]

By the beginning of the League controversy, the major ecclesiastical leaders of almost all American Protestant denominations had positioned themselves at the forefront of the campaign for an international organization so conceived. Many had joined some of the secular League advocacy groups established during World War I; many more became active in their own groups.[65] By 1920, all major Protestant denominations in the United States, save the Southern Baptist Convention and the several Lutheran synods, had endorsed the League. The Methodist Episcopal Church had acted first, on May 10, 1919, and when officially endorsing the League its bishops even claimed that not a single clergyman in that denomination was opposed. The General Assembly of the Presbyterian Church followed with its endorsement on May 15, the Philadelphia Meeting of the Society of Friends and the Christian Reformed Church soon after, the Protestant Episcopal Church in October 1919, the Congregationalists in November, and the Church of Jesus Christ of Latter-day Saints in September.[66]

The FCC endorsed the League once in 1918, twice in 1919, and once more in 1920. It advised its members to spread pro-League materials and to put pressure on recalcitrant senators during the ensuing League ratification controversy. It sent a delegation to Paris when the peace conference was meeting and delivered to President Wilson the urgent message that the League seemed to them nothing less than "the political expression of the

Kingdom of God on Earth." Thereupon, the FCC mobilized its own resources on the pro-League side, asking local churches to provide courses of study on internationalism and the League, to pass resolutions of support, and to designate specific days of prayer for the League. When the League Covenant was debated in the U.S. Senate, the FCC coordinated efforts with other churchly and secular pro-League organizations, sent pamphlets and petitions to senators and to clergy, and organized two major pro-League rallies in Washington, where the call went out for speedy ratification of the League Covenant.[67] Throughout these activities, it was the Social Gospelers who led the churchly campaigns. No matter the specific organization, the same handful of energetic men were likely to be found on their boards of directors, writing articles in their publications, and taking on the lecture circuit on their behalf.

Conclusion

The Social Gospelers never lost their faith in the inevitability and millennial beneficence of a very broadly conceived League of Nations. By the end of World War I, they had come to so intimately associate the promise both of Christian America and the Kingdom of God with international organization that they could not but believe in the eventual triumph of such organization. All well-meaning and properly ethically enlightened peoples, they thought, agreed with them, and they were convinced that the goal would surely be reached if such people but banded together under American leadership and used their accumulated, internationally coordinated power. Never were they as optimistic about it as in 1919, when they proclaimed anew that the world would be "evangelized" and the Gospel "socialized" in their generation.

This churchly optimism mirrored the confident expectancy of most of the American left at that time. By the end of World War I, practically all the members of that left—religious and secular—had come to see internationalism and international organization as peculiarly their own, intrinsic to their self-image and their aspirations. They were sure that they had the numbers and all the requisite historical determinants on their side. World War I had not shattered their optimistic expectations of humanity's progress; on the contrary, liberal internationalists had become more intent on pooling their strength to achieve their varied social goals. They could justify support of the war only if it would indeed bring about the new (social) democracy on which they agreed, and they convinced themselves that this was exactly what was going to happen, both because such was (still) the supposedly inevitable course of ethical evolution and because they themselves would make it happen. On such a confident, expectant basis, all the three generic strands of modern internationalism coalesced in the effort to create the League of Nations.

CHAPTER TWO

Dispensationalists: Prefiguring the Latter Days

The Protestant community's most active and passionate opponents of the League of Nations were the dispensational premillennialists. They were anti-internationalists long before the Covenant of the League of Nations had even been sketched, let alone publicly discussed, and much that the Social Gospel campaigns helped fuel their opposition, it is safe to assume that they would have resisted the League even had their liberal rivals not been its apologists. In the course of World War I, they developed a distinct premillennialist critique of internationalism from which few in later generations of prophecy thinkers diverged. This critique traced the League of Nations and all modern internationalism to modernist liberal theology, and it ascribed to all three the place that in premillennialist eschatology was reserved for the Antichrist and his allies. On that fixed doctrinal basis, the leaders of the most important organization of the early fundamentalists, the World Christian Fundamentals Association, set themselves against the League of Nations with a passion unrivaled even by the most strident political Irreconcilables.

Dispensationalist Premillennarianism

Most twentieth-century prophecy investigation took place within the dispensationalist premillennarian hermeneutic, and it was this hermeneutic

27

that gave the fundamentalists their utter self-confidence regarding the menace of the League of Nations. Rooted in the apocalyptic books of the Bible and the writings of the second-century theologians Irenaeus and Tertullian, premillennialism itself had been available throughout the church's history, but only after it was renovated in the late nineteenth century did it start to influence great numbers of Protestants. The renovation owed to the British proto-Pentecostal Edward Irving and his Catholic Apostolic Church (also known as the Irvingites) and to John Nelson Darby, the founder of the Plymouth Brethren, who were contemporaries influenced by each other's prophecy investigation and coequal originators of modern premillennialism. Especially in the United States, where Darby brought dispensationalism in the 1860s, their kind of prophetic speculation proved widely appealing, not least because of its power of explaining the rapidly changing world in persuasive, supernatural terms that brought order, predictability, and clear causality to modern chaos. By the time of World War I, dispensationalism had already conquered the thinking of many Presbyterians and Baptists, and to a lesser extent Methodists, Episcopalians, and the various Holiness churches that were then beginning to coalesce into Pentecostalism.[1] Thus it provided the doctrinal matrix for interpreting current events for a significant portion of American evangelicalism.

Dispensationalist eschatology taught that historical time was divided into seven distinct periods, each with its unique media for divine dealings with humankind (a given chosen people) and each with specific means of living a godly, satisfactory life (law or conscience before Christ, grace after Christ). Dispensationalists maintained that each of these periods culminated in disaster because each was suffused with human hubris, the sin-induced presumption to usurp the laws and the position of God and to assert humanity in the place of the divinity. In any given dispensation, only a minority—the "remnant"—would remain loyal to God, and it was to this minority that God had given the task of gathering in the small number of the saved. In the present dispensation (the Age of the Gentiles), which was the last, it was the Christian Church that was the remnant, and its God-given task was to preach the Gospel of Jesus Christ's atoning work on the Cross to as many people as possible. It was also to keep its mind fixed on the "Blessed Hope" of Christ's eventual, physical return, which at last would rescue humanity from its sin-induced, repetitive circle of hubris and disaster.[2]

On his Second Coming, Christ would establish the thousand-year reign of earthly peace and happiness known as the millennium. This would come about at the battle of Armageddon, where Christ himself would defeat Satan and his host. In the ensuing millennium—this was the first major addition that the dispensationalists made to traditional premillennialism—the Jews, having been converted by the returning Christ, would rule the Earth, the Christian saints assisting them from heaven. A thousand years into this state of affairs, Satan would be let loose for one last time, defeated, and cast into the pits of Hell forever. God would gather all the living and the dead for the Last Judgment and then create the new heavens and the new earth in which all believers would live in peace for ever.

Of particular importance, dispensationalists supposed that Christ's Second Coming would be preceded by some seven years by the secret, any-moment "rapture" of true Christian believers or their sudden ascension to heaven (1 Thess. 4:16–18). This rapture doctrine was the dispensationalists' second major eschatological innovation. Most of them believed that the rapture would take place before the Great Tribulation, which referred to the final period of the Age of the Gentiles—a period marked by increasing apostasy, war, and persecution that would end sometime after all the Jews had been restored to the Holy Land. According to the pretribulation rapture believers, this period would culminate in the emergence of an anti-Christian world empire, eventually headquartered in Jerusalem, that would be made up of the nations formerly belonging to the Roman empire (the "ten toes" of Dan. 2:41) and composed of "iron and clay" (Dan. 2:33, 41–43); that is, popularly supported but dictatorially led, and legitimated by a new prescribed religion, an apostate form of Christianity. In the last seven years before the Second Coming, this world empire would attempt the purification and perfection of the world by centralized, coercive human effort that had lost its relation to God.

Reformation period millennialists (the Chiliasts) had thought that the final empire's ruler would be a great Christian leader, the liberator not only of the Holy Land but also of all lands from the infidel oppressors of the true believers.[3] Modern dispensationalists, conversely, held that Satan himself— the Antichrist—would be the final empire's head. They supposed that once unleashed, Satan would use the empire for his anti-Christian purposes, which included increasing persecution of messianic Jews and postrapture converts to Christianity and the construction of a false humanistic religion that supposedly made peace, prosperity, and the unity of humankind at last achievable. But the redemption of nations was impossible until the returning Christ changed human nature and the conditions of the world, dispersed all human institutions as so much "chaff of the summer threshing" (Dan. 2:35), defeated Satan, and ushered in the millennium. Dispensationalists consequently stressed that nothing good or lasting could come of the final world empire.

Most dispensationalists assumed that the Antichrist's empire would come into existence in the period *after* Christians had been raptured, when Satan could no longer be restrained by the sole power on Earth that thus far had restrained him—the members of the Christian Church. However, the nearness of the empire could be gauged with the help of a number of prophetic "signs of the times" that had been given in the apocalyptic books of the Bible. In addition to the rapture itself, these signs included "wars and the rumors of wars" (Matt. 24:6–7); "false Christs" and false prophets (Mark 13:6, Matt. 24:4, 11); famines, pestilence, and earthquakes (Matt. 24: 24–29; Zech. 14:12–15); an explosion of secular knowledge (Dan. 12:4); the restoration of the Jews to Palestine (Luke 21:24; Jer. 23:7–8); and a general, growing apostasy in professing Christian churches (2 Thess. 2:1–10). All these developments, dispensationalists maintained, would coincide with the most imposing sign of all, the gradual emergence of the Antichrist's empire.

Premillennialists disagreed among themselves on only one major doctrinal point. A minority among them affirmed the so-called historicist interpretation of dispensations (the Catholic Apostolic Church formed the bulk of these), whereas most others (especially in the United States) were futurist dispensationalists. The doctrinal difference between the two groups was related to timing and dating only. That is to say that the historicists believed that the final period of the Age of the Gentiles was already under way and past events had already fulfilled some of the prophetic signs given in the Bible, whereas futurists believed that the unfolding of prophecy would all take place in the future, although in a future that could be at hand at any time. This divergence of views, as important as it was in theory, did not affect the broad interpretive framework that both groups used to correlate current events with their eschatological schemata. This framework came from the Catholic Apostolic Church and was perpetuated by the futurists, for even if the latter did not accept that specific, present trends necessarily fulfilled specific prophecies, they nevertheless accepted these at least as prefigurations and antitypes of what was surely to come.[4]

The interpretive framework was carried over to the United States, where it came to exert much more influence than it ever did in Great Britain. The transfer owed mostly to premillennialists in the Darbyite mould, and it was due to their efforts that futurist dispensationalism conquered in America. It came to cohere in much of *The Fundamentals*, those pivotal premillennialist essays that were published in 1910–15 and gave the popular name to the dispensational movement in the United States.[5] These early dispensationalists weighed constantly against the "false Christs" of Christian Science, Jehovah's Witnesses, Spiritualism and Theosophy, the Bahai, the Mormons, and even against an alleged onslaught of the ouija board. They saw the rise of ecumenism, Higher Criticism, evolutionary theory, and the Social Gospel as signs of churchly apostasy, and they interpreted the emergence of modern socialism and anarcho-syndicalism as fulfillments of the "clay and iron" motif. The rise of gigantic commercial trusts and holding companies was also depicted as an antitype of the gradual focusing of all human effort into a single controlling aggregate. Indeed, before World War I the dispensational-ists saw the budding anti-Christian empire prefigured in *all* forms of concen-tration—whether they be economic, political, industrial, social, or religious—and in all perceived deviations from the fundamentals of the Christian faith.[6]

But increasingly the dispensationalist polemic started to concentrate on the international dimension. This was hardly surprising, because the spread of dispensationalism in America coincided with the rise of modern churchly and political internationalism, the creation of the Hague Court of Interna-tional Justice, and the Social Gospelers' push for new structures of interna-tional cooperation. In the last full year of peace in Europe, leading dispensationalists therefore condemned the internationalist peacekeeping schemes that were proposed by the American Peace Society, the Church Peace Union, and other similar organizations, as well as by Pope Pius X and assorted American and European politicians. They also had nothing good to say about international cooling-off and arbitration treaties, about the Hague Court itself, or about calls for a "United States of Europe." The dispensation-alists saw each of these internationalist schemes as fallacious quests for per-petual but impossible peace rooted in that apostate belief in human self-sufficiency over which their eschatological scheme expected to triumph just before the rapture of Christians and the Second Coming of Christ.[7]

There is every reason to suppose that these kinds of sentiments would have continued to be voiced even if World War I had not intervened. The outbreak of that war, however, fueled an unprecedented worldwide surge of prophecy investigation that convinced those who read their Bibles dispensa-tionally that the end-time prophecies were being fulfilled. Rehearsed at three major American prophecy conferences in 1914–18, this message was brought in sermons and tracts to great numbers of ordinary congregants all across the United States, and it also spilled over into the more secular press that in wartime was eager to publicize apocalyptic themes. To those who partici-pated in this prophecy investigation, and to many an outsider influenced by the wartime mood of apocalypticism, international organization came to appear as one of the surest proofs of the approaching end of history, and internationalism was therefore indelibly soiled by its identification with the anti-Christian influences supposedly at work at the end of times.[8]

Early in the war, the dispensationalist community concluded that the putative League of Nations must be either the apostate empire's immediate precursor and antitype or the very entity itself. Together with the other "signs of the times," this empire's apparent arrival was important to dispensationalists because its predicted coming was the most evident, most imposing physical sign of the imminent end of history. Once it was forming, dispensationalists felt certain that presently their time on Earth would be up and that Christ would very soon—at any moment—return. All conceivable prefigurations of the final world empire were also useful as didactic and evangelizing tools in gathering the "remnant" that the dispensationalists believed had been enjoined on them. These theological convictions, academic until 1914, were greatly strengthened and specified by the world war's experiences, and the general interpretive matrix first offered by the Irvingites in the 1830s appeared to be confirmed in all its particulars.

Dispensationalists against the League of Nations

The first to essay into political contention over the prophetic portents of war events were actually British, not American, prophecy investigators. On an October morning in 1917, a relatively small group of British premillennialist preachers gathered for a breakfast meeting in London and founded the Advent Testimony and Preparation Movement, the single most enduring prophetic investigation group (which was later renamed the Prophetic Witness Movement International).[9] The founding of this—in a few years—2,000-member-strong association of conservative premillennialists was the first shot fired in the dispensationalist polemic against the churchly advocates of modern international organizations.

Under the direction of F. B. Meyer, a leading British Baptist of the period, the foundational meeting of the Advent Testimony movement issued a manifesto declaring that the Gentiles' era was ending, that the Jews were soon to return to the Holy Land en masse, and that the rapture of the church and the return of Christ were soon to be expected. Given this imminence, the manifesto stressed that "all human schemes of reconstruction must be subsidiary to the second coming of our Lord, because all nations will then be subjects to His rule." All Christians were advised to make this statement the guide and rule of their participation in any and all secular efforts to address "the pressing problems of the hour."[10] The result was a spate of frequent and passionate denunciations of the idea then being canvassed for a League of Nations.[11]

American fundamentalists applauded the Advent Testimony's manifesto, and at their own prophetic conferences they issued similar though less systematic statements, especially at those organized in wartime in Chicago, Philadelphia, and New York. Many of these conferences were coordinated with the Advent Testimony group, first by A. C. Gaebelein, the influential, originally Methodist editor of the dispensationalist journal *Our Hope*, and then especially by William B. Riley, the Minnesota Baptist leader and president of Northwestern Bible and Missionary Training School, who had long been in contact with some of the founders of the Advent Testimony group.[12] Having been greatly impressed by the doctrinal clarity of the British manifesto, Riley wanted to create out of the prophetic conferences an organized "Christian confederacy," a worldwide counterweight to the organizations of modernist theologians and their secular liberal allies. He hoped that this putative Christian confederacy would broadcast the premillennialist message on both sides of the Atlantic.[13] Before this goal was reached—in the World Christian Fundamentals Association of 1919—it was up to the prophecy conferences to contextualize prophecy to current events. As they proceeded with the task, the portent of a world association of nations as a key "sign of the times" was prominent in the dispensationalists' exegesis.

Most often, the prophecy conferees concentrated on two particular, interlocked aspects of end-times apostasy: the so-called church sign, and the "clay and iron" motif. They traced both back to modernist theology and forward to the great anti-Christian empire that they said the League of Nations idea, among others, prefigured. The church sign denoted apostasy in its broadest sense, but in the context of World War I, the dispensationalists equated it not least with the modernist clergy's apparent spiritualization and sacralization of the putative League of Nations. When viewed from the dispensationalist perspective, modernist theologies of divine immanence and universal, ethical incarnationalism appeared not just as that pursuit of universal human brotherhood and equality, which the liberals ostensibly advocated, but also as a dimension of the decay of human reliance on Christ alone. The goals and competencies with which the liberals invested their desired League allegedly exposed an overweening faith in the ability of the people, acting by the lights of their own ethical promptings and independent of divine instruction, to perfect the world. This, according to the dispensationalists, was nothing but an apostate conflation of humanity and divinity.

Wartime dispensationalists were not averse to spelling out their implication in the most explicitly antidemocratic terms. Riley was perhaps the most explicit of all, and he kept attacking the popular notion that World War I was being fought to "make the world safe for democracy"—an entirely fallacious, dangerous, and anti-Christian goal, as far as he was concerned, and one that helped perpetuate the lapsing of a proper Godward concentration and dependence throughout the Western world. It was no use fighting for democracy, Riley stressed repeatedly, "unless the democracy that now gets ascendancy in the world comes into the hands of men who are redeemed by the blood of the Son of God." Because "the man has never yet been born who, apart from God, could guide his own steps aright, how can we imagine that when you multiply him into thousands and millions, that power will be imparted by the multiplication?" But it was exactly the opposite that was taking place, Riley averred: Liberal theology had abandoned "the divinely appointed plan for 'Redemption'" and instead had made an idol of "that word of human coinage"—democracy. It had associated this idol with the ethical works of a particular political organization—"the parliament of nations"—which it saw as the hope of the world and then offered as the substitute for the orthodox Christian faith and the real Christian church. This was the anatomy of the church sign, of the prophesied false faith that was to break out upon the world before the millennium.[14]

The biblical reference, "Saying, peace, peace; when there is no peace" (Jer. 8:11), pointed to another aspect of the church sign. Apart from the regular refrain that the salvific message of the Christian Bible was denatured by the modernist sacralization of democracy and the League of Nations, this reference to the impossibility of humanly wrought peace was the most-often-employed description of the apostasy that allegedly underlay modern internationalism. That is to say, the prophecy conferees posited the liberal clerical quest for organized world peace as a principal aspect of the apostate belief in human self-sufficiency and ability. They stressed that the liberal clerics were entirely mistaken and that all hope for the attainment of a permanent and universal peace through a League of Nations was "delusive" and would "end in disappointment and dismay,"[15] because it entirely ignored original and persistent sin and the fact that both non-Christian and nominally Christian nations were in fact constantly engaged in the pursuit of selfish interests.

Some of the more charitable commentators (even Riley for a while) did acknowledge that a "temporary world truce" might be achievable through some such system of collective security as the League to Enforce Peace was proposing.[16] But even they stressed that only the returning Christ could effect a lasting peace and only after humanity had been redeemed. Riley therefore emphasized that all who would place their trust in "man-made thrones and administer man-made laws," rather than trusting in the returning Christ alone, were despising God and his law and were being counted on the side of the Antichrist.[17] Gaebelein echoed this charge by stressing that interest in "man-made peace," progress, and prosperity was indicative of the prophesized "'Man's Day,'" that ultimate stage of the "church age" when "man more and more defies God and His Word, and deifies himself." Gaebelein was assured that it was all "used by the god of this age, Satan, to lull a secure world to sleep," to convert ever more people into thinking that a secular world organization, without reference to the Christian plan of salvation, could solve all the problems with which the war-torn world was burdened.[18]

Gaebelein also exerted himself mightily to popularize the second major League-related motif of dispensationalism, the "iron and clay" prophecy of the Book of Daniel. To dispensationalists, the clay in this prophetic motif signified the latter-day rise of democracy and popular sovereignty, and the iron represented the actual, autocratic anti-Christian ruler who reigned behind the appearance of popular rule. This motif depicted socialism, the newer liberalism, and the Social Gospel as but many different forms of modern autocracy, legitimated through democratic catch-phrases but really predicated on a concentrating of coercive powers in a single directing center. When Gaebelein and others related this perception to wartime events, they conflated the increasingly collectivist practices of wartime administrations (including that of Woodrow Wilson), the churchly internationalists' calls for a socially reformist League of Nations, and the theories and practices of socialism and communism. Socialism came in this conflation to equal communism, and communism was understood as the modern form of exceedingly autocratic rule.[19]

Theologically, Gaebelein traced collectivist social reform to the modernists' immanentist theologies about human ethical insight. He stressed that the very dynamics of these theologies would inevitably produce a socialistic despotism. Because modernism put its faith in human ability and natural moral sense, it was by definition incapable of building safeguards against the misuse of coercive political structures that was as inevitable as humans were sinful. At the same time, modernist theology fostered entirely unrealistic expectations and predisposed peoples to accept any and all means for the satisfaction of such expectations. An inevitably ineffective regimen of collective security under the League of Nations would thus eventually develop into a futile attempt to control human sin and its international results through coercive agency. The socially reformist dimensions of the League would likewise yield a gradually ever more tyrannous directorate, still perhaps actuated by the ethical promptings of modernist theologians but forced to have recourse to unprecedented worldwide coercion because unredeemed humanity simply could not otherwise produce the expected millennial results.[20] According to Gaebelein, the inevitable culmination would be the eventual reorganization of the whole world into one great "World Communist Internationale, in which our civilization and religion will be totally destroyed."[21]

Dispensationalists therefore alleged, as Riley put it, that in their Social Gospel and League of Nations enthusiasm liberal clergy were redefining the Second Coming as "social service," "socialism," and "social reconstructionism" that could only be carried out by an international organization, replete with a "common king" and a "world's capital."[22] Or, as W. W. Fereday put it, the arrival of a socially activist League of Nations marked the beginning of the prophesied final era of earthly history, because it prefigured the premillennial world order where "government will control religion, trade, and the people themselves" and "will leave no room for freedom of thought, or independence of action in any direction whatever." It would end up under the control of "Satan's super-man," who would, in turn, grasp worldwide control.[23]

By making these kinds of claims, the dispensationalists endeared themselves to the burgeoning antisocialist and anticollectivist movement of secular conservatives. As of yet, the dispensationalists did not become politically active members of that movement but preferred instead to conduct their polemics in their own, rather isolated communities. Their message, however, was nearly identical to that which was proffered in increasingly shrill terms by secular conservatives. The wartime experience of greatly increased state powers, the rise of Russian Bolshevism, *and* the social reform plans offered by secular and churchly enthusiasts of the League of Nations were all aspects of a rise of collectivism that catalyzed the political right to oppose the League. To many a political conservative on both sides of the Atlantic, the League (and particularly its International Labor Organization) appeared to be the socialists' chosen, indirect vehicle for the socialization of all capitalist societies that socialists had thus far not achieved through regular electoral or legislative processes in their separate nation-states. For conservative politicians, the fight against the League was a continuation of their fights against socialism and collectivism at home.[24]

It was easy for dispensationalists to echo the secular conservative clamor in their own, separate communities of discourse. This was because most of them had imbibed in some ways the traditions of clerical laissez-faire, those social and political tenets of pre–Social Gospel evangelicalism that had celebrated capitalism and private enterprise as dimensions in God's law and natural law, and had restricted the churches' social effort to various kinds of local social service and charity work.[25] The anticollectivist argument flowed naturally enough also from the "clay and iron" motif of dispensationalist speculation, and once that motif was married with clerical laissez-faire, it proved a potent one.

Dispensationalist commentators employed one specifically war-related accusation when they advanced these various interpretations. Whether they were discussing collective social reform, collective security, or the broader implications of modernist theology, the prophecy conferees tended to conflate these with the German quest for world dominion. This linkage of their domestic churchly rivals with the nation's foreign enemies helped at once to affirm the dispensationalists' pro-war and anti-German credentials and to draw attention to their core charge that modernism was alien and as such as disastrous in its theological as in its political manifestations. It was a necessary conflation to make, because the dispensationalists' deprecation of slogans such as "making the world safe for democracy" and "ending all wars" had already led to prominent and well-publicized liberal accusations of unpatriotic defeatism.[26]

Thus, the prophecy investigators tried to turn the tables by painting the liberals' war enthusiasm as but another form of the disastrous deification of human culture and collective effort that had prompted Germany, in the first place, to start the war. Before the world war, Germany had been the nation most eager with this secular hope to regenerate the world, but all that its scientific and collectivist "Kultur" had in the end managed to yield was war and tyranny as the methods of change. This was inevitable, said the dispensationalists, because German "Kultur" had lost its touch with God and attempted to substitute purely human values and efforts in God's place. The same applied to all other products of German philosophy—to the so-called higher, or scientific, criticism of the Bible; to social evolutionary thought and collective social reform; *and* to collective international effort for whatever ends. Each was inevitably an anti-Christian and destructive proposition, no matter who endorsed it and no matter under what humanitarian justifications.[27]

The prophetic conferees were, in other words, convinced that whichever side won the war, it would form the world league that prefigured the Antichrist's world empire. They wanted to appear patriotic and thus predicted that Germany would not emerge victorious, yet they were equally unanimous in claiming that German ideas *would* win. German ideas would have their apotheosis in the coming world league, and it would be the clerical and political liberals, steeped in German science and philosophy as they were, believers in collective human ability, who would act as the agents. Liberal clergy had been the first to be corrupted by German theology and the initial media for its spread in the Anglophone world; therefore, they would also be the ones that would establish the sway of those ideas in new, purpose-built world institutions.[28]

Important as it was, the German motif remained, however, largely a wartime flourish. After the Armistice, modernist theology continued, of course, to be traced to its actual roots in German philosophy and natural sciences, but in other respects attention soon switched away from the specifically German dimension of prophecy. For example, wartime portrayals of the German kaiser as the Antichrist disappeared very quickly from dispensationalist discourse. What concerned the dispensationalists once the Paris peace conference began its deliberations were the substantive contents of their prophetic interpretation.

The Dangers of "Yoke Fellowship"

The plenipotentiaries of the victorious Allied and Associated Powers gathered in Paris for the making of the peace and the drafting of the League of Nations Covenant immediately after the dispensationalists' wartime conference series, in January and February 1919. It was, as the dispensationalists kept constantly reminding everyone, an assemblage of modernist or liberal Christians (Woodrow Wilson, Lord Robert Cecil, and David Lloyd George), professed atheists (Georges Clemenceau), and people of Catholic or pagan faiths (much of the rest). The dispensationalists drew attention to the facts that the conference was not opened with prayer, that it did not at any point beseech the help of the Almighty, and that neither the peace treaty nor the Covenant of the League contained the words "God" or "Deity."[29] Only eight predominantly non-Christian states were immediately admitted to the League (Japan, Persia, Hedjaz, Siam, China, India, Liberia, and Haiti), but many more were Catholic, and given the liberal terms for admitting new members, it was likely that the ratio of Protestants to non-Protestants would grow more and more unfavorable to the Protestants as time went by.

Given these facts, several leading dispensationalists began immediately to assail the emerging League Covenant as an unnatural "yoke fellowship" (2 Cor. 6:14) between Christians and pagans. In what turned out to be barely disguised fusions of dispensationalist theology and ethnic prejudice, they stressed that "God appoints lands and peoples to each other" and "assigns the races to their sections of the earth" and that all attempts to break or obscure these divinely set "primary lines of division" would inevitably lead to disaster. More particularly, as J. C. Massee, a New York Baptist pastor, put it, the "Malay and Mongol" belonged to Asia, "negroes (three varieties) to Africa," the "Slavic races—borderland between Asia & Europe," and "Semitic races to the Eastern shore of the Mediterranean." Europe and America were "divided in half—north and south," so that the "Anglo Saxon, Teuton" were to live in the north and the "Latin races" in the south.[30]

Whether so strictly segregated or not, dispensationalists averred that any mixing of the races and religions was bound to reduce the League itself to impotence, given the assumed racially and morally inferior qualities of the pagan member states. It was also bound to further erode the purity of the church and of all Christian nations. "How can God bless these nations," asked Gaebelein, "who continue in idolatries, who defy His laws? Can He bless professing Christian nations, banded together in pact with heathen nations? . . . And what will be the effect of such a league upon the conscience of the heathen nations? Will it make them more willing to turn to the true and living God. . . . Or will they, through being allied with professing 'Christian nations,' accepting the Western civilization, being part of a great brotherhood, think themselves right and in no need of that which is their greatest need, the Gospel of Jesus Christ?"[31]

It was that same notion that caused the Moody Bible Institute's James M. Gray to argue that the United States should not join the League lest its Christian nature be corrupted through a "partnership with nations over whose head the sword of divine justice is impending, that she be not a partaker of their sins."[32] John Roach Straton, a New York fundamentalist leader, was similarly prompted to decry all interethnic and interfaith cooperation that did not affirm "the sovereign Lordship of God Almighty,"[33] and J. C. Massee was inspired to brand the League of Nations "a deliberate effort to dethrone God in the earth," the linear descendant of the original Tower of Babel in that it attempted "to make the judgment of the crowd a moral law." "If I had any fear or trembling for my nation today," he wrote, "it would be this, that we are entering into alliance with all sorts and conditions of people. . . . We who are a professedly Christian nation are about to enter a league of nations, and into an international alliance, with nations that are altogether pagan." God would punish America for that, Massee was certain, for Christian nations were "under obligation to foreswear any alliance with a pagan nation."[34]

When the hit man of Southern Baptist fundamentalism, J. Frank Norris, went on to denounce the League as an organization controlled by mostly Catholic southern Europeans, and therefore ultimately beholden to the pope, he was developing yet another dimension of the same argument. Some others at the prophecy conferences followed Norris, and on occasion some of them even suggested that the Antichrist might well turn out to be the pope. The more the daily press reported on the Vatican's immediate postwar attempts to join the League (in which it failed), the more worried and shrill the dispensationalists became in their speech.[35]

The League membership of Catholic and pagan countries underlined the core dispensationalist prediction that the final world empire would establish a new, syncretistic false religion. This prediction was given apparent added corroboration by the fact that the Versailles conference coincided with the creation of the Inter-Church World Movement, the most ambitious interdenominational organization of the modernist Protestants thus far. The liberal clergy intended it for the worldwide application and dissemination of their Social Gospel agenda. This coincidence was of great consequence to the dispensationalists, given that many of the interchurch apologists portrayed their organization as the religious ally, arm, or concomitant to the political

League of Nations. As the dispensationalists saw it, these two liberal, modernist organizations would have at their disposal all the media necessary for the creation not only of the political empire of the world but also of the prophesized false religion with which this empire was to be imbued. The syncretistic nature of this emerging false world faith was only underlined by the presence of pagans in the League.[36]

Sometimes these fears were also linked to anti-Semitic utterance. This formed a minor additional strain of the League critique of some prophecy conferees, although it must be stressed that neither its tenor nor its proliferation yet approached the anti-Semitic conspiracism for which some dispensationalists became notorious in the 1930s. Yet dispensationalists sometimes had recourse to the *Protocols of the Elders of Zion*, the malicious concoction of Russian anti-Semites that purported to be the secret blueprint for world conquest of a cabal of what the evangelicals called "apostate Jewry," that is, secular, nonobservant Jews.[37] The *Protocols* dated to 1903, but they were republished after World War I, and only then did they have a major impact on Western Christian discourse, including prompting some dispensationalists to start seeing the Antichrist's empire as an apostate Jewish empire.

This interpretation violated traditional dispensationalist theory, which had taught that Jews would indeed return to their Promised Land in the latter days, unconverted, and would make a pact with the head of the Antichristian empire, only to be persecuted by this empire and almost annihilated before their Messiah would return. It had not been part of the traditional understanding of dispensationalism that the Antichrist himself would be a Jew or that his empire would be imbued with a Jewish form of religion. On the contrary, many dispensationalists had long been noted philo-Semites and had celebrated the wartime renascence of Jewish national spirit and the Zionist pursuit of a national return to the Promised Land. They had also testified to the eschatological role of religiously observant, Messianic Jews, even if they had also insisted on carrying out an aggressive conversion effort among them.[38]

But by World War I, some dispensationalists had begun increasingly to draw parallels between "apostate Christianity" and "apostate Judaism." Even philo-Semites like Gaebelein started to point out that modernist Christian clergy and Reform Jewish rabbis were appearing on the same platforms, and that both seemed to be endorsing collectivist schemes for world betterment. Also, much as the dispensationalists celebrated the Zionist revival of Jewish nationhood, many of them insisted on pointing out that most Zionists had no more use for the Triune God than the modernist Social Gospelers. Some dispensationalists suspected collusion between the founders of the League of Nations and the alleged Jewish world conspiracy, collusion pregnant with prophetic implications. This suspicion was later fed from the fact that through its Palestine Mandate (1922), the League was central in giving Palestine to the Jews as a National Home. Also, the role of Great Britain, a League member, in conquering Jerusalem and in giving out the Balfour Declaration, which promised a "Jewish National Home"—both in 1917— came to be seen as portents of a specifically Jewish League of Nations.[39] One Congregationalist minister even claimed that the League was likely to be headquartered in Jerusalem and that President Wilson would head it from there, together with the Zionists.[40]

With time, there developed out of these general, groping ruminations the clearly anti-Semitic conspiracism to which some of the leading dispensationalists—William B. Riley, most prominently—resorted in the interwar years. By then, "apostate Jewry" was increasingly seen as the mastermind behind most of the socialist, communist, and New Liberal movements, often allied with "international finance" and with some sinister Masonic and occult directorate (it usually went by the name Illuminati). The League of Nations, too, came to be lumped in with these schemers.[41] Thus, Riley was representative of the dispensationalist form of conspiracist anti-Semitism when in the 1930s and 1940s he claimed that the *Protocols* proved the existence of a "diabolical plan" by a secret directorate of apostate Jews. According to him, these Jews had befriended Gentile politicians and, for some time, dictated policies; ultimately it was they who were responsible for the spread of communism and all spiritual degeneration. All of it, Riley affirmed by the 1930s, was designed to assist in the eventual takeover of the world by the "Zionist lord" and world dictator of the great final Antichristian world empire.[42]

When these anti-Jewish arguments were added to the anti-Catholic, antipagan, and antisocialist arguments, the dispensationalist case was complete. This took place during World War I, and once that war ended and the League of Nations began to be set up, most dispensationalists believed that the final world empire was imminent and that the League anticipated it. The League was not, however, taken to be the final empire itself. Christians had to be "raptured" from the Earth before the Antichrist could set up his dominion in such an empire, it being impossible to fully subordinate the world to transcendental evil as long as converted Christians remained in the world. There would also have to emerge an alignment of nations that was "wholly different" from the then-existing war alliances; for if based on these alliances, the coming League would contain nations not formerly parts of the Roman Empire. Such nations did not play a role in prophecy and could not therefore be in the final world empire.[43] With a few exceptions, the dispensationalists stressed that the United States, in particular, was not destined to be a part of the League, because it had not been part of the Roman

Empire. Although in the present it should continue to witness for the Christian religion, it did not play a role, as a nation, in the end times.[44]

With such qualifications, the dispensationalists did not believe that the formation of the League could be prevented. Whether it was the prophesied final world empire in embryo or an immediate forerunner of it, the dispensationalists were convinced that its emergence had been foreordained and was beyond human power to prevent. In their own communities, they nevertheless sided with those in the political arena who fought against the League, and especially against American membership in it. Aspects of their separationist cultural posture and theology militated against direct political activism, and they were agreed on the inevitability of American nonparticipation in any case; yet the dispensationalists still insisted on relating their wartime prophetic commentary to the specific League that was being debated in the secular sphere after the League Covenant had been drafted in mid-1919. This was because they deemed it sinful to assist the coming of the Antichrist in any way and therefore felt duty-bound to arouse awareness about the League in as many people as possible, so as to strengthen the "things that remained" of a remembered, truly Christian America unentangled with heathen nations. The reverse was also true: It was positively righteous to save people from being corrupted by the liberal theology that undergirded the League's idea of internationalism. As Gaebelein put it early on, even if Christians could not influence the final result, "our God does not forget our work, our faithfulness and the love we show."[45]

Most secular politicians knew little about the flurry of dispensationalist commentary on the League that coincided with the League fight in the Senate, for few of them read dispensational journals. In secular newspapers, the dispensationalists' statements were only rarely given attention. In letters that they sent to politicians and conservative publicists, some dispensationalist-minded constituents did repeat the arguments that were advanced by their preachers, and sometimes copies of such preachers' sermons found their way to political opponents of the League. But it was not as a direct influence on the secular League polemic that the dispensationalist conversation mattered; rather, this conversation laid the ground, set the categories, and devised the rhetorical constructs for a distinct dispensationalist form of anti-internationalism that would continue to influence the thinking of a sizable portion of devout American Christians into the twenty-first century. After World War I, popular and diluted versions of prophecy thought lodged themselves in American popular culture as an apparently permanent deposit, which was to have significant political repercussions.[46]

The World Christian Fundamentals Association in the League Fight

No major fundamentalist luminaries became members of the secular anti–League of Nations organizations, because that would, indeed, have violated their emphasis on Christian separateness. But many did echo these organizations' message in their sermonizing, pamphleteering, and article writing. This took place as soon as the League advocates moved from theory to implementation and was sustained throughout the political debate on the ratification of the League Covenant. The League was now denounced not just as an eschatological portent, an idea, or a symbol, as heretofore, but as the specific organization whose structures and areas of competence had been settled, and for which the United States' adherence was asked. The polemic also found a new organizational umbrella that magnified its impact as it took the message to every local community where dispensationally minded individuals were to be found.

It was of some importance for the spread and perpetuation of dispensationalist anti-internationalism that the final draft of the League of Nations Covenant reached the United States just when the organization of the fundamentalist movement into the World Christian Fundamentals Association (WCFA) took place. The WCFA's foundational conference was held in Philadelphia from May 25 to June 1, 1919, just after the content of the final League Covenant had become public and only ten days before President Wilson formally presented it for senatorial debate and hoped-for ratification. Given the dispensationalist promptings of the bulk of its membership, it was inevitable that the WCFA would at such a time focus on the final world empire and its apostate faith.

Being strictly a doctrinal document, the manifesto which the WCFA conference issued on the five fundamentals of Christian doctrine did not itself touch on international or political matters, and of course not on the League of Nations specifically. Given the interpretive matrix that the prophecy conferences had already established, even apparently purely political issues such as this were, however, affected by the manifesto's frame of reference. In other words, the WCFA's doctrinal statement's denunciation of liberal, modernist theology and social action implied a denial also of churchly political internationalism. Had not the dispensationalists been saying that throughout the war? Had they not been stressing for years that the pursuit of perpetual peace and social advance through an international political institution was one aspect of the fundamentals of faith being ignored and violated?

At the conference, Riley, who was chosen as WCFA president, pegged his explanation of the fundamentals on the distinction between those, like himself, who believed that the church was "called out" of all worldly pursuits, no matter how ethical, and those modernists who held that the church was on the way to becoming "co-extensive with the world," already fast transforming the world's structures through its own agency. The difference, Riley stressed, was not just that between believers and nonbelievers on biblical inerrancy, the Virgin Birth, or the existence of Satan. It was about two diametrically different approaches to solving the problems of the world—one approach trusting the agency of a returning Christ, and the other trusting unredeemed human nature.[47]

Riley was echoed by George E. Guille, an originally Southern Bible teacher from the Moody Institute, who stressed that Satan was not in Hell at all but rather busy at work in the world, in all its human-made institutions, and the author of all its schemes of improvement, including those of modernist Christianity. Guille did not mention the League of Nations by name, but he did imply it when he denounced all "world-mending" by political institutions. John Roach Straton condemned all "earth-bound, time-limited, humanitarian program[s]" and world-bettering social service organizations, whereas I. M. Haldeman stressed that it was not for the church to "condone" or "convert" the world, nor to reform it through "ethical culture" or "government by righteousness." The church could only "condemn" a world that trusted its own failed reason and did not admit that it needed Christ's direct rule to solve its problems.[48]

This kind of general juxtaposition of world mending by human institutions and of world change by the returning Christ continued after the WCFA's founding conference. It continued in denominational newspapers and theological journals and, most important of all, on the nationwide speaking tour that Riley and several of his closest associates undertook soon after the founding conference. Though planned in advance, the six-week, eighteen-city, 7,000-mile tour happened to coincide with the much better known tour on which President Wilson embarked soon after the final League Covenant had been submitted to the U.S. Senate. Riley and others visited most of the places where Wilson presented his arguments, and most often their appearances took place right on the heels of the departing president. Thus, on September 18, Riley spoke in Seattle and in Tacoma, only five days after Wilson's visit there. On September 20 he visited Portland, again just five days after Wilson, and on September 25 he followed on Wilson's heels to Berkeley, a week after the president's visit. Riley's tour of the West culminated at a meeting in Los Angeles where Wilson had spoken eight days earlier. After this, Riley's entourage moved back to the Midwest and eventually to the East Coast, again stopping at many of the places where Wilson had spoken on his way westward. Had he not suffered a stroke on October 2, Wilson would also have continued on to the Eastern states.[49]

With his trip, Wilson intended to convert the American people to the League of Nations. The WCFA, conversely, was touring to spread the word about premillennialism and to encourage conservative laity to rise up against the modernists not in politics but in their denominations and their schools. It did not intend specifically to trail or hound the president, or to concentrate on the League of Nations.[50] But Riley and his associates did address audiences that would just have read in their daily newspapers what Wilson had been saying or that may even have themselves listened to Wilson in person. Whether they wanted to or not, they could not but leave their hearers with a clear juxtaposition between the fundamentalist and the modernist/liberal visions of the world's future on their minds.

President Wilson concentrated on the technical aspects of the League Covenant that had raised the most opposition in the Senate. This meant that Wilson's main focus was on questions of collective peacekeeping and economic sanctions, the Monroe Doctrine, and national freedom to set tariffs and institute immigration restrictions. But he claimed also that there existed a "common will of mankind," which had come to insist on the precise institutions and procedures that the Covenant entailed, a will so sublime and irresistible that no responsible nation or leader could defy it and not "break the heart of the world." According to the president, the Covenant was the embodiment of this collective moral opinion of the world and indeed nothing less than the "instrument of divine Providence," for so fully had the peoples of the world internalized what was highest in Christian ethics that they were now its principal champions, and the politicians only the followers. Wilson therefore stressed—"with all the emphasis that I am capable of"—that the structure and substance of the League was "Christian and not pagan," that it was the only possible "program of civilization," and that it alone could banish distrust and war and better all aspects of the life of humankind. Above all, the president claimed that the peace and happiness of the world depended on this League and on its American ratification and leadership in particular, and that no worthy goals at home or abroad could be reached before the League had been placed in situ and had started working.[51]

Throughout, the president put special emphasis on the labor provisions of the International Labor Organization (ILO), a core part of the liberal churchmen's League concept. As finally structured, the ILO did not go as far as many of its churchly, socialist, and liberal protagonists had hoped. But by recognizing collective bargaining and the coequality of labor and employers, it devolved more political and industrial power to the working class; and by instituting a new charter (Article 427 of the peace treaty) of labor and industrial standards, it created a new, universally valid set of labor rights that it intended to enforce and police the world over. These were potentially revolutionary changes in how Western societies worked, and Wilson therefore pronounced the ILO not only a "great humane endeavor" but actually the single most important aspect of the new postwar world order. In most of his addresses, Wilson went to great lengths to stress that it was the ordinary working peoples of the world who understood the highest Christian and humanitarian ideals the best and how therefore they, in particular, were supremely entitled to that increase in political and economic power that only international social reform could give.[52]

Whether he believed it himself or was using it as a tool of persuasion, Wilson enunciated the very case that liberal theologians had been making ever since they had first discovered the global implications of the Social Gospel and of immanentist theology. His was an argument for perpetual peace and social alleviation born out of an organized humanity acting from a set of universally shared ethical values.

Riley on his tour, conversely, said that he pitied men who had "linked their fortunes to a failing enterprise." One such failing enterprise, stressed Riley, was the Social Gospelers' effort to infuse Christian ethical principles into the secular institutions of the age and thereby to reform the world. "Men talk about a civilization dominated by the spirit of Christ," Riley reminded his hearers. But "that is not the need of the hour! A civilization that professes to be Christian cannot save! Any program which proposes the exaltation of civilization despises the prophecy of Daniel to the effect that the civilization of this age will be ground to powder and driven from the face of the earth, as the chaff of the threshing." Furthermore, Riley put it that the only enterprise worth linking to was the enterprise of Jesus Christ and the only institution assured of success was that of the church that restricted itself to preaching the Gospel and to converting by the power of the Holy Ghost. All those, therefore, who would chain the church for the purposes of "advancing civilization, effecting world improvement, and giving the crown of such accomplishment the name of Christianity" were but trafficking in the "false prophecies of those who scorn His promised return to establish in the world a reign of righteousness—produced *not* by the propagation of culture but by the personal rulership of the Lord Himself."[53]

Put differently, Riley was saying that the more liberals tried to define their world improvement attempts with the name "Christian," the more they were obscuring the true fundamentals of the saving faith and actually crucifying Christ anew. Their transference of humanity's hopes from the returning

Christ to purely human institutions utterly denied the sole efficacy of Christ's work. The biblical reference to the "chaff of the threshing" (Dan. 2:35, 41) that Riley used in making this argument could not have left a shadow of a doubt in the minds of committed dispensationalists but he was referring also to the League of Nations—for those who knew the locus and dispensational interpretation of this quotation also knew that it, and therefore the whole line or reasoning that was pegged on it, referred to the prophecy on the Antichrist's world empire. Riley's listeners would have left his meetings with the idea firmly implanted in their minds that the time was, indeed, one for choosing (just as Wilson was saying it was), but it was the time for choosing between the "false prophecies" of world progress through human institutions that were the fruits of the Antichrist and the promise of a returning Christ and his millennial "world reign of righteousness."[54]

The clarity of this message notwithstanding, Riley's own conversation on the WCFA trip was not explicitly geared toward the League of Nations. A number of the other dispensationalist preachers who joined Riley on the tour *did* make the reference explicit. During and after the tour, several key leaders of the WCFA issued unambiguous statements in which they opposed the ratification of the League Covenant, either under all conditions or in the form in which it then stood. Exposed in many of these men's commentaries were not only the doctrinal dispensationalist bases of their anti-internationalism but also the surviving remnants of their belief in America as a Christian nation, now losing its self-knowledge because of the Social Gospel's redefinition of "Christianity" and "America" but still "the climax of all human efforts at government" and still with the God-given task of helping in the spreading of the true Gospel. These men still harked back to the days during the Spanish-American War of 1899 and the Chinese Boxer Rebellion of 1897 to 1901, when their advice had been heeded and America had acted unilaterally in support of the church's traditional missionary work.[55]

The most explicitly supportive of American unilateralism was James M. Gray, the Reformed Episcopalian head of the Moody Bible Institute. In his editorials in the widely circulated *Christian Workers Magazine*, he advised all Christians to send for the anti-League materials of the League for the Preservation of American Independence, the main publicity organization of the Irreconcilable camp. This organization advocated universal military training instead of the League, and Gray explicitly sided with this alternative program. By 1920 he even stated editorially that no Christian should support League ratification, because to do so would be tantamount to committing "national suicide." Instead, Gray advised all Christians to do all that they could to prevent the United States from joining a League that undermined its independence and was a prefiguration of the Antichrist's world despotism.

He did not deny that the United States should play a major role in world affairs (including a military role); only, he queried, "Did not her power in the late war lie in this, that she was free to arise when the crisis came, and to throw in her great influence on the side of the right as she saw it at the time?"[56]

Less pointedly but nevertheless significantly, *Our Hope*'s editor, A. C. Gaebelein, applauded the speeches of Henry L. Myers and Lawrence Y. Sherman, two senators critical of the League, and of the late President Theodore Roosevelt, the champion of great power nationalism and merely ad hoc international alliances. He attacked the pro-League speeches of the leader of the League to Enforce Peace and the National Committee on the Churches and Moral Aims of the War, former president William Howard Taft (whom he pointedly identified as a Unitarian). Furthermore, Gaebelein advised everyone to listen to the League's political opponents, whom he called "wise" and "very sensible" men of "the most intelligent class."[57]

Gaebelein had recourse to anti-Catholic and antipagan arguments as well, and he even issued a book-length denunciation of the League, *The League of Nations in the Light of the Bible*, which came out just as the Senate was immersed in its League debates. The book traversed all available dispensationalist arguments against the League but was held together by the core accusation that all schemes of purposive, collective reform betrayed but the "great delusion . . . that man, by his power, by using his resources, financial and otherwise, will succeed in making the world better, and find a way out of the horrible conditions which the race is now facing in every direction." According to Gaebelein, the "monster league" therefore obscured the "root of the whole matter," that is, that terrible world conditions were the result of sin and could only be removed once Christ himself had arrived to finally obliterate sin itself. The League must not be entered into lest the contrary, fallacious belief be thereby spread.[58]

In addition, J. C. Massee, one of the WCFA leaders who traveled with Riley on his tour, had recourse to antipapal and antipagan arguments. In his late 1919 sermons, Massee stressed that for Christian nations to build postwar reconstruction upon a new system of "international relations" was just as wrong in 1919 as it had been "forbidden to Israel" long ago to mix with the Gentiles. Christian America had to retain its "aloofness" and freedom of action, for it was no more allowed to compromise "its moral value to the world" than Israel of old; if it did compromise, it would be just as severely punished as ancient Israel. Similarly, it was wrong for a Christian America to be, as he implied President Wilson was doing, "kissing the Pope's toe," which was what membership in the League would amount to, because it was a papally controlled League that imperiled free churches, free speech, free schools, and free marriages the world over.[59]

In a book published in the middle of the Senate's League fight, Massee further denounced what he called the "man-made programs of peace," among them "the organization of the league of nations," that were constructed by "dreaming idealists." In particular, he demanded that the League's collective security regimen not be accepted, that the United States not be forced to carry that "big stick" that others were proposing to put in American hands, "with which to police and protect the world and maintain the permanence of peace." America must not consent to this, Massee stressed, for with it would go enormous expenditures for maintaining the army and the navy, universal military training, and militaristic teaching as part of school curricula. All of it was "foolish" and a "vain thing"; it would be much better if the United States just kept lending its protection and assistance to Christian missionaries.[60]

Finally, Massee's fellow Baptist, Cortland Myers, came out with the most extreme denunciation of all things connected with the League, its Covenant, and the broader Versailles peace settlement. Speaking at a special conference of Baptist dispensationalists in June 1920, he denounced the Covenant as "the most atheistic, infidel document that was ever printed in this world," the product of a "sordid, selfish transaction" by a group of "infidel" politicians acting more like animals than like the Christians that some of them professed to be. It was "a farce from beginning to end," averred Myers, and if the Senate would have accepted it, one would have been led to question "whether God had not dropped His scepter. . . . You would have had to change every page of human history, if God did not pass judgment on such a bit of infamy as that."[61]

These kinds of statements littered the road to the final defeat of the League Covenant in the Senate on March 19, 1920. After that defeat, they were heard less regularly but did occasionally crop up during the presidential election campaign that Wilson had dubbed the "great and solemn referendum" on the League. At that time, New York's John Roach Straton claimed to have toyed with the idea of running for president himself; and if he had done so, he said he would have offered a dispensationalist alternative to the League of Nations. This would have substituted for that political and interfaith organization a voluntary cooperative arrangement between Christian states. The U.S. government would come, Straton promised, "to the best possible understanding with all other nations of the earth, would seek cooperative efforts with them, under covenants and agreements that would recognize the sovereign Lordship of God Almighty and would seek to move the nations forward as subjects and servants of the Most High." Because "wars never settle anything," Straton would also have done everything possible to forward disarmament and discourage preparations for war, and he would have sent copious amounts of food and other humanitarian assistance to Europeans, "thus to win them to us by the bonds of that love which 'never faileth,' rather than by the fear and force which always fail."[62]

Similarly, other dispensationalists continued to insist that any and all future efforts to usher in a pacified and perfected world through human institutions were going to fail. They claimed that only "infidel" and "ignorant" preachers and politicians could still repose faith in the League, and they demanded that dispensationalists exert themselves in the public dissemination of the premillennial hope as the only alternative to a popular acceptance of the "world-betterment" ideology.[63]

Moreover, by this time some Pentecostals had started to echo the WCFA in their own separate polemic. The WCFA leaders absolutely refused to regard Pentecostals as Christians, because it was part of their beliefs that speaking in tongues and other charismatic occurrences had ceased after the passing of the Apostles and that therefore satanic forces probably used the Pentecostals. The WCFA would, therefore, have nothing to do with the Pentecostals. However, the Pentecostals were just as rooted in premillennialist dispensationalism as the evangelicals of the WCFA, and therefore they, too, joined in making all the arguments of dispensationalist anti-internationalism.[64] And because the Pentecostals were even more separatist and nonpolitical than non-Pentecostal dispensationalists, the Pentecostals did not enter the political debate at all, nor did they tend to approve of voting in elections. But even though their polemic was intramovement, it also significantly augmented the dispensational argument's reach among the faithful at the crucial moments in late 1919 and 1920 when the League of Nations Covenant was defeated in the Senate and then in the presidential poll.

Conclusion

The fundamentalists' and the Pentecostals' passionate engagement of the League of Nations idea exposed the tension that existed in both traditions between apolitical separatism on the one hand and continued interest in wielding culturalist power on the other. Pentecostals most emphatically, but also all dispensationalists in some form, maintained that Christians needed to separate themselves from the institutions of the secular world and from all its preoccupations and hopes. One should concentrate all one's thought and effort, they kept stressing, on the Triune God alone, and nothing else should either matter or impinge on one's existence. This requirement was at the very core of the dispensationalist worldview; and it was also at the very core of the dispensationalist argument against a League of Nations that they saw as a purely human device, the ultimate testament to human pretensions of self-sufficiency. They did not want any Christian to have anything to do with such a League.

Consistent with such a separatist posture, the dispensationalists organized no such political pressure groups like those that they would create later on in the 1920s and subsequently. Nor did they directly affiliate themselves with any existing political group of League critics. Nevertheless, in their own journals and at their prophetic conferences, they offered an unceasing, very passionate, and widely disseminated barrage of religious arguments against the League, and they often asked Christians to do everything in their power to oppose the League. No dispensationalist, indeed, thought that their polemics could prevent the creation of the League, nor did they set out to act in ways that tried to achieve that goal. On the contrary, dispensationalist theology regarded the establishment of an Antichristian world empire as inevitable. But it was entirely conceivable that if the dispensationalists publicly attacked the League, many of the spiritual issues that they thought were associated with this coming Antichristian empire and with its apparent precursor, the League, could be exposed and more and more people could be pried away from being deceived by its lures. That is why the League debate occasioned a rare explosion of culturalist polemic by ostensibly separatist and apolitical dispensationalists.

But there was another side to this: In their polemics against the League, the dispensationalists of the WCFA were also sketching a vision of an American political order and of America's proper place in the world that, they said, would take the place of the League once Americans returned to the "true" fundamentals of the Christian faith. That vision, as Straton suggested in his presidential plan, was a vision either of an America cooperating with like-minded Christian nations for godly ends or, as J. C. Massee preferred, an America that remained a separate, exemplary Christian nation shining its light onto the world, beckoning others to follow, and never consenting to have its freedom of action circumscribed by any other nation. Simply by sketching such alternatives for the League of Nations, the dispensationalists were beginning to assume cultural pretensions that militated against their purported apolitical stance. A few years later, this renewed culturalist interest translated into direct political work over the teaching of evolution in public schools, but the preconditions for that later participation in politics were, in fact, laid during the religious League controversy.

The importance of the dispensationalists' prolonged campaign against the League of Nations can therefore hardly be overestimated. Even if it was mainly rhetorical, the campaign took place at that crucial juncture in the history of the world, and of American Protestantism, at which the perimeters were set for the twentieth-century encounter with all aspects of an apparently triumphant modernism. What the dispensationalists then learned formed the irreducible core of their approach to international organizations and to internationalism as an idea, symbol, and aspiration. They then forged an abiding conflation of modernist theology and newer political liberalism. The whole fundamentalist/modernist controversy—arguments, enemy images, alliances—was in fact rehearsed during these debates on the League of Nations, and these debates also created that dispensationalist Christian anti-internationalism that was to abide ever after as a potent subspecies and undercurrent to much of American nationalism. That it was based on the premillennialist view of history, which expected little good from human efforts, did not alienate the dispensationalists from public engagement. Rather, it was precisely because their opposition to modern internationalism was based on such fixed doctrinal grounds that the dispensationalists became such passionate anti-internationalists that before long they would take their fight into politics. For them, opposition to modern internationalism was just as important a part of Christian defense and propagation as any other.

CHAPTER THREE

〜〜〜〜⌒

Calvinists: Contesting the Public Means of Grace

The creedally oriented conservatives of the Calvinist tradition were just as critical of the League of Nations as were the leading dispensationalists. Their contributions to Christian anti-internationalism issued from a biblical literalism rooted in the traditional confessional orthodoxies of the Reformed tradition. Being highly church centered, these Calvinists outlined their case in theological journals, scholarly sermonizing, and denominational pamphleteering—of which the majority of Americans was largely unaware. They joined the political debate over League ratification no more than did the dispensationalists, but in their own community, they did develop a cogent confessional version of Christian anti-internationalism that supplemented and redirected the dispensationalists' argument.

Three distinct varieties of this uniquely Calvinist anti-internationalism were evident in the League debates. These largely mirrored the confessional distinctives of the three main clusters of the Reformed tradition in the United States. First, the Presbyterian Church (North), the Reformed Presbyterian Church (the "Covenanters"), and the Christian Reformed Church formed the most traditionalist and strictly confessional grouping, rooted in the Westminster and Heidelberg Confessions, in the public theologies of Princeton Theological Seminary, and increasingly in the so-called Kuyperian or Dutch school of Calvinism. Their stress was on the Christian's cultural mission to conquer the world. Second, the Southern Presbyterian Church stood for largely the same confessions but modified them in favor of a distinctively sectional aversion to corporate churchly essaying into politics. Third, the Northern and Southern Baptist conventions, which always contained a strain of Arminianism but were predominantly Calvinist in theology by 1919, proffered a rather weaker Calvinist argument that was significantly shaped by Baptist distinctives. In addition, there persisted a definite Calvinist minority in the Protestant Episcopal Church, but its ecclesiastical structures had been so fully taken over by various strains of liberalism that it yielded practically no conservative Calvinist argument.[1] This limited conservative Calvinist anti-internationalism to Presbyterians, the Christian Reformed, and some Baptists.

Their very real doctrinal differences aside, conservatives in each of these three major clusters of Calvinism put forward a case against the League of Nations and against modern secular internationalism that cohered around a very specific Calvinist worldview. Given that each of these denominations, except the Southern Baptist Convention, officially supported League ratification, the existence of this distinctly theological counterargument within their fold can be seen as an aspect of a conservative fight to take back control of their denominations and the self-definition of the Calvinist tradition from the modernists. In addition, Calvinist anti-internationalism must be seen as the expression of deeply held theological suppositions on the illegitimacy of all the organizations in the secular world that were engaged in such expansive projects of world reform as the liberals envisioned for the League of Nations.

Varieties of American Calvinism

There were many Calvinists in the World Christian Fundamentals Association, but on the whole the confessional Reformed tradition did not lend itself to the dispensationalist view of the League of Nations as the end-times world empire. This did not mean, however, that Calvinist anti-internationalism was any the less rooted in a highly prescriptive eschatological view of history. Conservative, nondispensational Calvinists tended to be postmillennial; that is, they expected the physical reappearing of Christ to be preceded by the prophesied Kingdom of God, during which the entire world would become Christian and would remain at peace for a thousand years. Postmillennialist Calvinists maintained that God had not only preserved the elect through personal, saving grace but had also sufficiently restrained the operations of evil through "common" and "public grace" to make it possible for the elect gradually to transform the world into an ever-fuller approximation to a perfected Creation. On the basis of the core Calvinist tenet of the sovereignty of God, they saw common grace as an aspect of redemption that was parallel to the redemptive operation of the Holy Spirit in the elect—the universal principle complementing the individual, so that all Creation would tend toward its ultimate teleology in restored unity with God.[2]

A significant number of Calvinist traditionalists were preterist in their eschatological orientation. The term "preterition" meant, quite simply, something that was past or beyond. It was primarily used to denote the past election of some and not all, but in the traditional Calvinist interpretation of prophetic writings it also referred to the already fulfilled character of the specific prophetic signs that were given in the Bible. More often than not, the preterists believed that the crucial point in time had been the destruction of the Second Temple (70 C.E.) and the attendant wars and persecutions; what remained thereafter was the gradual evangelization of the world and the final conquest over Satan that a personally reappearing Christ would complete. However, the period between Christ's first Advent and His final appearing (or *Parousia*) was not a period free of evil. According to the preterist interpreters, it was a period during which the power of evil was being constantly more and more circumscribed and bound by the church, yet also a period when the enemies of the Christian faith would eventually become emboldened and would try to usurp the prerogatives of the church. This development was expected toward the end of world history, just before the Second Coming.[3]

Those Calvinists who did not subscribe to this view tended to be so radically postmillennial that they believed the biblical sketch of the pre-*Parousia* "signs of the times" to be more in the nature of allegories or symbols of spiritual realities than historical signposts. Those individuals who affirmed this view, like Benjamin B. Warfield, the influential spokesperson of the Princeton Theology, regarded the millennium as but a description of the state of believers after death and before resurrection (the "intermediate state"), or they used the term to refer to the church's work of bringing the world into an ever-closer approximation to the blessedness that awaited believers at the end of history, when they would be in full inheritance of the Kingdom of God.[4] In other words, the radically postmillennialist Calvinists agreed with the preterist ones that the Kingdom of God was already present in the world in a "now, not yet" fashion. They believed that the Kingdom was being gradually constructed "by the work of the Holy Spirit in the church and through the Gospel" and that this construction would be completed once Christ returned.[5]

Conservative and liberal Calvinists alike subscribed to this view. Many a version of Kingdom Theology grew out of the concept of common grace, and many Social Gospelers continued to employ the concept as they pursued world change through domestic and international social reform. The difference between the liberal and conservative renditions was that the conservatives insisted on a literal, church-centered approach whereas the modernist liberals increasingly immanentized the public means of grace; redefined the competencies of the church; and injected other, extra-ecclesiastical instruments into the basically shared effort. That modernist redefinition was at the very core of the profound, prolonged, and pervasive intra-Calvinist contention that characterized the denominational discourse(s) of most kinds of Calvinists well into the twentieth century. This ecclesiastical, soteriological, and public theological contention—played out in debates over Higher Criticism versus biblical literalism, over modernist missionary efforts versus traditional evangelism, over the proper nature of Christian education, *and* over the League of Nations—went to the very core of the Calvinist self-image and was therefore both prolonged and often exceedingly bitter.

Distinct differences of emphasis were evident between Presbyterians, Christian Reformed, and Calvinist Baptists. The least consistent were the Baptists, who did not operate from a generally accepted confessional text and were therefore attracted by mild Calvinism. The Baptist distinctives of soul liberty and congregational autonomy militated against unambiguous and authoritative doctrinal statements, and even those Baptists who did affirm a given confession (most often a Calvinistic confession) tended in practice to move into the Arminian orbit.[6] However, these very emphases lent themselves to a conservative theological position just as easily as they could be used to argue for the Social Gospel.

Thus, conservative Baptists could feel that they had firm doctrinal grounds for their aversion to all public theology that proposed new, organized, or coercive centers of authority, whether these be domestic or international, ecclesiastical or temporal. This aversion was especially pronounced in the Southern Baptist Convention, which was more conservative than its Northern counterpart and much less affected by modernism and the Social Gospel. Their relative conservatism meant that Southern Baptists did not need much to combat modernist or internationalist clergy within, but they did regard it as their duty to warn others of the deleterious effects of the Social Gospel. Among other things, this tended to make conservative Baptists into opponents of socialism and champions of a traditional, laissez-faire, and individualistic case for national habituation in conservative Christian thought forms. Their view of the church's cultural role was understated and predicated on the expectation that American freedoms would gradually, almost imperceptibly tend toward ever-fuller approximations of Baptist ideals.[7]

The Presbyterians and the Christian Reformed, conversely, being groups rooted in a specific written confession, had throughout American history championed a most direct and aggressive culturalism. In the mid–nineteenth century, this had led many of them to the Christianization campaigns of the so-called benevolent empire. And after the Civil War, it led many of them to the detailed legislative program of the National Reform Association, which had stood for sabbatarian, school prayer, and antidivorce legislation and had demanded the emendation of the Constitution so that it acknowledged the Christian God as the final authority in the land.[8] Alongside this "New School" enthusiasm for churchly social activism (part of which coalesced into the Social Gospel), there persisted throughout an "Old School" theological resistance. But even those erudite theologians under whose direction this resistance unfolded almost invariably affirmed that it was indeed the church's duty to infuse all areas of life and thought with the Calvinist message. The Old School disagreed with the Social Gospel redefinition of the message, and on some of the methods to be used, but it did not deny the primacy of the church in transforming temporal society and thought. By the late nineteenth century, the leading theologians of the Old School—those of the Princeton Theology—were, indeed, to be found in the forefront of those Calvinists who called for moral legislation and Christian education, and some of them even wanted the church corporately to take part in changing social and class conditions.[9]

Conservative culturalism was significantly further strengthened after the 1880s, when the one-time Dutch prime minister Abraham Kuyper began to exert his influence on both sides of the Atlantic. Kuyperianism, the early-twentieth-century rendition of confessional Calvinist culturalism to which he gave his name, demanded a return to aggressive culturalist campaigning and idea dissemination by confessional Calvinists. Because it combined a strictly traditionalist theology and a faith-based social reform agenda, it was acceptable to the Old School at Princeton. Moreover, Kuyperianism insisted on radically differentiating between the public and private spheres, on disallowing state authorities' interference in the latter, and on defining the private sphere so broadly that it encompassed all economic activities. This denial of the Social Gospel went to the very core of the conservative Calvinist position and was thus welcome among conservative Presbyterian and Christian Reformed activists.[10] Southern Presbyterians remained somewhat less enamored of the Kuyperian thesis, because their sense of Calvinism, like that of Southern Baptists, remained rooted in a sectional aversion to all churchly essaying into politics.[11]

When placed in this context, the liberal clergy's pursuit of world peace and progress through political institutions and sociopolitical reform appeared to conservative Calvinists as a usurpation of the culturalist mission of the church that insinuated into ecclesiastical discourse inappropriate human-made thought forms, aspirations, and expectations. Eventually, conservative Calvinists came to accuse liberal Protestants of having fastened upon the League of Nations as yet another secular vehicle for the spread and perpetuation of a modernist, Social Gospel theology that was in contravention to the fundamentals of the Reformed message and therefore likely to redound to the detriment of the Calvinist project of world Christianization. In other words, conservative Calvinist anti-internationalism emerged as one aspect of a confessional fight against the Social Gospel, and it was throughout infused with all those eschatological presuppositions that configured modernism and the Social Gospel as parts of a latter-day apostasy of Christendom. This view of modern internationalism had a well-formulated doctrinal expression decades before the League controversy broke out. And no one more clearly expressed its essential assumptions than Abraham Kuyper himself.

In his widely read 1898 Stone lectures at Princeton Theological Seminary, Kuyper denied the legitimacy of international political organizations that pretended to universalize Christian civilization through worldwide legislation. He traced churchly calls for these kinds of organizations to the alternate, non-Christian worldview of "modernism," the origins of which he, too, placed in the French Revolution and the radical Enlightenment. Like those premillennarians who were rooted in the dispensationalist matrix, Kuyper thought that this alternate worldview was taking over the Calvinist faith community under the names of the Social Gospel, modern philosophy, and New Theology, and that it included a definite deification of purely human competency, including the competency of the state and the international association of states. According to Kuyper, it was part of the modernist heresy that led to the construction of dictatorial regimes of coercion and to their false legitimation with Christian rhetoric and aspirations.[12]

This was an essentially "pagan" and "pantheistic" undertaking, Kuyper stressed: rooted in a "worship of the creature," explicitly challenging the Calvinist reposing of all trust in God alone, and offering a "ghastly caricature" of the Calvinist project of placing all life and thought under Christian control. No "one State could embrace the world," nor could all humanity be associated in "one world empire," because after the Fall, the universal sinfulness of humanity made impossible all such ideational unity of humanity that internationalists presupposed. Given the facts of unredeemed human nature, all attempts to bring about a pacific "world empire" were therefore bound to fail and could lead only to centralized coercion in such economic, scientific, and family matters for which internationalists had begun to call. All coercion in these matters was illegitimate, for God had specifically removed them from the competence of governments and reserved them for freely interacting individuals. To underline the world scale of the perceived menace (and exposing his ethnic prejudices in the process), Kuyper even borrowed the dispensationalist motifs of yoke fellowship and the Tower of Babel when he further stressed that ethnicities, which he labeled in the terms of the times as "Hottentots" and "Kaffirs," were incapable of self-government and democracy. They could not, therefore, be trusted with the coequality of power that an inclusive world empire would entail. All these facts pointed, according to Kuyper, to only one possible conclusion: "A world-empire neither cannot be established nor ought it to be."[13]

Thus, Kuyper insisted that the Christianization of all life and thought could take place through only two instruments. It could take place directly through the church, itself engaged in transforming all areas of human activity, or it could take place through the voluntary activities of individuals, all acting through their own vocations, who had been imbued by the church's message. Christianization could not, however, take place either through the (secular) state or through an international association of (secular) states. It was a rather radically anticollectivist agenda that he sketched, and theologically it refused to accommodate in any way the core assumptions and goals of the modernist Calvinists who championed the League of Nations. Indeed, by Kuyper's definition these modernist Calvinists were not Calvinists at all.

Whether in this Kuyperian rendition or in one of its other versions, the Calvinist bent for Christianizing all life, social and political as well as personal, obviously retained universalist presumptions. It was not opposed to internationalism on such an a priori basis as was dispensationalism; rather, it opposed one type of political and theological internationalism but not any number of other conceivable internationalisms. Given this internal tension, conservative Calvinists constantly had to renegotiate, restate, and contest the terms of their engagement with world change, and especially so after the Social Gospel had come out with its case for the League of Nations. By redefining the Kingdom of God not least in terms of international social reform, the Social Gospelers had explicitly challenged traditional Calvinist postulates; yet much as their conservative counterparts disapproved of the new interpretation, they could not issue blanket denunciations of the universal culturalist vision except to say that it involved a compromising of their own witness.

Therefore, once liberal Protestants began to offer their specific programs for a socially reformist and peacekeeping League of Nations, conservative Calvinists had a profound quandary to negotiate. They had to explain their long-standing deprecation of secular and modernist churchly world improvement, and they had to denounce the modernists' League proposals on a culturalist basis yet at the same time retain a culturalist orientation for themselves. The anti-League case(s) that arose out of that effort were far less obvious, far more complex and circuitous, than those offered by the dispensationalists—yet no less significant. Like the dispensationalist one, it was to be perpetuated into the twenty-first century.

The Conservative Calvinist Quandary

The conservative Calvinists' quandary was evident, first of all, in the editorial stance taken by the *Presbyterian*, the leading voice of the conservative section of Northern Presbyterianism. This journal, usually consistently conservative on theology and cultural issues, was the flagship of orthodox, traditionalist Calvinists, and it did more to disseminate strictly doctrinal confessionalism than probably any other comparable publication. But when the *Presbyterian* came to assess the early sketches for the League of Nations, it was rent by its confessional deprecation of secular institutions and its urge to infuse all institutions with Christian content.

At first the *Presbyterian* endorsed President Woodrow Wilson's Fourteen Points, including the final point, which talked about a postwar association of nations. It also voiced support for all other plans that aimed at war prevention and the reduction of international mistrust, and it pronounced the proposed League a good project "if properly constructed" and if kept "simple." When the Versailles peace treaty was presented to the world, the journal predicted optimistically that the treaty might usher in "a period marked by life, liberty, and joy," and it even opened its pages to profoundly immanentist guest articles that celebrated the League as a road to a new world "united by the ties of universal brotherhood, animated by one spirit, one common life, and one hope."[14]

At other times, the *Presbyterian* claimed that the League of Nations might instead turn out to be "the nation's danger." If it was entered into "in undue haste" and "on any condition," the journal stressed in August 1919, the United States might be bound to obligations from which it would later be impossible to disengage and that might seriously harm national interests. "A wrong action here may bind the nation hand and foot," the journal's editors supposed, and they counseled vigilance and careful consideration.[15] In this context, the League to Enforce Peace plan, which centered on the codification of international law and consortia of the major Western powers, seemed both safer and more realistic as a national policy than any League with legislative, administrative, and executive powers.[16]

More important, the *Presbyterian* argued that League enthusiasts were bound to fall short of their goals because these goals contravened essential Reformed dogma and, therefore, the laws of nature. The League enthusiasts' aim, in other words, was a "universal domain" that simply could not come to be as long as human sin remained in the world. "The attempt is not worth the trial," the *Presbyterian*, therefore, stressed in January 1919, because "universal domain might be successful in the hands of angels, but where will be the angels? Who would be the chief executive? Gabriel has not applied." The whole scheme reminded the editors of the "universal effort of the Tower of Babel to end world floods"; and it, like the tower episode, was bound to result in "failure and confusion," for "universal domain and perfect peace are beyond the reach of man. They will never be accomplished save by the power and personal presence of him who has the right to reign."[17]

Any attempt, moreover, to create a universal domain by the human efforts of an "international organization" would necessitate the creation of an overwhelmingly powerful "centralized power in the hands of a few." These few would have to coerce popular submission to their schemata on a global scale, which, in turn, "will mean the realization of the German idea by another and less direct route."[18] In the *Presbyterian*'s considered opinion, proper internationalism should therefore be confined to the traditional missionary effort, which set out to convert all and which, incidentally, would also increase the number of people who behaved virtuously in worldly pursuits. The League of Nations might indeed prove a blessing but, stressed the *Presbyterian*, this was of relatively small import in comparison with the blessings that would flow from a real conversion of the world to the Christian faith and the consequent comprehensive transformation of its structures and modes of thought. This did not mean that the League was without hope or validity; it meant only that its mechanisms for peacekeeping and reform could be but temporary, groping, and inadequate in themselves unless practiced in a world that had already been converted to Christianity.[19]

The Southern Presbyterians' counterpart of the *Presbyterian*, the *Presbyterian of the South*, publicized very much the same reservations. This journal never endorsed the specifics of the League of Nations Covenant's collective security arrangements, but it did deem a peacekeeping League "a great blessing to the world." However, the *Presbyterian of the South* stressed that collective security notwithstanding, the League could work only if it was composed exclusively of Protestant nations and even then only if it assured first of all that there would be absolute freedom of operation for those church and proselytizing efforts that alone could create peaceable and cooperating nations.[20] Because the Senate's debate was prolonged, the journal concluded that the League was slated for "signal failure" because it included "heathen nations," because it allegedly ignored the ineradicable fact of human sin, and because it refused to ground its structures, operations, and governing ideas in the supremacy of God. No permanent good could come from a "Peace Conference of merely human invention," one of the journal's contributors stressed in September 1919, for peace was not a human product, not something "that can be made to order at will" or "compelled into existence and safeguarded by the force of arms." Rather:

> [Peace] is a work of divine grace in the souls of individuals and thence to society and nations. So, then, until the effective peace-producing dynamic is introduced into the heart and will of man and he becomes "a new creation in Jesus Christ"—"created unto good works that God ordained that we should walk in them," there can be no peace of any lasting value. . . . The League of Nations is doomed to signal failure for the simple reason that there has been a most conspicuous ignoring of the fact of God on the part of any, and all, of the men at the peace table.[21]

The Presbyterian vacillation—both North and South—was still evident in January 1920, after months of very public deliberation on all aspects of the League Covenant. It was revealed clearly in an article contributed to the other major Northern Presbyterian publication, the *Princeton Theological Review*, which like the *Presbyterian* was edited by some of the Princeton faculty. In thirty-three pages of text on the "Problems of Peace," Daniel S. Gage managed to denounce the League of Nations on two different theological grounds and also to endorse it as a "majestic" experiment. On the one hand, the League appeared to Gage to be full of "transcendent glory" and "in reality, if not in name" to have established "as the world's future standard, the Law of Christ." Yet on the other hand, he felt compelled to warn that all human-made "empires and social structures"—and he specified the League of Nations as one of them—were doomed to eventual and utter failure because they refused to ground their ideology and activities in the Christian Gospel and in it alone.[22]

By thus welcoming human efforts at world pacification and reform and yet by also constantly offering the full-scale Christianization of all nations as the only ultimately workable solution, Presbyterian conservatives managed to witness to the essentials of their confession yet not appear out of touch with the popular aspirations of the moment. The same applied to leading Baptists' comments. On the whole, conservative nondispensational Baptists were somewhat more sympathetic to the League's collective security and social reform regimen than the *Presbyterian* and the *Presbyterian of the South*, but they too hedged their early and sustained endorsement with caveats about the ultimate insufficiency of peacekeeping efforts that were not grounded in the Christianization of the world. Conservative Baptists tended to argue that unredeemed humanity was incapable of meeting the ambitious goals that liberal League champions had sketched for international cooperation yet to also stress that precisely because the majority of humankind was unredeemed, it was necessary to maintain a powerful controlling center of collective international power. This fundatum led most conservative Baptists to embrace what came to be called the mild Reservationist position, that is, approval of collective security in principle but insistence on its limitation in practice. More often than not, Baptist conservatives also advocated the future further development of collective security in the direction of a distinctly alliance-based, Anglophone consortium of cooperating Christian powers.[23]

Revealingly, even the official (and rather liberal) journal of the Northern Baptists, the *Standard*, decided to endorse the League to Enforce Peace's (LEP's) plans rather than Wilsonian collective security. Although it came to acquiesce in the Wilsonian model, the journal never deviated from its preference for the LEP alternative.[24] The independent Baptist publication, the *Watchman-Examiner*, also endorsed the LEP program, particularly its advocacy of a world court. It publicized the LEP's activities on its pages and insisted that an aggressive propaganda and publicity campaign should be undertaken to persuade the American people of the need for LEP-style security cooperation.[25] The Cincinnati *Journal and Messenger*, the Richmond *Religious Herald*, and the *Baptist World* of Louisville were also supportive of a League of Nations in the mold of conservative rather than liberal internationalists. The *Journal and Messenger* was the most coherent of the three, with its unwavering endorsement of a Rooseveltian association of nations, one that would build on the wartime alliance and be limited to the further codification of international law.[26] So strong, indeed, was the Baptist sentiment on this point that even one leading premillennialist among them— Amzi C. Dixon, formerly with Spurgeon's Tabernacle in London—felt compelled to break ranks with the dispensational consensus and to endorse such a new collective security regimen.[27]

This embrace of an alliance-based collective security regimen also meant that conservative Baptists showed almost no sympathy toward the Irreconcilables, those sixteen senators who wanted to prevent League ratification on any and all terms. Throughout the League controversy, editorials and guest articles in all leading Baptist journals depicted and criticized the Irreconcilables as partisan politicians devoid of principles, actuated by revenge and spite, incapable of offering any constructive alternatives, and in default of a manifest need to construct some structure of organized international peace-keeping.[28] The *Watchman-Examiner* bemoaned their "puerile and childish" maneuverings, and the *Standard* claimed that they persisted in "narrow intellectual valleys" and made all "forward-looking men sick at heart."[29] The Baptist call, therefore, went out almost invariably—first, for the ratification of the League Covenant with reservations; and second, for the gradual further development of the League toward a more alliance-based organization more fully controlled by the Christian great powers.

One key exception to this rule was the controversial minister at the Temple Baptist Church in Philadelphia, Russell H. Conwell. This noted Christian nationalist and apologist for the Spanish-American War of 1899 absolutely refused to countenance a League of Nations, even on the alliance plan. Instead, Conwell insisted that many of the nations that would join the United States in the proposed League were of such weak Christian faith that cooperation with them was pointless. With non-Christian nations no cooperation was, of course, possible. So Conwell demanded that the United States—the only nation in the world that truly approximated the Baptist definition of Christianity—proceed unilaterally to reform the world. "If this nation is to be Christian," he thundered in a sermon, "we will build a Christian navy, . . . and we will have a Christian army . . . that shall ever set its face against the infidels and against the heathen, and never, never, permit them to weaken us."[30]

Conwell's advice was an exception to the predominant Baptist opinion, more rooted in American nationalism than in anything else. Nevertheless, in his eclectic way he did fit in with the never-relaxing conservative Baptist emphasis that tempered their basically supportive comment on collective security, their emphasis on the fatuity of collective security short of the Christian conversion of all nations. It was all very well, stressed the *Watchman-Examiner*, to speak of the Baptist concepts of spiritual liberty and individual freedom as lending themselves to institutional world democratization, and to talk about this project as the modern face of the missionary effort. But it was necessary to be "careful and precise" when conclusions were drawn and institution building was undertaken. The journal insisted that any international organization that included nations other than those actually rooted in a Christian understanding of these concepts—and the *Watchman-Examiner* acknowledged only the United States, Great Britain, and France as so rooted—was bound to fail ignominiously. If, say, the Japanese and the Chinese were part of such an organization, they would inevitably frustrate its Christian goals by injecting their "not yet sufficiently ethical and theistic" beliefs into its activities. Therefore, stressed the *Watchman-*

Examiner in March 1918, no lasting or beneficial "universal state of federation of the world" could be created before human nature had been changed through rebirth in Christ. At the very least, the leaders of each member nation of the putative League would have to be professing Christians if the League was to solve the world's problems and institute a real democracy.[31] This was clearly not the case; therefore, the League could be seen neither as the fruit of the Christian mission nor as its likely forwarder.

To those conservative, Calvinistic Baptists who wrote thus—and most of them did—it remained a given that unless all nations based their international behavior on the Ten Commandments and actually, not nominally or symbolically, affirmed their dependence on the Christian God, it was pointless to hope for peace, comity, or progress. No matter what the number or the scope of collective security provisions or international social reform agencies, as long as nonredeemed nations were party to their operation and maintenance, they would not work. The best chance for peace, countless Baptists stressed instead, lay in the universal spread of their version of Calvinism, a moderate Calvinism based on soul liberty and individual freedom.[32]

This demand actually became part of the Northern Baptists' convention resolutions in 1919, which demanded that the proposed League Covenant be amended to assure religious and proselytizing freedom.[33] "A league of nations in an unregenerated world cannot long keep in leash the hellish hounds of national jealousies and rivalries," the *Standard* therefore concluded in March 1919. "No constitution of a world league, however carefully framed, can bring this about in and of itself. Only God can put within the nations this willingness. We must seek Him."[34]

On the whole, then, the leading Presbyterian and Baptist periodicals arrived at a guarded acceptance of the collective security regimen that the League of Nations proposed to establish. But it was always a grudging acceptance, riddled with reservations and limitations. Most of these related to questions of ethnicity, interreligious cooperation, and what were believed to be the sinful ineradicables of human nature; and all were rooted in the felt primacy of the church as the dispenser of grace and progress. Few conservative Calvinists ever advocated ratification without reservations, for they did admit that the League's critics had genuine grounds for opposing some of the central articles of the League Covenant. Nor did they tend to accept the contention that a political institution, no matter how well its collective security mechanisms were structured, could reach the goals of world peace and cooperation if it were not first imbued by the Christian spirit of brotherhood. It was constantly stressed that only the churches could provide this. Yet those Calvinists who argued thus did not choose to denounce all international cooperation, nor did they condemn the idea or necessity of a political world organization or the usefulness of much that the League Covenant incorporated for collective security tasks.

Kuyperian Calvinists and the League of Nations

Others were rather less accommodating. Even as the leading Calvinist periodicals negotiated the technicalities of collective security and international social reform, several of the most respected Princetonian and Kuyperian theologians of the day embarked on a separate and much more hostile discourse. For the most part, they did this in tangential remarks inserted into their articles and sermons on entirely different matters. That procedure itself testified to the strength of their beliefs and grounded their anti-internationalism in specific confessional beliefs even more explicitly than the daily or weekly commentary of Reformed journals could do. As the political debate on the League heated up in the course of 1919 and early 1920, the tone of these theologians' separate discourse also heated up. It left a legacy whereby some leading Calvinist theologians were predisposed to remain very skeptical of all further projects of their liberal fellow believers.

The Christian Reformed theologian Geerhardus Vos, a professor of biblical theology at Princeton Theological Seminary from 1893 to 1932, was among those eminent Calvinist divines who threw themselves into League-related commentary of this kind. Vos was very much the scholar and very much centered on his work as a biblical theologian, and his writings rarely addressed topical matters outside the academic study of scripture. Indeed, he took a hardly noticeable part even in the denominational contention that so much characterized the four decades of his scholarly career.[35] This makes it all the more significant that he did, nevertheless, choose to argue against several of the aspirations with which conservative evangelicals felt the League of Nations had wrongly been invested. The words "League of Nations" did not appear in his writings, but he nevertheless tackled the core ideas, paradigms, and sets of goals that churchly and political internationalists had set for that organization, and he offered a cogent Calvinist countertheology.

Throughout his exegetical and preaching career, Vos had placed especial emphasis on the futility and illegitimacy of all purely human efforts at world betterment. His theology was radically God centered and pietist in that he defined the Christian as one elected by God to live in a mystical union with Christ in the spiritual Kingdom of God. This Kingdom was but approximated in the temporal churchly community and had its actual locus in the transcendent realm. For Vos, in other words, the Christian life was one spent entirely in the presence of God; one that excluded everything except God-ward concentration; and one that in every sphere of life was directed to the glory of God, never to any merely human task, aspiration, or valuation. This premise led Vos to repeatedly take to task both the secular social reformers and the nominal Christians who reinterpreted the church's mission in terms of reforming the social and political conditions of temporal existence.[36]

As a Kuyperian, Vos believed that Christians were meant gradually to conquer more and more spheres of life for the Kingdom of God. Yet he stressed that this very procedure, necessary in itself, always ran the risk of confusing the redemptive-soteriological purpose of world conquest with a purely humanistic "improvement of the present world" where a profane "creature-betterment" usurped the place of proper Godward concentration. "Everything that is cherished and cultivated apart from God (in such a sense that it cannot carry it with us in the Godward movement)," he underlined to a Princeton audience in 1902, "becomes necessarily a hindrance, a profanation, and at last a source of idolatry." This included the "good works" of world betterment, because in the process of bringing the world into an approximation of the divine plan, the truth stating that "sin is a spiritual thing and it must be paid for in kind by the life of the sinner" tended to be obscured. The sinner who engaged in good works was forever in danger of falsely concluding that atonement could be had by bringing the world purified to God as ransom.[37]

This rather abstract line of reasoning had definite political implications. Vos came to sketch these once World War I was under way and once liberal Calvinists began to speak of the need for new world organizations to speed up ethical evolutionary development and world conquest by enlightened Christians. At this point, Vos insisted that the fruition of God's work could be effected by God alone, not by humans. He felt impelled to scold both the premillennarian dispensationalists and the postmillennial Social Gospelers and to take both to task for what he saw as their opposite yet equal forms of weakening Godward concentration. The premillennarians were wrong in thinking of the millennium in material and literalist terms, but they were correct, Vos claimed, in regarding the Antichrist as a "politically organized world-power under a supreme head" and in teaching that before the Second Coming there would emerge a powerful apostate form of Christianity.[38]

The Social Gospelers, conversely, were wrong in thinking that the church was tasked with the full and final Christianization of the world and wrong in positing a spiritualized millennium of ethically acting humanity before the Second Coming of the Lord. Vos was especially scathing about the postmillennialists' stress on churchly essaying into social reform, and he insisted that "no amount of evangelization, no degree of success in the conversion of men, or in the reconstruction of social or political life, can ever change the constitution of nature or eradicate the physical forces of evil at work in the kosmos." In believing or suggesting otherwise, the Social Gospelers were not only optimistic in a way wholly unwarranted by a proper understanding of the Bible; they were also, alleged Vos, so enamored of purely human competency that they had forgotten that God alone could provide redemption and perfection for the world.[39]

Thus, as far as Vos was concerned, even the public means of grace had definite limits. The instrumentalities of the church were intended to reach "no absolute, but only relative results," he stressed in 1916, and the final perfection of the world was still reserved for the returning Christ. The world could be redeemed not by Christians acting ethically in humanitarian reform causes at home or internationally; rather, it could be redeemed only through a direct eschatological, divine intervention.[40]

By early 1920, Vos was ready to carry this analysis one step further and to identify the churchly liberals' idea of a League of Nations as an aspect of illegitimate creature betterment through purely human effort. In an article in the *Princeton Theological Review*, he stated in no uncertain terms that the "modern movement for world-reconstruction, . . . of making over of things," which was offered by many a cleric as the postwar mission of the church and as the producer of "an absolute and ideal future," was in fact "more humanistic than religious" and derived "its motives and ideals from man rather than from God." In his studies of the Psalter, Vos had found a "certain striking resemblance to the desires and ideals of this eminently modern drift of life . . . [toward] reconstruction on the grandest scales . . . projected on the stage of earthly existence." He had concluded that those who championed the reconstruction of the world through purposive political change were merely perpetuating the Old Testament fallacy that configured the temporal as the anticipation of the eternal and the eternal as the prolongation of the temporal. The temporal did not lead into the eternal, not without a direct supernatural interposition, Vos underlined, but it was instead up to the church to insert its supernatural power into the midst of all that was temporal, and only in this way could the world be "made better." He stressed, therefore, that the liberals' plans for institutionalized world betterment meant only that the churches were being subsumed under secular institutions and were losing all that was distinctive, unique, and truly salvific in their public mission. In short, Vos was convinced that such "human endeavors or performances are not credited with bringing the world-change," no matter the scope or intensity of the effort, that "not through evolution from beneath, but through descent and theophany and interposition from above . . . the face of the earth is to be renewed."[41]

Vos was unique among the leading Reformed theologians of the early twentieth century in that much of his work concerned eschatology. He was thus poised to relate the Calvinist public means of grace to the apocalyptic mood that during World War I had seized not just dispensationalists but also, in a different way, the liberal Social Gospelers. Moreover, as a systematic theologian, he had been formed through his discipleship with Kuyper. Thus he stood at the very juncture where Calvinist eschatology met the Kuyperian concept of transforming all aspects of life and thought through the agency of the church. Vos was at Princeton Seminary in 1898 when Kuyper said there that a world empire neither could nor should be established, and he saw to it that generations of Princeton seminarians were indoctrinated in Kuyperian concepts of the culturalist mission of the church.[42] Yet Vos was always insistent that the church itself could never entirely subjugate the world and that a direct, cataclysmic intervention by God was needed before the Kingdom of God would come into its own. Both these emphases were related to modern churchly internationalism, and both led irresistibly to opposition to the churchly liberals' idea of a League of Nations. Few Princetonian Calvinists were as capable of arguing a strictly theological, strictly God-centered case against the League of Nations, and few did this in as uncompromising and coherent terms as Vos.

One who did pick up the cudgels in much the same way was John M. Foster, a Bostonian clergyman and a Kuyperite who represented the small Reformed Presbyterian Church (with roots in the strict "Covenanter" section of Scottish Presbyterianism). A veteran of the National Reform Association, he was not as influential a figure as Vos, but he engaged the League of Nations issue much more explicitly and even more passionately than his fellow Kuyperite. Foster had been one of the contributors to *The Fundamentals* of 1910–15, where he had forcefully criticized the papacy as a "foreign despotism" that allegedly endeavored to spread its dominion over the United States by insinuating its false doctrines into American politics.[43]

Ever since the late nineteenth century, Foster had insisted that collectivist social reform threatened the culturalist tasks of the church in that it conspired to create a new, overwhelming center of power—the secular legislature—which was subservient only to the changing passions of the electorate. This, as far as Foster was concerned, was likely to supplant God-given rules of social and political organization with purely human, forever fickle ones and so to hinder the church's culturalist mission. He stressed that all states derived their powers from God and had to legislate according to rules laid down by God; indeed, because states existed "for the sake of and to serve the interests of the Church," they would be severely punished by God for all idolatry. Every aspect of organized life had to be brought under subjection to

God, and the principles enunciated by the church had to be the be-all and end-all of organized life.[44]

Once the League controversy erupted, Foster felt compelled to relate these assumptions to it. He wrote a pamphlet titled *The Covenant Treaty: Humanity's Despair* and issued it when the Senate deliberated on ratification. This pamphlet, which was sent to some senators, called the League Covenant a "fatal departure" and "the devil's temptation," denouncing it as a purely "secular World Covenant" and its drafters as men who "defy the Almighty" by trying to have the world "organized without God." As far as Foster was concerned, the League was based on a denial of the core Calvinist tenet that Satan had been conquered at Christ's first coming and that ever since then Christ and His Church had been the kings and rulers of the world. Instead of accepting this fact and building the postwar world order firmly on Christ's sovereignty and kingship, League enthusiasts seemed to be suggesting that it was still up to human beings and human organizations to reform the world and its inhabitants, that the fixed rules of conduct and organization imposed by the Decalogue should yield to whatever humanitarian projects happened to seize the imagination of the ethicists and the social reformers of the moment.[45]

This was nothing if not satanic defiance of the Almighty, Foster stressed, a new means to surrender the world to "Satan and his followers."[46] It was unworkable, too, given the fact that some nations remained pagan and therefore could not meaningfully contribute to Christian progress. The nations in question—all Catholic nations; all Greek Orthodox nations; and all Muslim, Buddhist, Confucian, Brahmin, Taoist, and Zoroastrian nations—remained a "menace to themselves and to others," Foster opined, and they needed through proselytizing to be "emancipated from these false religions and brought into the glorious liberty wherewith Christ makes His people free." Until then, "there is no hope for them except in a limited imperialism which will have in view their benevolent development and a preparation for free government." No yoke fellowship of the redeemed and the unredeemed could bring about the desired results, for no mere intermingling of the redeemed and the heathen could rub Christianity off on the unredeemed. It would be patently impossible to curb the non- and anti-Christian passions of the unconverted except through an "instrument of autocracy" if the mistake had once been made to give them coequal power. The League Covenant was, however, predicated on just such a transference and coequality of power and if ratified, Foster claimed that "like the former experiments it will fail, and this time break the heart of humanity." Whether ratified or not, it was in any case in direct disobedience to the will and law of God.[47]

Foster's argument cohered around an alleged nexus of centralized social reform, irreligion, and the League experiment. He conflated the League's pagan members and the Social Gospel reform program, and he concluded that as a result of these two joining hands, the public means of grace would be abandoned and a secular, autocratic world power would emerge instead. In a slightly different, less sophisticated way, Charles Wadsworth, the president of the Presbyterian Board of Education, witnessed to this effect as well. His pamphlet on the League of Nations, published sometime in 1919, accused the preeminent political advocate of the League, President Wilson, of betraying his Presbyterian roots and having become a new Nebuchadnezzar by having constructed a new "deity for all mankind—internationalism" and now trying to force all peoples to worship this "grotesque absurdity," "crazy contrivance," and "indescribable device." "No longer content with domineering over the external activities of his subjects," alleged Wadsworth, Wilson "was seized with an irresistible yearning to prescribe their ideas for them," to "unify the races" and to force all nations to "accept the same ideals, to worship the same deity." The League effort, being analogous to the Tower of Babel, was certainly not Christian, Wadsworth stressed, but rather a case of "playing politics with a holy sentiment" and of proffering a secular way to "lift the race to heaven," an example of political "graven images" usurping the prerogatives of the church.[48]

Most important of all, as far as Wadsworth was concerned, was the social dimension of the Wilsonian internationalist effort. The League of Nations was not only a peacekeeping organization but also a new center of executive and legislative power, an international and irresistible center, which according to Wadsworth would subvert the U.S. Constitution and set up in its stead a "hybrid" derived from Marxian theory, German authoritarianism, and American secular and religious radicalism.[49] Being confessionally Calvinist to the core, Wadsworth would not accept any blending of internationalism, socialism, and theological modernism, and he regarded each of the three as practically identical and the League of Nations as the preferred twentieth-century tool and instrument of each. This was indeed the generic view of the League of Nations for all those Princetonian and Kuyperian commentators who engaged the theological, rather than the purely technical, level of League commentary.

⌐⟶ *J. Gresham Machen and Southern Anti-Internationalism*

Vos's, Foster's, and Wadsworth's culturalist statements were further echoed by Vos's Princeton colleague, J. Gresham Machen, a professor of New Testament from 1906 to 1929 and perhaps the best-known scholarly expositor of the fundamentalist case. Unlike Vos, Machen was very much the polemicist and political campaigner. Starting in the immediate post-1919 period, he fought a long, ultimately losing fight against the seepage of modernist theory into Presbyterian mission boards and education institutions, which culminated in his resignation from Princeton Seminary and ouster from the Presbyterian Church. To spread the traditional Calvinist message, in the mid-1930s Machen formed instead the Orthodox Presbyterian Church, complete with its alternative to Princeton, Westminster Theological Seminary.[50] Although a member of a Northern presbytery when on the Princeton faculty, he was a representative of the Southern Presbyterian tradition, having been born, raised, and indoctrinated in Calvinism in its fold. This background imparted a peculiar complexion to Machen's public theology and made him a prime spokesman for the Southern Presbyterian version of Calvinist anti-internationalism.

Privately, Machen was very critical of all aspects of the Versailles peace settlement. He regarded this settlement as a "terrible crime against the Truth," a crime, as he put it to a friend, "whose effects will be more permanent than all the other ravages wrought by the war." He believed that the whole peace treaty was an "almost unparalleled example of bad faith and sordid cruelty," rendered only worse by the "high professions that preceded it." The way in which President Wilson nevertheless defended it was, according to Machen, a grave error and a shame.[51]

The passion of this assessment was partly explainable through Machen's distinct and very personal aversion to most things British, an aversion that had roots in his Southern upbringing and in the years that he had spent studying in Germany. There he had acquired a lifelong affinity toward what he regarded as the German way of perceiving the world. This pro-Germanism contributed to his support of the neutrality policies of President Wilson in 1914–17, to his opposition to preparedness and universal military training, and to his instinctual blaming of World War I on a supposed effort by Britain to spread the "satanic" dominion of its imperial system.[52] Of course, there was nothing theological in this anti-imperialism and partiality toward Germany. On the plane of theology, the biblically literalist Machen detested German Higher Criticism and fought against it as avidly as anyone. But his private, strongly held pro-German sentiments undoubtedly formed a strong impulse that colored his entire stance toward the League of Nations and the punitive peace settlement of which it was part.

Yet distinctly Calvinist, theological factors also figured in Machen's detestation of the Versailles settlement and the League of Nations experiment. It seemed to him that the post–World War I world was evidencing a profound, and dramatically misplaced, "satisfaction with human goodness." This manifested itself in a whole range of projects that together amounted to "the substitution of paganism for Christianity as the dominant principle of life." Without using the designation "League of Nations," Machen repeatedly intimated that wartime and immediate postwar attempts to perfect the world, especially by those who tried to set up an overarching "man-made authority," issued from this new paganism that had raised purely human goals and self-sufficiency in the stead of God. He accused liberal clerics of "trying to produce a decent, moral life in their world while denying the basis of morality in the being of God." He accused them of an embrace of international social reform as "a god manufactured to serve the social needs of man," "a god of our own making," of religion as "a useful thing" and a "mere means to an end"—in other words, of the idolatry of spiritually legitimating world-bettering secular organizations.[53]

Personally, Machen could not decide whether postmillennialism or amillennialism was the correct biblical interpretation, but he did always stress that the world was not degenerating, as per premillennialism, and that the church still had a function in making it better. Politicians, however, did not have that function, nor did the liberal theologians who had imbibed secular modernist notions on nonevangelical means of world perfection.[54] Though he never directly, publicly joined the political anti-League forces, privately he felt that League ratification would be a "calamity."[55]

Whenever Machen argued this case, but especially after the League had already been defeated in the Senate, he exposed his anticollectivist promptings. He even joined a small Massachusetts association called the Sentinels of Democracy, a group dedicated to civil libertarian and anticollectivist publicity work, which was led by the president of the American Shoe Machinery Corporation, Louis A. Coolidge. This man was also one of the directors of the main political organization opposed to the League of Nations, the League for the Preservation of American Independence, and a close friend of Henry Cabot Lodge, the chief senatorial opponent of the League. The Sentinels campaigned against all concentrations of political and administrative-bureaucratic power, which they tended to lump together under the rubric of "communism," and they refused to endorse either the League of Nations or the World Court.[56] Under the auspices of the Sentinels, Machen himself campaigned against a proposed constitutional amendment forbidding child labor (a core item in the charter of the International Labor Organization, as well as a long-standing aim of most liberal clergy) and against a federal department of education. He even opposed laws against jaywalking and municipal regulations for compulsory city lightning, as well as Prohibition and the registration of aliens.[57]

All this anticollectivist campaigning was based on the Christian grounds that all forms of statist "materialistic paternalism" (as Machen put it) violated the Christian's basic freedom of choice and put in the place of what was properly a personal, conscious decision to do good an impersonal, externally institutionalized, and vicarious mending of the world. Such a supplanting of individual decisions with collective organization, no matter the intentions, smothered the very life out of the Christian's faith and could not be countenanced. Indeed, stressed Machen, it was only Christian fundamentalism that could defeat "the soul-killing collectivism which is threatening to dominate our social life. . . . It must fight the great battle for the liberty of the children of God."[58] So strongly did he feel about this that by the 1930s he took the symbolically significant step of abandoning his lifelong affiliation with the Democratic Party and voted against Franklin D. Roosevelt.[59] Regarding the president as a dangerous collectivist, he could not have done otherwise if he was to stay true to his felt Christian duty to fight all forms of collectivism.

Machen's fight against domestic and international collectivism testified to his civil libertarian and Jeffersonian political beliefs. But it was also an aspect of his Southern Presbyterianism, a theologically impelled defense of traditional views on the state's limited competency and an assault on the presumptions of secular power to dictate in areas properly reserved for individual and church action. This found official expression at the 1919 General Assembly of the Presbyterian Church South. By the time the assembly met, the church's moderator, James I. Vance, had been to Paris as a member of the Federal Council of Churches (FCC) delegation, which meant that the Southern Presbyterians had indirectly endorsed the FCC's pro-League work.[60] However, their critique of the FCC's League campaign both persisted after and overshadowed this semi-endorsement.

At its 1919 assembly, the Southern Presbyterian Church lodged an official protest with the FCC. This protest took the FCC to task for having confused the church's purely spiritual mission with the issuance of authoritative statements on "political relations, *international relations*, labor and capital problems, wage questions and working hours, woman's work, race problems, the making of laws and the enforcement of the same, *treaties with foreign powers*, women's full political and economic equality" (italics added). Southern Presbyterians refused to regard FCC statements on any of these matters as in any way binding. The denomination repeatedly insisted that churchly endorsement of any and all of these aspects of the League of Nations' social reform agenda was inappropriate.[61]

There did exist a tension between the laissez-faire traditions of Southern Presbyterians and the more aggressively culturalist promptings of the Kuyperian paradigm; yet in both cases it was the church and the individual believers formed by the church—never the state or the League of Nations—that were put forward as the real source of solutions for current problems. Both the Kuyperians and the Southern Presbyterians agreed that all concentrations of secular power like the League—especially when infused with expansive, essentially spiritual goals—dangerously hindered the church's true culturalist mission. They were, therefore, to be denounced.

Southern Baptist Conservatives

Much the same was affirmed by some representatives of the other major focus of Southern Calvinism, that of the Southern Baptist Convention. There Richard H. Edmonds, a leading conservative layman who edited the *Manufacturers Record*, a major laissez-faire journal, avowed that he was "much afraid" of the League of Nations, "tremendously impressed with danger of proposed league," and of the view that it was "one of the most dangerous propositions ever put before the American people."[62] Racist, nationalist, and class prejudices clearly played a role here, but at the core of Edmonds's concern was just as much his stated fear that membership in the League would dangerously compromise both the churches' work and what he regarded as the United States' essentially Baptist national witness to soul freedom and individual liberty.[63]

On that basis, Edmonds denounced the League as an unnatural coequality of Christians and pagans, as an alien-dominated organization that would force the United States into wars not in its interest, as a Vatican-dominated instrument for the suppression of civil liberties, and as world autocracy that would interfere in all manner of domestic social, economic, and political questions. For all these reasons, the League could only lead to Christianity being submerged under the tide of pagan philosophies and agendas. The whole organization, Edmonds also stressed, was analogous to the planned organic merger of all Protestant denominations, for which modernist clergy inveighed as passionately as for the League. But just as Baptists should never accept the abandonment of their distinctives that such a church merger would involve, so should they and the United States never accept the merger of Protestant, Catholic, and pagan nations.[64]

Though a Northern, not Southern, Baptist publication, the Cincinnati-based *Journal and Messenger* also thought so. Throughout a very skeptical League commentary, it emphasized the dangers of including in the League's remit domestic social and industrial questions and immigration, and it expressed fear from early on that the true intentions of the League's formulators were those socialist reforms enunciated by the socialist Berne Conference.[65] So passionately did the *Journal and Messenger* feel about this that toward mid-1919 it began to praise Senator Philander C. Knox, one of the Irreconcilable League opponents, and to charge President Wilson with socialist tendencies and autocratic dreams. Then, in November 1919, it explicitly branded the League "a super-state which should in fact rule the world." The journal alleged that "a more ambitious project than that of the Kaiser William" was not just the end result but that it had always been Wilson's aim, carefully hidden from view. Wilson, claimed the *Journal and Messenger*, fully intended to become the first president of his centralized, socialist world state.[66]

Even the two influential League supporters among the Southern Baptists, E. Y. Mullins, professor of theology and president of the Southern Baptist Theological Seminary, and his colleague, William O. Carver, gave frequent voice to their concern about the ascendancy of socialism that they perceived in the postwar world, America included—which, according to them, would lead to highly oppressive "bureaucratic government" and a "new kind of slavery."[67] Carver insisted that in the form in which President Wilson had presented it, the League of Nations Covenant should not be ratified, for it contained too many dangers to free, voluntary development and sociopolitical interaction to justify the risk.[68]

Against this background, it is understandable that the Southern Baptist Convention never officially endorsed the League of Nations Covenant.[69] It could not shake off the impression that the League constituted a threat to individual freedom and thus to the Baptist witness. The anticollectivist presuppositions that were thereby exposed were practically identical to those of Machen's Southern Presbyterian witness. That both these versions of Southern Calvinism issued such similar anticollectivist critiques of the League was partly, of course, a commentary on sectional distinctives that were not primarily theological. But it was also a theological commentary in that, whatever the original reasons, both types of Southern Calvinism had embraced anticollectivism as a religious message. Both had proffered a concept of the church as only a spiritual body, one that should not become engaged in political or social organization but should instead offer its own, more promising alternative to all secular efforts at world betterment. By transferring these beliefs onto the debate over the League of Nations, Southern Calvinists managed both to reaffirm their denial of the Social Gospel and to highlight the truly global, universal nature of the threat that they perceived in its formulations. These conservative Calvinists warned of an international, more clearly political plane to the perceived menace. And they regarded both these planes as equally menacing.

Calvinist Anti-Internationalism Summarized

Strict Calvinist confessionalism impelled a fight against the secular ethical ambitions of the League of Nation's proponents. For Calvinist conservatives, the crux of the matter was that only the church and only those shaped by the Gospel possessed the ability to change the world. Such a promise could not be associated with the state nor with an international organization of nation-states. As far as conservative Calvinists were concerned, both these entities were based on a profoundly non-Christian worldview, a materialist, force-based weltanschauung that ignored the primacy of spiritual truths, offered essentially idolatrous, purely human schemes of redemption, and thus deflected attention from Godward movement. For this reason, conservative Calvinists saw the Social Gospel and the League of Nations as enterprises that were equally anti-Christian in conception and equally likely to weaken Christian allegiances in practice.

Nor was the League's proposed admixture of Christians and non-Christians admissible in the Reformed tradition. Conservative interpreters of that tradition held tenaciously to the belief that there was nothing in pagan civilizations that was worthwhile or beneficial. They challenged all modernist attempts to equate ethical international cooperation and Christianity and saw these as but new forms of the modernist secularizing of the public means of faith. This meant that the Calvinist polemics apparently over the League of Nations were part and parcel of the debate over the definition of missionary activity that came to constitute the first stage in the modernist/fundamentalist conflict among Presbyterians and Baptists. It was the most theological plane of ostensibly League-related contention, the least connected to the League's formal structures and aims, but as far as the conservatives were concerned, also the most central. They not only doubted that peoples of different cultural and religious traditions could meaningfully cooperate, but many of them directly denied the very legitimacy of such cooperation, of "yoke fellowship" and a "mixed multitude" of Christians and pagans working together by the light of their disparate consciences.

Conservative Calvinists could not accept the right to equal power or consideration by peoples who had not accepted the Gospel, and they could not abide an international organization that by its composition did so recognize such peoples. Nor could they accept the proposition underlying all international organizations: that Christians and non-Christians should be bound together in a common effort or endeavor, whatever the relations of power within such an endeavor. This position was rooted in traditions spanning the entire history of Christianity and in first principles, the prescriptive powers of which were taken to be as strictly binding as any speculations on a premillennial anti-Christian world empire. There was not the slightest possibility, even in the absence of dispensational prophetic speculations, that a strictly orthodox, traditionalist understanding of such traditions would have yielded anything but opposition to the League of Nations.

Theologically, the positions of conservative, confessional Calvinists were certainly at variance with the anti-League stances of leading premillennialists. Yet both these and conservative, nondispensationalist Calvinists were in like measure critical of "Man's Day," of the secularization of the Christian eschaton and of that palpable politicization and transference onto secular world institutions of the public means of grace that churchly League enthusiasts allegedly proposed. Conservative Calvinists were also just as insistent on the futility and danger of human-made projects for world perfection as were the dispensationalists. As was evident in the commentary of the *Presbyterian* and the leading Baptist journals, conservative Calvinists clearly were not opposed to the collective security aspirations of moderate League advocates, but they perceived profound spiritual dangers in the larger liberal aspirations and therefore felt propelled to criticize the entire enterprise.

Thus, while they engaged in their separate denominational, creedal, and doctrinal contention, Calvinist conservatives and the dispensationalists of the World Christian Fundamentals Association were drawn together by a shared awareness of the Social Gospel's international plane of activity. This, too, the conservatives had to challenge if they were to defuse the modernist challenge. Therefore conservative Calvinists in the Presbyterian, Christian Reformed, and Baptist communities entered the fight against the liberal clerics' League of Nations no less forcefully than their dispensationalist antimodernist allies. The Calvinists took no more clearly political sides in the League fight than did a James M. Gray or an Arno C. Gaebelein. But like those dispensationalists, throughout the political League controversy they did sustain a coherent and continuous, parallel anti-League commentary in their leading theological journals. This commentary pointed out several profound causes for Calvinist concern over the expansive aspirations of the League. More often than not, it concluded that the ideas and goals with which liberal clerical internationalists infused the League were grave threats to confessionally orthodox Calvinism. The League of Nations controversy must, therefore, be seen as a significant aspect of the defense of a traditional, God-centered, church-centered Calvinist worldview.

CHAPTER FOUR

⌒

Lutherans: The Two Kingdoms and the Antichrist

S ince the mid–twentieth century, the Lutheran confessional tradition has been known for the pioneering internationalism of its
Lutheran World Federation. Under the auspices of this organization, Lutherans have involved themselves in international cooperation in a range of ecumenical and secular fields, and, with some exceptions, they have acquired a
worldwide reputation as a group particularly open to interfaith dialogue and
to cooperation with secular humanitarian organizations. It may therefore
appear surprising that when the League of Nations was being debated in
1919 and 1920, of all the major nonfundamentalist clusters of evangelicalism, American Lutherans showed the most pervasive skepticism and aversion
toward modern internationalism.

In the course of League of Nations controversy, Lutherans built up a considerable corpus of theological and other commentary on the issues of public
theology that they saw as intertwined with the League and, more particularly, with the clerical Christian apologias for that organization. Almost all
of this was distinctly hostile to modern internationalism. The result was that
no Lutheran synod endorsed the League during the ratification debates of
late 1919 and early 1920, or in the run-up to it, or for quite some time
afterward, or, in many cases, ever. In this nonendorsement, Lutherans were
joined by only one other denomination, the Southern Baptist Convention,

and by the interdenominational movement of the dispensational fundamentalists proper. They were therefore at the very forefront of the Christian anti-internationalists.

Contemporary Lutheran accounts tended to explain their nonendorsement of the League by the long-standing confessional proscription against the church entering into politics or stating anything authoritative about purely political matters. As set out in the foundational confessions of the Lutheran community that were collected into the Book of Concord in 1580, this proscription had not always been followed in those lands where Lutheranism was an established church, but the demographics of American Lutheranism in the early twentieth century were heavily slanted in favor of those who had emigrated in protest against this very failure. Consequently, Lutheran clergy in America tended to be more strictly apolitical than many of their European brethren.[1] Insofar as this was still the case in 1919, Lutheran nonendorsement of the League of Nations would not have been a commentary at all on the merits of the League but a silence imposed by confessional fundamentals.

This interpretation is, however, unsatisfactory. The defense of their confessional group had, in fact, led many American Lutherans to violate their self-imposed proscription long before the League of Nations controversy. Some of them had vocally opposed efforts to have the United States enter World War I on the side of the Allied nations and then, after the United States had after all entered the war, some of them had joined those of other denominations who invested the war with religious meanings.[2] After the United States had joined the war, Lutherans went on to create a number of national bodies, which further involved them in political matters on a range of topical questions. The Lutheran Bureau (1917) was led by a pastor from the most apolitical and theologically conservative of all the Lutheran groups, the Missouri Synod, and it engaged in propaganda and publicity work on various civil rights issues of interest to Lutherans. The National Lutheran Council (1918), the joint lobbying agency of eight different Lutheran synods, cooperated with non-Protestant interdenominational bodies and carried on its own activities in social, economic, and political spheres.[3] Even earlier (in the 1890s), several Lutheran synods had essayed into a profoundly political, organized fight to assure continued freedom of operation for parochial schools. This campaign was resumed in the wake of World War I.[4]

The League of Nations involved some issues related to defending their confessional group and, therefore, it led some Lutheran organizations to engage in direct political lobbying. This was the case especially, but not only, in the more nearly liberal sections of the denominational family. More typically, however, the Lutheran participation in the League of Nations debates was of the same kind as that by dispensationalists and conservative Calvinists; these debates provided them with a space for contesting the Social Gospel definitions of Lutheran confessionalism that their tradition's modernists had put forth and a space for arguing their own version of Christian anti-internationalism as a nonnegotiable dimension of the confessional witness. Though ethnic prejudices and loyalties played a rather more prominent role among Lutherans than that in the more fully Americanized denominations, this Lutheran version was also emphatically theological, impelled by a strictly literal interpretation of the historically accepted reading of the Lutheran foundational books. The Lutherans who argued the case partook of generic evangelical arguments against modern internationalism, and they added ones uniquely their own. Practically all Lutherans across what was an extremely fractured denominational terrain took part.

The Conservatism of American Lutheranism

At the time of World War I, there were some twenty self-governing Lutheran synodal groupings in the United States, and together they represented approximately 2.25 million members. In fact, by the early twentieth century there were more Lutherans in the United States than there were Presbyterians; only the numbers of Baptists and Methodists surpassed those of Lutherans.[5] But these Lutherans were divided on a range of ethnic, cultural, and doctrinal lines, much more so than the other major Protestant denominations. A basic doctrinal aversion to public theology conspired with a separatist cultural-ethnic posture and with the persistent internal divisions of their faith community to isolate Lutherans from the mainstream of American life, depriving them of a discernible, authoritative single voice on public questions. Consequently, their public prominence was far below that of traditions much smaller than theirs.

In their own communities, the Lutherans formed one of the most conservative religious entities anywhere in the United States. Doctrinally and culturally, the faith community was rooted in specific Lutheran confessional writings, in derivative cultural attitudes, and (often) in the European prejudices and practices of their original communities. These differed from those of revival-shaped American Protestantism in many significant ways and, on the whole, tended to push Lutherans toward more conservative postures than other Protestants.

Above all, Lutheran confessionalism recoiled from the essentially Calvinist Christianization of all life and thought—including social, political, and cultural life and thought—which had become a prime characteristic of American churches' public theology. Here was a major reason for the

Lutheran proscription against taking positions on political issues, but it never meant disinterest in political affairs. Rather, Lutherans tended to teach that law and order were divine ordinances given to the state to maintain and to citizens to support. If so maintained and supported, these ordinances would create a safe and stable framework in which the Gospel could fruitfully be preached and spread by the church. It would then be up to the individuals transformed by the saving Gospel (but never to the corporate church) to act rightly in temporal, political affairs. More than any other Protestant tradition, Lutheranism utilized the concept of adiaphora, of things that were not necessary for salvation and therefore were nonessential—things not enjoined on Christians regardless of their possible ethical worth or beneficence. Concerned above all to fight all works-righteousness doctrines of salvation, Lutherans thus tended to content themselves with those two Christian activities that they regarded as explicitly enjoined by the Bible: the preaching of the Gospel and the administration of the sacraments.[6]

Accompanying this self-limitation of the Christian effort was the Lutheran preference for a largely amillennialist eschatological doctrine, that is, for a doctrine teaching that the much-adumbrated thousand-year reign of Christ was either an allegory or a description of the already existing spiritual kingdom of believers. Many a Calvinist may have hoped to set up the millennium through the church's conquest of the world, and dispensationalists may have looked for it in a future separated by a supernatural catastrophe, but Lutherans denied the relevance of the whole concept for present public concerns.[7] Taken together with the overarching distaste for the purposive Christianization of social structures, amillennialism further conspired to distance Lutherans from any but the most conservative views of the political world.

Geography and ethnicity supported this conservative theological orientation. The most significant section of Lutherans resided in the traditionally isolationist Midwest, from which hailed many of the League of Nations' leading political opponents, and ethnically they tended to be relatively recent immigrants, often from those parts of Central Europe against which the Allied and Associated Powers had fought in World War I and which were not initially allowed to join the League. This meant that German American pressure groups, such as the Steuben Society, which contained significant numbers of Lutherans, were distinctly hostile to the League of Nations and among the earliest organized campaigners against its ratification.

Moreover, in the early twentieth century most of these Midwestern Lutherans were still engaged in agrarian occupations but had not shown any marked sympathies to the spate of Populist agitation that spread throughout their communities in the 1890s. Even the hard times that befell the countryside in the later nineteenth century did not make a major dent in this

Lutheran aversion to the politics of the left. Even then many a synodal authority had seen to it that Lutherans on the whole stayed clear from farmer radicalism and from labor unions, and on the whole Lutherans tended to vote with the main party of order, the Republican Party. This preference seems to have been especially pronounced among the more recent Lutheran immigrants, the Scandinavians and those from German-speaking lands, while longer-established and more assimilated groups sometimes tended toward the Democratic Party.[8]

All in all, American Lutherans were a people, as Martin Marty has suggested, who preferred to live quiet lives under the canopy of their tradition, rather than embark on ambitious schemes for world betterment of any kind.[9] The tradition was nothing if it was not conservative. It is hardly surprising, then, that by the latter part of the nineteenth century, the Lutherans were participating in the fight against Higher Criticism and all other aspects of modernist theology. This critique came, in fact, to be so all-pervasive that even the most ethnically German of all American Lutheran groupings, the Missouri Synod, came to denounce the "heathendom . . . made in Germany" to which it said modernism amounted.[10]

As Milton Rudnick has shown, most Lutherans were so concerned about the rise of modernism that they tended to welcome the fundamentalist movement. Some leading fundamentalists—such as J. Gresham Machen—in turn applauded the Lutherans' persistent, unadulterated bibliocentrism. Late-nineteenth-century Lutherans were just as alarmed as the fundamentalists by the inroads that the Social Gospelers were making in the legislative sphere, especially in the areas of public education, drink, and collective social reform. Even if their confessional beliefs prevented all but one conservative Lutheran from joining the World Christian Fundamentals Association, and even if they tended to strongly disapprove of the millennialist doctrines of the fundamentalists, conservative Lutherans could not but acknowledge that their affinities must lie with a movement that assailed theological rationalism and its social and political concomitants.[11]

The Lutheran church bodies could not be "indifferent to the conflict now going on," stressed the Lutheran member of the World Christian Fundamentals Association's executive, Leander S. Keyser, a Midwestern pastor and professor of systematic theology at Hamma Divinity School in Ohio. It had, rather, to throw itself on the side of the fundamentalists, despite their premillennialism. Keyser felt strongly because, in the years bracketed by World War I, it became apparent to him that if the modernist liberals were not stopped, they would "cut the heart out of Christianity." To them, he charged, reason and not the Bible was the "final arbiter," and the "ethnic religions" were just as praiseworthy and inspired as historical Christianity, whereas the "good deposit" of the dogmata—verbal inspiration, the Virgin Birth, the deity of Christ, His vicarious atonement, His bodily resurrection, and His visible Second Coming—seemed insignificant. Such heresy, he argued, had to be fought, and people had to be kept from falling into their error and "ruined for ever." Therefore, though it was out of the question to effect any organic union with the dispensationalist and Calvinist conservatives, it was equally wrong to persist in calling them "false prophets" and to refuse to join them in the actually shared fight.[12] The persuasiveness of this line of argument was shown in the fact that even the Missouri Synod's official publication, despite its denial of premillennialism, expansively praised the dispensationalists' wartime prophecy conferences and "rejoice[d] to find so much Lutheranism in men of non-Lutheran denominations."[13]

Though this level of explicitness was rare, important clues on Lutheran views of the League of Nations are in fact exposed by this Lutheran approach to the fundamentalist defense of the faith. There was no reason why this burgeoning opposition to the doctrines and campaigns of the liberals would not have included the League question; on the contrary, there was every reason why it should include it, because the League's apologists were the same people who challenged traditional Lutheran theologies and practices at home and whose rationale for the League was the same as their rationale for these domestic demands. The opposition to the League that was evidenced in the conservative sections of Lutheranism arose from a merging of growing culturalist fears and once-and-for-all settled doctrinal assumptions. This aversion to the Social Gospel yielded itself easily enough to a growing suspicion about the motives, goals, and impact of liberal clerical advocacy for internationalism. It was, in fact, the main proximate conduit of Lutherans to polemics against the League. There were, however, distinct differences of emphasis within this generally cohesive community, and these led to two slightly different postures toward the League.

In the so-called Eastern tradition of Lutheranism, centered on the General Synod and, after 1918, in its successors the United Lutheran Church in America (ULCA) and the Evangelical Lutheran Church of America (created in 1988), a muted and limited sympathy for the Social Gospel and even for some forms of "higher" biblical criticism was evident. The ULCA was made up largely of those Lutherans who had either been born in the United States or had resided there the longest, and it had become the most Americanized of all strands of American Lutheranism long before the League of Nations debate. Its some 800,000 confirmed members were greatly influenced by the pietistic revival that nineteenth-century Germans had brought to the United States and that in many ways was analogous to the more typically

American forms of revivalism and social action, those Calvinist forms out of which the Social Gospel developed.[14]

The mid-nineteenth-century efforts of the General Synod's influential head, Simon Samuel Schmucker, to create on such a basis a truly "American Lutheranism" had, indeed, been denounced by more traditionalist Lutherans as nothing more than Calvinist syncretism. Eastern Lutheranism had not, in fact, embraced the modernist project (even the ULCA refused to join the Federal Council of Churches), but its apologetic did incorporate elements of evolutionary and scientific thought, and in its cultural posture it did wish to remain firmly in the mainstream of American theology and social action. By the early twentieth century, this also applied partly to such smaller, ethnic-based Lutheran synods as the (Swedish) Augustana Synod and the Synod of the Norwegian Lutheran Church in America.[15]

In opposition to these relatively liberal groups stood the very conservative Lutheran Church–Missouri Synod with its million confirmed members, the Wisconsin Synod, and the Iowa Synod, as well as a multitude of tiny, ethnically based synodal organizations. All these tended to clung tenaciously not only to their separate, bibliocentric educational institutions but also to a strictly literal understanding of their confessional books, and they militantly opposed the embrace of extrabiblical authorities of interpretation. These conservative synods also tended to be culturally more out of the American mainstream and ethnically more cohesive than those of Eastern Lutheranism.[16] Both these clusters had their own distinct views on the League of Nations, even as they shared a more general commonality that set them apart from non-Lutheran approaches to internationalism.

Eastern Lutheranism and the League of Nations

When representatives of Eastern Lutheranism came to discuss the issues of war and peace, international cooperation, and morality, they tended to carry their qualified liberalism over to their foreign policy commentary. They consciously discussed these matters as secular, not theological, issues, but their involvement in nontheological fields of inquiry made them also regard such issues as worthy of attention. During World War I and in early 1919—before the text of the League of Nations Covenant was out—many representatives of Eastern Lutheranism put on record views sympathetic or supportive of a League of Nations, and sometimes these views were couched in terms just as optimistic as those of the Social Gospelers proper. The more these relatively liberal, initially sympathetic Lutherans came to learn about the details of the League Covenant, however, the more they began to waver and reassess their early position.

When it still existed as an independent body, the General Synod led the way for Lutheran pro-League sentiment. Throughout 1918, its *Lutheran Church Work and Observer* was explicitly supportive of the Federal Council's and the Church Peace Union's wartime campaign for what it called "a larger democracy, international justice, and a league of nations." It equated Woodrow Wilson's stated war aims with the trope of "Christianizing international relations," and it preemptively assailed those "strong, selfish, greedy" people, the munitions manufacturers and militaristic nationalists, whom it expected to fight the League once adherence to it would start to be discussed. Contributors to the journal even celebrated the prospect of a "United States of the World," called the putative League the "first practical step which is before us to bring on peace on earth," and repeatedly insisted that Lutheran traditions aside, the churches should forcefully speak out in its support and "enlist the sympathy and active interest of all good people" for it.[17]

By early 1919, other writers had joined in broadcasting the General Synod's type of reasoning in the other journals of the groups that came to form the ULCA. By that time, the editors and many contributing writers in the *Lutheran*, the *Lutheran Church Review*, and the *Lutheran Quarterly* agreed that the League of Nations was "not a visionary, impracticable project" but rather "the one wise, and the only reasonable course" to take. More specifically, many in the ULCA endorsed the arbitral and juridical goals of the League to Enforce Peace, the sanctions regime of collective security, and the equality of economic rights and opportunities that Wilson had outlined in his Fourteen Points. Some of them even suggested that a distinct world legislative assembly should be part of the League. Confidence in the durability of a peace based on such mechanisms tended to be predicated on that duo of very liberal authorities, history and "scientific advancement," and those Lutherans who appealed to these authorities contended that whatever faults the League yet possessed, these lay not in its core idea, in its structures or mechanisms, but in the insufficient public support and moral clout upon which the managers of these structures could depend. When the U.S. Senate refused to ratify the League Covenant, some of these individuals denounced that body as "timid" and as "reactionary and jealous."[18]

One of these individuals, who was supportive of the League in principle and well versed in and influenced by the secular philosophical currents of the age, was John A. W. Haas, a New York pastor and president of Muhlenberg Seminary, one of the leading institutions of Eastern Lutheranism. He had been partly educated in Germany and had acquired there some modernistic theological notions, including a basic willingness to accommodate evolutionary theories.[19] In discussing the League, Haas revealed the influence of this education. He sympathized with those who saw human history as a gradual evolution toward more pacific and collaborative—more "Christian"—types of order, and he felt that liberal League enthusiasts were correct in trying to limit the sovereignty of nation-states. They were correct, he averred, because German war making had shown the bankruptcy of all notions that reserved to the state the final authority in matters affecting others and because the whole concept of unlimited state sovereignty was, in any case, a "remnant of mistaken truth inherited from the Middle Ages," a residue of papal imperialism and domination. He thus guardedly endorsed the core precept of modern internationalism, the idea that there was more security for all nations and all peoples, including Christians, in a new world order that subjected its operations to an impartial supranational authority.[20]

Yet even in the ranks of the Eastern tradition, these kinds of pro-League statements issued from rather irenic individuals and not from synodal authorities. League supporters had almost no success in translating their sentiments into official pronouncements. Even Haas could not inject his personal views into the official "General Proclamation" of the ULCA, although he was one of its drafters in November 1918. The ULCA proclamation did endorse "such an agreement of nations as shall be entirely unbiased and just to all who obey the laws that make for the common good of humankind, and as shall have adequate power to protect and defend the nations against any and all aggressions." It added, however, that "the root of war is sin" and that a "final unity of mankind" could come only after all nations were converted to Christianity.[21] At its next meeting, in 1920, the ULCA president, Frederick H. Knubel, insisted on further tempering this semi-endorsement of the League by pointedly criticizing all efforts at world-bettering by "law or force" and by demoting what he called the reigning popular "emphasis on great organization" that was predicated on the supposition that "all actions must be mass movements and nations must stand as units."[22]

The official reticence was further highlighted when two of the ULCA's three constituent members, the old General Synod and the United Synod of the Evangelical Lutheran Churches in the South, that held last-minute premerger conventions failed to place the League issue on the agenda. Both of them did come out with detailed statements in support of President Wilson's Fourteen Points—but neither included in this endorsement explicit support for the plank on the League of Nations. The convention proceedings of neither mentioned the League by name, and both insisted that world peace was possible and democracy safe only if imbued with the principles of the Gospel and practiced by Christian states.[23]

Even the National Lutheran Council, the collaborative organ for wartime public activities that was dominated by Eastern Lutheranism, decided not to petition the Senate in favor of League ratification. It then dismissed the whole committee that had been considering such a move. Instead, the council issued a statement on the League debate in which it stressed that a reconciliation of nations could come only through a preceding reconciliation of all peoples with the Christian God. The only one of the council's members that took a clear position was the (Swedish American) Augustana Synod, but when it did so, it refused to endorse the League Covenant because it did not feel that its provisions went far enough in a truly Christian direction.[24]

Apart from these ambiguous statements, official Lutheran sympathies simply were not voiced for any kind of liberal Christian internationalism. Just as important, those individuals who did voice a muted personal version of such sympathy, such as Haas, took care to add significant and persistent caveats that set them distinctly apart from the League's main clerical enthusiasts. As the major political fight over the League came closer in the course of 1919, these warnings tended to take the place of their earlier statements supportive of the League.

Typically, Haas equivocated between the benefits of limiting state sovereignty and the dangers of allowing the establishment of new supranational centers of economic control and direction. Even as he apparently contradicted Lutheran traditions on subjection to temporal authority—by welcoming a world state that limited national sovereignty—he nevertheless kept insisting that expansive concepts of a "world union" contained the dangerous potentiality of future transfers of power to a new international "social abstraction" with well-nigh-unlimited powers. This he could not countenance, and he insisted, in particular, that the League of Nations not be permitted to expand its authority to cover economic matters. He also stressed the need to maintain the "variety of mankind," and he opined that its national cultures, traditions, and "racial inheritances are of value" and should in no wise be suffered to be overwhelmed by internationalist ideas or organizations.[25]

Similarly, many Lutherans who were in principle supportive of the League of Nations kept insisting that to be effective, the League needed to be backed up by an entirely new moral opinion of the world. This world moral opinion had to be first constructed, disseminated, and maintained before the mechanisms of the League could work. Moreover, only the churches—not politicians, the League itself, or the modernist clergy—could manufacture such a world moral opinion. It had to be based on the "Christian spirit" and on it alone. By that spirit, as Theodore E. Schmauk, the leading theologian of the relatively conservative General Council (the third, more confessionally traditionalist of the ULCA's member bodies), emphasized, one could not understand the spirit of those Social Gospelers who would "absorb the whole significance of the gospel into social work" and who saw it as the church's task to legislate men into morality. Many Eastern Lutherans indeed warned that the League, if not infused with a Christian spirit other than that of the Social Gospel, was likely to turn into a new socially and economically dictatorial "world empire" that would be "a menace to society." If so, it would not be that different from Russian Bolshevism.[26]

The liberal Lutherans who spoke thus also stressed that the needed world moral opinion could not be had by way of a "new Tower of Babel," not through any such "mixed world" of Christians and pagans in which these two groups cooperated by the lights of their separate faiths. No matter how liberal, even those Lutherans who were most supportive of the League of Nations still agreed that the necessary precondition for the League's success was the evangelization of all member states and their resultant, habitual performance according to the principles of Lutheran confessionalism.[27] Even the writer who in the *Lutheran Quarterly* had pronounced the League worthy of "hearty endorsement" had immediately gone on to stress that Lutherans should, of course, countenance no kind of "idolizing" of temporal competencies in solving the problems of the age. His support for the League, he had underlined, was based strictly on the assumption that only men and women who had "Christ in [their] hearts" could profitably operate the League.[28]

Finally, even the ULCA's *Lutheran Church Work and Observer*, which had been so effusive in its praise of the League idea only months before, by March 1919 had come to different conclusions. Now it believed that no matter how "desirable" and "noble and worthy" the League of Nations was in theory, its attempt to "actualize a Christian ideal" by political means was sure to fail in practice. Prayers for its success should still be said, but the *Lutheran Church Work and Observer* now felt that

> if men generally were born again by divine grace and were filled with the spirit of love to God and to man, we should expect [the League's] success. But as long as the majority of the citizens and the leaders of nations are unregenerate and are controlled in action by selfish and narrow-minded and sordid motives, they are sure to nullify at least partly, the noble ideal of peace. . . . The presence of human sin militate[s] against the complete or even partial success of the League of Nations.[29]

These caveats and reservations resembled those that issued from the fundamentalist movement more than they resembled liberal internationalism of howsoever moderate or subdued a variety. The League of Nations commentary of even the relatively most liberal Lutherans confirmed that Lutherans and fundamentalists shared, to a significant degree, the culturalist posture that utterly rejected Social Gospel methods and definitions of world Christianization. Even the most liberal Lutherans absolutely denied that a secular world institution in which Christians and non-Christians cooperated for purposes of peacekeeping and mutual social progress could advance the purposes of Christ. All of them insisted also that an overweening supranational authority could not possibly be safe unless administered by Christian men and by them alone.

The League of Nations as Works-Righteousness

The similarity between Lutheran and fundamentalist thinking was particularly clear in the League-related discourse of Eastern Lutheranism's opposite pole, which was made up of the conservative Wisconsin Synod, Iowa Synod, and Lutheran Church–Missouri Synod. Of these, the Missouri Synod was the largest and also the most forthright in making its views nationally known. Its views were particularly firmly grounded in the theology and doctrines of Lutheran confessionalism as interpreted by its own authoritative tradition and organs. The synod owed its origins to nineteenth-century immigrants who had left Germany because they felt that the territorial state churches, or *Landeskirchen*, which in their areas had merged Lutheran and Calvinist groups into one, were violations of true Lutheran confessionalism. Since then, the Missouri Synod had been among the most consistent critics of what it regarded as the confessional laxity and corruption of most other forms of American Lutheranism.[30]

Strict Lutheran confessionalism made for a conservative anti-internationalist position that incorporated all the generic Christian arguments against the League of Nations and added original contributions of its own. These latter were rooted in three theologically based suppositions. The Missouri, Iowa, and Wisconsin synods criticized the League because that organization seemed to them, first, to confuse the Kingdom of God with temporal legal polity, thus violating the doctrine of the two kingdoms; second, to include and legitimate dangerous notions of human self-sufficiency, that is, social perfection through law and without God and personal conversion, and a works-righteousness doctrine of salvation; and third, to be conducive to future Roman Catholic domination over the nations of Christendom.

Articles V, XVI, and XX of the Augsburg Confession were by far the most-used confessional reference points for the Missouri, Iowa, and Wisconsin synods' argument against the League of Nations. These articles adumbrated the doctrines of the two kingdoms, in America often renamed the separation of church and state, and of justification by faith alone.[31] These two core doctrines were felt to be relevant to the League of Nations issue, for two interlocked reasons.

They were relevant, first, because the Lutheran conservatives saw the League's churchly protagonists as having invested this temporal legal polity with competencies belonging only to the church; and second, because the very fact of churchly embrace of a temporal authority, regardless of its nature, was felt to be inadmissible if done in the way that the liberal churchmen did. Lutherans tended to ascribe both errors to the Calvinism dominant in much of American religiosity and politics, that is, to the Calvinist doctrine of the "public means of grace" that even the League's Presbyterian critics put forth. The resultant attempt at making men moral through legislation seemed to Lutherans both counterproductive and contradictory to the Word of God, under the best of circumstances, but when applied to the League of Nations, it seemed a renaming of the works-righteousness doctrine of salvation.

As argued by Martin S. Sommer and Theodore Graebner, the influential editors of the *Lutheran Witness* and *Der Lutheraner*—two leading Missouri Synod publications—this "mixing of politics and religion" characterized the Social Gospel as a whole, its international dimension included. On the international level, the Calvinistic Social Gospel led to an investing of secular international legislation with definite salvific purposes. These purposes violated both the separation of church and state and the doctrine of justification by faith alone. It was bad enough, these two men suggested, that this kind of Calvinism held sway in domestic politics; to now expand it also to the international plane was worse still. For the fact was that the League of Nations was a "purely secular, political" institution, dealing with temporal matters—not indeed unworthy for that, given also that the authorities of the temporal realm were a divine deposit. But it was wrong to try to make these authorities transgress the decreed limits of their competence. Temporal authorities could only assure peace and security, no more; and thus a League of Nations should therefore be assessed solely on its ability to meet those limited tasks. [32]

However, it was not for churchmen to make this kind of assessment, because "such subjects do not come within the purview of the Christian pulpit." When churchmen did try to define the competencies of purely secular institutions, domestically and internationally, investing them with the semblance of a salvific function, they were contributing a new institution that was of neither the temporal nor the churchly realm. On those criteria, implied Graebner and Sommer, the expansively envisioned and legitimated League of Nations failed. [33]

Lehre und Wehre, the theological journal of the Missouri Synod, was just as clear on this point. American society and politics had always been "dominated" by the Calvinist worldview, it claimed, a worldview that was based on "rationalism" and not on a loyal, literal interpretation of the Bible's message. The result was an endless series of attempts to reform society through "the Gospel of good works"—through a "Doology" (the doctrine of doing things), which had also spawned the recent quest for a "Christian world order," "a Christian democracy" of cooperating and peaceable nations. Impossible to attain though they were in the light of original sin, by the time of World War I these kinds of "Calvinist" visions had so deeply burrowed into all Protestant denominations, including some Lutheran groups, that, according to *Lehre und Wehre*, they were obscuring the whole purpose and mission of the church.[34]

The journal gave as a case in point a mid-1919 appeal issued by the National Lutheran Commission for Soldiers and Sailors' Welfare (a constituent of the National Lutheran Council), where this supposedly Lutheran organization had inveighed in favor of using collective action to right "individual, social, industrial, political, racial, and *international* wrongs." Such a "sad" undertaking, *Lehre und Wehre* was convinced, did not belong to the church. The churches existed simply to preach the doctrines of sin and of salvation through Christ alone, and whenever they taught the "false doctrine" of partaking in human redemption through world-bettering works, they were lost to God.[35] The League of Nations was not mentioned here by name (it rarely was in Lutheran theological discussion), but the implication was nevertheless clear.

Der Lutheraner even appealed directly to Martin Luther to make the point. In an editorial titled "Luther über einen Völkerbund" (Luther on a League of Nations) and published some months after the Senate had refused to ratify the League Covenant for the final time, its editors quoted from Luther's 1523 tract *Von weltlichen Obrigkeit* (Temporal Authority) to contend that even if the Calvinist project of making nation-states Christian through legislation were successful in the first instance, there would inevitably come a later reckoning and backlash that would shatter all that had apparently been achieved. According to Luther, there would always exist "wicked people" (*bösen*); thus, even if an earthly Christian power were to take over the entire world, the wicked would always frustrate even the best-prepared and most consensually accepted plans for world pacification and harmony. They could not but abuse the "Christian liberty" that by definition was a by-product of legislated world Christianization, for they were natural men overwhelmed by their sin. "Therefore," wrote Luther,

> it is out of the question that there should be a common Christian government over the whole world, or indeed over a single country or any considerable body of people, for the wicked always outnumber the good. Hence, a man who

would venture to govern an entire country, or the world, with the gospel would be like a shepherd who would put together in one fold wolves, lions, eagles, and sheep. . . . The sheep would doubtless keep the peace and allow themselves to be fed and governed peacefully, but they would not live long, nor would one beast survive another.[36]

The editors of *Der Lutheraner* concluded from this that even if a new world order that was allegedly, or even really, rooted in the principles of the Gospel was forced upon a world that remained more un-Christian than Christian, the natural inclinations of unredeemed humanity would before long break out and defeat the experiment.[37]

The Iowa Synod's *Kirchliche Zeitschrift* agreed. It maintained that as much as the world boasted of its high ethical ideals, short of conversion and rebirth in Christ, no one in the world was capable of "mercy and neighborly love" nor, therefore, of establishing durable world peace. The works of the ethicist and the world reformer were "like the flowers that lack the vitality to develop into palatable fruit," for they wanted the fertilization that God only could provide. Therefore, stressed the Iowa Synod's leading exegete, Johannes Michael Reu, it was worse than futile to place a nation's trust in "human works and performances and [to] laud them as being instrumental in effecting one's salvation." Among these human works, Reu classed "fasting" and "monasticism, prohibition, humanity, *peace congresses*," and he maintained that those who trusted any of these were in the grip of that prophesized "willful delusion and self-worship," which would take the world over in the last days when the "world dreams of a golden future in which all things shall be perfect." This advice was also related to the Paris peace conference that was then under way, for as Reu underlined in mid-1919, it was also based on faith in human self-sufficiency, and it would also fail because its participants and champions were blind to God and to the fact of ineradicable sin.[38] In a January 1920 sermon, Reu was as explicit on this point as any conservative Lutheran of the time:

> The main characteristic of our times is men's trust in themselves and their rejection of the Word of God. Alliances are formed today, alliances with one's own strength and wisdom; and He who is the only helper is ignored. . . . The future is to be made secure by political wisdom, built on the principle that "might makes right." The age of abiding peace is to be brought about by a league of nations. God's Word and testimony are considered too insignificant to be of any effect in our days.[39]

In other words, conservative Lutherans maintained that it was false doctrine to teach the possibility of perpetual peace short of universal personal conversion to Christ. It was also false doctrine to expect world peace and harmony from a forced, political, and legal subjection of the peoples to an abstract system of ideals and mechanisms, no matter how nobly actuated, which they did not actually, spiritually, endorse. Therefore, all political attempts to abolish or outlaw war were futile as long as unredeemed human nature remained what it was: evil. Jesus did not come into the world to bring peace, *Der Lutheraner* never tired of stressing, nor did He ever teach that by human effort the world could be rid of sin and turned into a paradise.[40]

Disarmament was therefore out of the question, and any League Covenant that removed from nation-states their divinely granted rights to self-defense was in blatant contravention to the Word of God.[41] Equally suspect were the collective security mechanisms that had actually been codified in the League Covenant, for these were unlikely to keep the peace and likely to breed only more wars, more revolutions, and more bloodshed. According to the *Lutheran Witness*, these mechanisms only fooled the peoples of the world into a false sense of security without actually producing safety.[42] Conservative Lutherans, Eastern Lutherans, thus showed practically no interest in or appreciation for the arbitral and collective security regimen that was espoused by the League to Enforce Peace; rather, they placed their trust in national armies and in military preparedness and charged all alternatives with obfuscation of the patent, immovable facts of temporal life and sinful human nature.

Moreover, the Lutheran conservatives maintained that whenever churchly leaders did, despite such warnings, become involved in politics and whenever they did endorse a specific political program or institution, they were weakening the salvific power of the church. This applied especially to clerical activities on behalf of the League of Nations. Given the immensity of the unrequitable hopes of humanity that already existed after World War I, hopes that were bound to lead to profound disillusionment, Lutherans insisted that church leaders should have known better than to promise an imminent peace, plenty, and harmony on earth. By investing the League of Nations with just these promises, and by sacralizing the whole institution in the process, liberal churchmen were helping to pave the way for that popular abandonment of the Christian faith that must follow the collapse of their internationalist utopia. For if the Christian faith became identified with a given political program and organization that failed, as the League was bound to do, the churches would be blamed. Already, the editors of the *Lutheran Witness* had heard an (unnamed) senatorial critic of the League of Nations state that he was so shocked by the political activity of leftist preachers and by their investment of the League with sacral imagery that he was minded to vote against it "even if Jesus Christ Himself appeared on Earth and commanded that the Senate should cast its vote in favor."

Such "blasphemy," felt the *Lutheran Witness*, was an inevitable concomitant of a Calvinist churchly essaying into political contention.[43]

Lutherans made another theologically based observation on the likely results of the churchly embrace of the League. Like the dispensationalists but on different theological grounds, they implied that the liberals' League concept was part and parcel of their rejection of the traditional doctrines of the reformed Protestant faith and of their quest for an entirely "new religion." Incarnationalists of a social and somewhat pantheistic kind as they were, ready to also allow for manifestations of deity in non-Christian cultures and philosophies, the liberals' quest could only yield, as the New York pastor William Schoenfeld suggested, a new version of the "old pagan and pharisaic formula of self-salvation through the Law." This quest should not be seen merely in terms of the Social Gospel as currently constituted, Schoenfeld stressed, but as encompassing all collective pursuit of political, social, economic, and industrial improvement with the stated goal of "heaven on earth" and with human agency as its sole instrument.[44]

Others stressed that the inner dynamics of the Social Gospel inexorably pointed toward a new universalist religion with an ever-clearer salvific rationale of its own. Their coming modernist, secular religion was not unlike that which had permeated a Germany imbued with materialist Darwinism and the sacralization of the state. Any such quasi-religion would be inadmissible, no matter how nobly actuated or how closely modeled on Protestant ethics, because (in the words of J. W. Behnken, a future president of the Missouri Synod) the true Protestant religion "challenged the right of every other religion to exist, and has set for itself the claim that it is the only right religion."[45]

All this, according to the Lutheran contention, would be the result of Calvinism in politics; of violating the separation of church and state; and of confusing the public, administrative functions of temporal authority and the personal, salvific functions of the church. Not only the safety and liberty of nation-states would be thereby compromised but also the very salvation of individuals themselves, for justification by faith alone was nowhere to be found in modern internationalism's new doctrines of earth-perfecting and redeeming works. It was a case against the League of Nations that only Lutherans could have made in quite these terms, for it flowed directly from their confessional writings, especially from the doctrine of the two kingdoms.

So strongly did the *Lutheran Witness*, the leading English-language conservative Lutheran journal, feel about this that in the early months of 1920—when the Senate was embarking on its final ratification debates—it decided to depart from the principle of never taking an explicit stand on a purely political question. For the only time in the course of the League controversy, the journal explicitly and emphatically stated that no Lutheran should join the other Protestants' campaign in favor of the ratification of the League Covenant. The journal was prompted by a circular petition that was sent in late 1919 to all religious journals by the National Committee on the Churches and the Moral Aims of the War. This petition appealed to "every Christian" to write to his or her senators, asking for speedy ratification, and also to arrange community meetings and mass protests in favor of the League and to persuade at least ten of one's closest Christian friends to join the campaign. Clergy were further asked to preach a sermon on the subject of the League. Some fear must have existed that some Lutherans would follow this advice for the *Witness* to have made such a major issue of its demand for abstention. However, the journal said it was glad that, as far as it knew, not a single Lutheran minister had thus far given a single sermon on the subject.[46] All the available evidence suggests that this was indeed so.

Lutherans, the Antichrist, and the Pope

Embedded in the historical legacy of Lutheran confessionalism was not only a distinct anti-Calvinist polemic but also an equally pronounced anti-papism. This, too, remained a specifically Lutheran subtext in most discussions of the League of Nations. To a degree both striking and unique, conservative Lutherans chose the religious League controversy as a plane on which to rehearse their prejudices against all things Roman Catholic. Anti-Catholicism was, of course, present in many a dispensationalist and Calvinist critique of the League, but in those circles it was never developed systematically, at length, or over a long period of time. But in a Lutheran context, the ancient grudge against Rome was still so acute and festering that it could not be kept from intruding into most commentaries on political matters. In writings dealing specifically with the League of Nations, the antipapal motif was particularly prominent, given that Popes Pius X and Benedict XV had campaigned for such a league since before the war and wanted the Vatican to join it.[47]

The American Catholic hierarchy was actually just as divided on the League as other Christians, and some of its most luminous bishops even appeared on joint platforms with anti-League senators and demanded non-ratification of the League Covenant.[48] But given the clear papal endorsement, this did not convince Lutherans. They could point, too, to the Catholic hierarchy's much noted Bishops' Program of Reconstruction (1919), which had endorsed a most comprehensive postwar rearrangement of socioeconomic and political life. The National Catholic War Council—the official war agency of the hierarchy, which was told to popularize and implement that program—had enthusiastically joined the liberal Protestant clamor for an international organization. Other Catholic agencies had done likewise, and when so doing, they had sided with the broadest, socially reformist agenda for postwar international reconstruction. They had indeed suggested, repeatedly, that a socially reformist League of Nations was an essentially Catholic conception.[49]

In Lutheran anti-League writings that were predicated on anti-Catholicism, Rome was still sometimes referred to as the eschatological Antichrist and the League of Nations seen as the Antichrist's demonic institution. This equating of the pope with the Antichrist was the single instance of Lutherans accepting the eschatological categories of thought that were normative for premillennialists. It was based both on Article IV of the Schmalkald Articles and on Luther's own writings.[50] Throughout its existence, the Missouri Synod had championed this traditional Lutheran tenet, and it continued to do so in the World War I period.[51]

It was more normal by 1919, however, for Lutheran antipapists to make reference to the extant temporal powers and supposed future ambitions of the pope, quite apart from any explicit eschatological motifs. They contended simply that the League of Nations was a dangerous papal instrument of power, deliberately structured to serve this end and endorsed by the Vatican with a view to forwarding its quest for temporal world domination. Lutherans stressed that even if the Vatican managed to fully chain and subordinate the League to its ambitions, it could not indeed exercise such dominion for long—because, as Lutherans were wont to stress, the divine intervention of the Lutheran Reformation had shattered the power of the Antichrist forever. But any attempt by the pope to challenge that state of affairs could still cause grave harm to all Protestant nations of the world, and it was up to Lutherans especially to make everyone aware of this possibility.[52]

Theodore Graebner of Condordia Theological Seminary was particularly vocal on the supposed Catholic domination of the League of Nations. As the editor of the *Lutheran Witness* and *Der Lutheraner* in addition to his faculty duties, Graebner had open to him more influential publicity outlets than any other single individual in American Lutheranism, and he used them to run anti-Catholic commentary on the League. This commentary unfolded, it would appear, according to a considered plan.[53]

As Graebner argued, both the Vatican itself and all the national hierarchies subservient to it were still bent on "world-dominion." All of them were incessantly endeavoring to "crush out the light of the Gospel," and temporal domination was "only the means" to that end. The papacy seemed to have settled on the League of Nations as the most promising agency because the

League afforded unprecedented global means of prescribing legislation and also because Vatican membership would allow its diplomats to directly interfere in the internal politics of member states. This was especially the case, Graebner averred, in the new nation-states that had arisen out of the imploded German, Austro-Hungarian, and Russian empires, where papal representatives were reputedly busy at work, sowing the seeds of still more confusion and chaos. The deliberately engineered chaos was to act as the backdrop to the Vatican's offer, sure to come before long, of its own agency as a calming and controlling influence. The new nations were especially susceptible, Graebner implied, to having their internal and international policies dictated by the Vatican. He feared, indeed, that "rivers of blood" would yet have to flow before the pope's alleged machinations were voided.[54]

The prediction was thus dire because Graebner also believed, or claimed, that the pope's repertoire of subversion included many additional tracks. The multipronged approach was allegedly designed to subject the Protestant nations to such a barrage of pervasive pressure that they could find no respite and would succumb before long. The other papal tools, he argued, included international finance, world Freemasonry, and the Interchurch World Movement, as well as the subdued but not truly changed German nation, which recent history had shown was especially open to manipulation by the Vatican. Russian Bolshevism also appeared somehow to be linked to all this; Graebner claimed that the pope still had additional, sinister plans ready "for world-conquest through new wars and revolutions."[55]

Graebner offered his most comprehensive exposition of this anti-Catholic argument in 1921, after the Senate had already refused to ratify the League Covenant. Then the League was no longer a matter of immediate political controversy. But he had seen to it that the same set of charges was repeated at regular intervals from the beginning of World War I through the Paris peace conference and into the Senate's deliberations. At the very beginning of the war, the *Lutheran Witness* had denounced Pope Pius X's 1914 offer of the good offices of the Vatican to settle the war, which offer it had branded as but a part of the pope's unending quest for world domination.[56] There followed the charge that if Vatican representatives were allowed into the coming postwar peace conference, they would dominate the proceedings by manipulating and misleading, as only Jesuits could, any Protestants present.[57] The apparent wartime rise of Catholicism in Britain, France, Italy, and Spain was also bemoaned, as was the granting of government recognition to Catholic social reform and war relief organizations in the United States.[58]

Many conservative Lutherans tended to see all these phenomena as but the different aspects of the quest for world power that the League of Nations would culminate. This was so whether the Vatican was allowed to join that organization or not. For even if it was not allowed to join (and it was not), Lutherans were certain that the predominance of Catholics in many of the League's member states would still make it possible for the pope to reach his alleged nefarious goals.

The Catholic Church, summarized Weert Janssen, a Missouri Synod pastor, in January 1919, "casts longing eyes upon the thrones of kings and is incessantly at work to realize its most ardent desire: the gaining of temporal power. . . . [A] society of nations under the control of the Pope, that is the aim and hope of the Catholic Church to-day." All true Christians ought to act to frustrate such plans, Janssen insisted, but this should take place primarily through earnest prayer for such a direct intervention from God as alone could prevent the creation of any Catholicized League of Nations.[59]

Their Lutheran critics did not, of course, regard Roman Catholics as real Christians. In this the Catholics were, after a manner, classed together with the League of Nation's many pagan member states and projected future member states. Although it was a minor and not dominating strain in Lutheran critiques, laments over the membership in the League of such non-Christian peoples and nations sometimes figured in their commentary as well. Though not as pronounced as in some of the dispensationalist and Calvinist circles, this lament yielded similar exhortations against "yoke fellowship" and a "mixed world." Even representatives of Eastern Lutheranism distinguished themselves with racialist remarks. Thus, quite apart from all their primary, theological grievances against the League, many a conservative Lutheran felt that even if, in the operations of the League, all these could somehow be mitigated—unlikely as that was—there was still the matter of the League's composition. Christians and non-Christians simply could not meaningfully cooperate, could not keep the peace or further any worthy goals, because they did not share the values and insights that membership in the spiritual Kingdom of God imparted.[60]

Lutheran Political Lobbying

One final, minor strain of Lutheran critique of the League of Nations—but the only one that prompted some Lutheran clergy into organized political lobbying—was that relating to the Versailles peace settlement's terms on religious freedom and the future of the mission stations formerly belonging to German churches. An Anglo-American delegation of Protestants had pressured the Paris peacemakers to assure that the freedom and safety of missionary activity was guaranteed in the peace treaty. Although they had succeeded in having a general statement inserted into the League Covenant on this matter, many conservative Christians remained far from satisfied with the relevant Covenant article. Another campaign was therefore launched to prompt the League's American congressional critics to insert stricter guidelines into the Covenant before it was ratified. The apolitical Lutherans, too, organized themselves to reach the shared Christian end. They violated their theoretical strictures against political lobbying and legislative activity by joining Calvinist activists in pressuring U.S. senators. Even the Missouri Synod did this.[61]

However, conservative Lutherans were even less satisfied with what was happening to the German mission stations. The British and other allies had taken over these stations as they had conquered German colonies in Africa, and the missionaries themselves had been repatriated. In early 1919, it seemed likely that the Paris peace conference would proceed to confiscate the stations along with other German assets. That would have disadvantaged the Lutheran mission effort, given that most of the stations in question were Lutheran, and this neither the ULCA nor the Missouri Synod could countenance.

To sort things out, a delegation of the (Missouri) General Synod Board's representatives went the rounds of senators' offices while the Senate was deliberating on the League Covenant's ratification. The delegation did not do this in order to endorse or not to endorse ratification but simply to impress on the League's opponents that if they did attach reservations to the ratification instrument, these ought to include guarantees on religious liberty and the continued freedom of operation of German mission stations.[62] As the delegation's head, the Reverend D. H. Steffens stressed that there was "grave danger to our country if it became a party to any scheme of government which would place difficulties or hindrances in the way of Christian people who are earnestly striving to carry out our Lord's missionary command." The delegation also told senators that the Covenant's lack of explicit guarantees for religious liberty was proof that the League was not the "culmination of Christian ideals but of the gross materialism of our age."[63]

Agreement was eventually reached on the former German missions. A number of them did fall into the hands of Calvinist missionaries from Europe, but American Lutherans undertook to take over the maintenance and care of the rest in a trustee arrangement. This was a significant financial and practical burden, but it also helped foster a major Lutheran missionary movement in the interwar years.[64] Thus the sole entrance of American Lutherans into political lobbying about the League underlined the general Lutheran juxtaposition of traditional missionary work as the hope of the world and the Social Gospelers' vision of international reform through a League of Nations. Politically unadvertised though it was, this spoke volumes.

Lutheran Anti-Internationalism Summarized

This political lobbying for the German missions and for inclusion of the principle of religious freedom in the League Covenant was the exception that confirmed the rule. The rule was a Lutheran proscription against the churches ever essaying into political controversy, and the exception was their own essaying into the League of Nations controversy. The Lutherans did not, indeed, set out to influence the political fight over the League (except on the two issues that they felt touched their church witness directly); what they did instead was participate in the parallel religious debate over the religious implications of international organization that was being effected on the basis of the modernist Social Gospel agenda. Missouri Synod Lutherans denounced all aspects of this agenda, and those of Eastern Lutheranism only some, but both regarded modern internationalism with unease. In the process of articulating this unease, both contributed to the creation of a Christian anti-internationalism that would in future years become overtly political even in their own denominations.

It is moot to ponder whether American Lutheran spokesmen actually believed all the more lurid theses that they proffered on the Catholic conspiracy or on the threat to salvation posed by the putative new religion of the League of Nations. These theses may also have been offered out of habit or as didactic tools in a continuing effort at self-definition. The point is that the League of Nations idea *was* comprehensively denounced and that practically all Lutheran clergy *were* kept from assisting in any way the coming of modern internationalism. Moreover, the case against the League was most emphatically doctrinal, not prompted by polemic linked to any battle for denominational control (as with Baptists or Presbyterians), for there was none to speak of. Nor was there any desire to insert into the debate any alternative conceptions of a League of Nations (as in some Calvinist circles), for Lutherans on the whole had none. Lutherans simply argued that the lack of world peace and social justice were "not caused by inadequate laws but by an unregenerate heart" and that one needed only to adhere to "the preaching of the Gospel—those verities which never need revision, and which bring to the hearts of men the peace of God which passeth all understanding."[65] No international organizations were needed for this.

The existence of a distinct and uniquely Lutheran critique of the League of Nations supports the contention that the American Protestant experience has been much more varied and nuanced than the historian Martin Marty's long-consensual two-party paradigm about the ubiquity of the fundamentalist/modernist divide, in all denominations, would suggest. This further appears to validate the alternative thesis on a distinct Protestant center, or a third party, that was made up of separate, strongly confessional traditions unaccommodated either by pietistic fundamentalism or by the socially activist Social Gospel.[66] Lutherans had their own unique interpretation of the League of Nations that built upon their confessional distinctives, and it led them to emphasize the two-kingdom concept in ways no one else could, as well as to a running anti-Calvinist commentary that was distinctly theirs. Also, the Lutheran commentary on the League's Catholic menace was without exact parallels elsewhere.

At the same time, conservative Lutherans had frequent recourse to general evangelical arguments that resembled those of the dispensationalists. Some individuals in the camp of Eastern Lutheranism did indeed voice a very diluted version of the liberal and Social Gospelers' enthusiasm for the League of Nations, but even these individuals tempered their support with significant, fundamentalist-like caveats and reservations. The Lutherans' case, therefore, was never truly in line with that of the Social Gospelers, but did show a considerable affinity for dispensationalist fundamentalists and a susceptibility to cooperate with them, or at least to mount polemics parallel to and supportive of theirs. In the League of Nations controversy, this did not yield practical, organized cooperation—certainly not in joint organizations even of an ad hoc nature—but it did lead to a Lutheran argument that significantly bolstered similar dispensationalist and Calvinist arguments. As a prompter for the pooling of the strength of all kinds of conservative evangelicals, which in real terms took place in the fundamentalist/modernist controversy some years later, this Lutheran anti-internationalism was no less important than its other, better-known catalysts.

The emphatically confessional nature of the Lutheran anti-League case should also disprove any suggestions that what really mattered was the ethnic prejudice that a denomination with predominantly German origins felt toward an international organization of which Germany was not a part and that imposed drastic punishments on Germany. This argument simply was not heard in American Lutheran discourse during the League controversy. There may well have persisted some such ethically based animosity toward the League; but if it did, it was channeled through secular German American organizations such as the Steuben Society. It simply did not figure in clerical discourse. What American Lutherans did do was to deduce from the alleged results of modernism in Germany the contention that the League of Nations, based on similar modernist notions, was likely to yield equally anti-Christian outcomes. In this core contention, American Lutherans fell firmly in line with other conservative evangelicals. Their critique of the League of Nations idea was just as pronounced, just as theologically grounded, and just as persistent as that of other conservative evangelicals.

CHAPTER FIVE

Methodists and Episcopalians: A Few Dissenting Voices

Among the denominations that were most supportive of the League of Nations were the Methodist Episcopal Church and the Protestant Episcopal Church. Probably no other denominations yielded as many passionate protagonists for Christian internationalism as these two, and nowhere was the anti-League position weaker and less influential. These two denominations also happened to be the ones that in 1919 were the most fully suffused by the presuppositions and goals of the Social Gospel, of which they had been the leading pioneers and corporate advocates from the start. Both denominations prided themselves on the significant role they had played in shaping American culture and in exporting American ideals around the world. Neither looked askance at direct political advocacy, for both had long defined themselves as the guardians of the nation's civil religion, which they tended to equate with their own public theologies. Their enthusiastic embrace of the cultural and political means of Christianization also helped explain their passionate work on behalf of the League of Nations.

The two denominations, of course, shared historical and theological roots in the worldwide Anglican Communion. But because the Methodists had left that communion in the late eighteenth century, they had eyed the Episcopalians with particular suspicion, and the Episcopalians had returned the apprehensive glare in full measure. Internally, both denominations had divided into several doctrinal strands, and externally they were so confident of their own calling that by the time that the League controversy erupted they allowed for no significant points of contact between them. The only reason to deal with them together is that both were dominated by the Social Gospel and both contained a small, conservative evangelical section that opposed this domination and, with it, Christian internationalism. In the process of battling their denominational powers that be, these Methodist and Episcopalian conservatives enunciated yet another version of Christian anti-internationalism.

~~~~~~~~⌐ Methodist Debates

By 1919, the Methodist Episcopal Church was the single largest Protestant denomination in the United States. With its some six million members, its highly decentralized structures, and its weak systems of doctrinal authority, it was hardly a group amenable to the kind of central direction that confessional Calvinists or the dispensationalists of the World Christian Fundamentals Association could use to enforce their views. Methodism thought of itself as a uniquely American religious group, indeed as *the* religious group that had defined the American interpenetration of religion and culture since the breakup of the colonial-era Calvinist ascendancy. At the core of this self-image lay a distinct preference for *action*, for doing things rather than doing theology, which defined Methodism to most Americans. By the early twentieth century, the Social Gospelers had managed to appropriate this preference for action so fully that the remaining Methodist conservatives felt shunned, marginalized, and out of tune with the majority of their brethren and sisters. Many of these conservatives had chosen to work with the World Christian Fundamentals Association instead, whereas others had separated into two Methodist offshoots, the Holiness churches and the Free Methodist Church, both of which disagreed with the modernist Social Gospel and claimed to be the "real" Wesleyans. Thus dispersed, conservative Methodists never could mount significant denominational challenges on any major issue of contention, the League of Nations issue included.[1]

Theologically, the Methodist majority's embrace of the League of Nations rested as much on the definite Arminian streak that persisted in post-Wesleyan theology as on the theology of action. Both these factors made the denomination susceptible to a certain heterodoxy, allowing as they did wide latitude for the right of private judgment. Indeed, traditional Wesleyan doctrine had always laid its emphasis on individualism—on the free availability of divine grace regardless of one's status or knowledge of doctrine, on the individual's free choice to accept grace, and on the individual's responsibilities after conversion and sanctification to pursue perfection in all areas of life.[2] Put simply, Methodism encouraged social and political effort more than most other forms of Protestantism—indeed, it defined itself through such effort. Because its Arminian core allowed its adherents to define the perimeters of this social and political effort largely as they wished, it was somewhat a foregone conclusion that once political Progressivism emerged as an option, many Methodists would interpret their duties as Christian guardians of the nation in terms of a Progressive and Social Gospel agenda.

The same individualistic dynamics applied also to those various Holiness churches that in the latter part of the nineteenth century had begun to separate from the Methodist orbit. In the case of these churches, however, the dynamics of Arminianism produced outcomes entirely different from those of the mainstream Methodism of the twentieth century. The Holiness churches remained extremely individualistic, entirely uninterested in corporate political or cultural effort, and their alternative to the increasingly collectivist Social Gospel was so-called social holiness, an essentially individualist and church-centered program of social alleviation and charity on the local level. The Salvation Army was the preeminent manifestation of this social holiness, a clear alternative to all programs of centralized and legislative world change, whether national or international. The Holiness churches, of course, also inveighed in favor of peace, progress, and equity, but they would not endorse any means of seeking such goals that removed social duties from the individual's sphere of action and placed them in a separate institution.[3]

In this latter insistence, the Holiness churches differed completely from the métier of most Methodists proper. That difference had, indeed, been a key reason for the Holiness groups' exit from the Methodist fold, for they could not abide the ascendancy of either modernist biblical theory or the institutional and increasingly secular orientations of the Social Gospel. In this, the Holiness churches shared the outlook of the few conservatives who stayed in the Methodist Church, and it was no surprise that these two groups also came to share the same attitude on the question of international social reform.

Among the Methodists proper, the Social Gospel triumphed because it, too, could be presented as the culmination of the denomination's lengthy engagement with radical social change. Early American Methodists had often been extremely radical socially and politically, and even if they became more respectable and conservative as they went about establishing their denomination as a national force in the pre–Civil War decades, the early example and inspiration lingered on. Even in the 1820s, some Methodists had advocated the use of state legislation for the redress of social grievances and for the redistribution of economic rewards. Later, Methodists had enthusiastically embraced the early Republican Party as a moral force for Christianizing the politics of the United States, and in the early twentieth century they remained firmly committed to that project.[4] There did abide a profound tension between Methodist individualism and pietism on the one hand, and the urge to reform society through collective agencies on the other hand. But it was also true that most leaders of the twentieth-century Methodist movement had very little difficulty in solving this tension in favor of the Social Gospel.

In this regard, and with a view to the League of Nations debates, the most representative and important Methodist organization came to be the Methodist Federation for Social Service. Under the direction of Harry F. Ward—a socialist-minded minister, a professor at Union Theological Seminary from 1914 to 1944, and an early leader of the American Civil Liberties Union—it was untiring in propagating the Social Gospelers' internationalist visions of radical reform. The federation's programs for radical social reform included a distinct sympathy toward Russian Bolshevism, for which Ward personally and through him Methodism in general became symbols distinctly notorious to all anticommunists. Indeed, Ward was wont to depict the Bolshevik experiment as an expression of the Christian search for a cooperative commonwealth and the Kingdom of God on Earth.[5]

Radical as this message was, the Social Service Federation's programs were, in theory, binding on Methodists. The relatively slight critique that they received from inside the denomination (until the mid-1920s) clearly showed how thoroughly the Social Gospel had won out among the Methodists. This was also evident in the definite underrepresentation of Methodist clergy in the World Christian Fundamentals Association, a fact noted and bemoaned by that organization's leader, who often tried to coax conservative Methodists to join in the group's activities.[6]

The result was that the Methodist Episcopal Church endorsed the Covenant of the League of Nations in May 1919. It was the first major denomination to give its endorsement. In 1920, it renewed the call.[7] Even before that official act, leading Methodist bishops and journals had been engaged in a passionate campaign for a "federation of the world" and a "league of free peoples" where, they averred, the Social Gospel would be implemented and the church would fulfill its mission as a worldwide "Social Redeemer." When opposition to the League began to increase, some preachers even compared President Woodrow Wilson to Christ, called him the leader of a "divine movement" who was being "crucified" by the "sheer selfishness" of the League's opponents.[8]

Even one book-length exposition of the Methodist case for the League appeared, Bishop Richard J. Cooke's *The Church and World Peace*, which came out in mid-1920. Cooke's case was typical: The world was inexorably moving toward a common "international mind," he claimed, and part of this process was the rapidly unfolding "moral and social unity of the race," under which the nations were beginning to perceive the insights of Christianity and on that basis to construct "perpetual peace." The League of Nations, though imperfect in some regards, was a mighty step toward the evolutionary goal, and it was up to the churches to sustain, nurture, and further inspire it. If the churches did not thus "mix in politics," they would be conquered by the world rather than vice versa; wherefore it was time to replace all "narrow view[s]" of the church's competency with the affirmation that "the world's social and political redemption" was indeed the church's business.[9]

According to Cooke, it was up to both the church and the League of Nations, working in tandem, to solidify the emergent moral unity and perpetual peace of humanity, and the millennium—but another name for the same—would surely come if the church persisted in its nurture. The church needed, however, to keep in mind that the League might relapse into a mere "old-fashioned alliance" and, above all, that "the League cannot become an effective institution or restraining force in future history, without the power of religion to support it." Cooke therefore stressed that "there must be moral sanction, there must be the compelling power of conscience, a spiritual, collective purpose unifying the masses of a nation, generated and sustained by religious inspiration." The only way to assure the availability of such a collective purpose for the League was to establish a parallel "Christian league, a league of Christendom supplementing the political League of Nations."[10]

This is as far as Methodist leaders were ever willing to go in expressing reservations about the League of Nations. Obviously, the reservations were minor, and they made but the slightest concessions to the evangelical anti-internationalist case. Not much hope beckoned for those few Methodist conservatives who refused to accept the evolutionist presuppositions and goals that were immanent in Cooke's analysis.

The case of one well-known and influential individual illuminates the difficulties under which Methodist conservatives labored. E. L. Shumaker was a Methodist preacher who acted as the superintendent of the Anti-Saloon League and who opposed the League of Nations. Shumaker thought the League perpetrated a "great moral wrong," and therefore he tried to block a pro-League proclamation at one Methodist conference. He asked for a show of hands of those preachers present who had actually read the League of Nations Covenant that they were proposing to endorse (12 out of 250 raised their hands). Then he asked for another show of hands of those who had understood what the Covenant was all about (none raised their hands). So entrenched was the Methodist preference for internationalism, however, that this display had no effect. After some laughter, the conference in question approved a pro-League proclamation with only a couple of dissenting voices.[11]

Such, by all accounts, was the fate of most of those others who in their local Methodist conferences tried to drive through resolutions opposed to the League or to prevent pro-League resolutions. But it is known that in some localities anti-League Methodist preachers were indeed successful and that congregations sometimes yielded even 90 percent votes against the ratification of the League. One Methodist opponent of the League in the U.S. Senate claimed that he had received countless petitions and reports of anti-League resolutions from fellow Methodists, as well as letters opposed to the League even from Methodist bishops, presidents of theological seminaries, and "dozens" of individual ministers.[12]

Among the Methodist laity, there were those who were much disturbed by the weakness of the conservative side in League-related debates. Some prominent laymen, such as Albert J. Beveridge, the former U. S. senator and leading League critic from the heavily Methodist state of Indiana, denounced their own clergy for having embraced every conceivable reform cause short of the simple doctrine of Christ's atoning death. Beveridge called the League "that unholy scheme," bemoaned the way in which his church's leaders "got wrong on this question very early in the game," and encouraged clergy to oppose the League in their area conferences and conventions.[13] Others took to writing shrill articles, letters to the editor, and privately printed pamphlets. None was more forceful than Eugene Thwing, a Southern YMCA activist and Methodist layman, whose 1919 pamphlet *The League of Nations as a Moral Issue* was eventually read into the *Congressional Record* by a sympathetic senator with a Methodist background.[14]

Thwing took issue with clerical depictions of the League as something so inherently Christian that every Bible believer was enjoined to support it. Instead he called the League un-Christian and anti-Christian, a "device of man's contrivance, which was built without recognition of God's governing hand in the affairs of men." He insisted that it was "in direct disobedience with the will of God as given many centuries ago to His people." The relevant Bible passage was 1 Thessalonians 5:3 and the teaching that there must be no "yoking" of Christians with the "unrighteous," but rather a "separation between the nations whose God is the Lord and the nations who will have none of Him." Going against this divine command as it did, the League of Nations was "foredoomed to utter failure" and "nothing good can come out of this unequal yoking together, but only evil." Thwing's solution was to convert the pagans and to adhere the United States only to such an alternative League that accepted God as its ultimate leader and righteousness as its "governing principle."[15]

Thwing's message was in no wise particularly Methodist. It was a generic Christian argument predicated on a literal understanding of the Bible. But it proved appealing among conservative Methodists, at least insofar as it brought into focus the one aspect of the League Covenant that even some of their liberal internationalists came to criticize: the coequality of Christian and heathen nations in the League's structures and decision making.

Most of the Methodists who addressed this issue did so with reference to the League Covenant's granting of suzerainty to heathen Japan in the Chinese province of Shantung and in Korea. Even Methodist journals that were supportive of the League, such as the influential *Sunday School Journal*, made an exception in this matter. Such were the Methodist sympathies toward the Chinese, fostered by long missionary contact with that people, that they insisted that the League Covenant be amended at least in these provisions. Even the Social Gospel–dominated Methodist Episcopal Board of Missions officially requested that the relevant article in the Treaty of Versailles be rewritten before League Covenant's ratification. The Board of Missions was ready to accept other reservations as well if these were necessary for speedy ratification, but it specifically demanded the elimination of the Shantung provisions.[16]

Only one nationally known Methodist spokesman took to public campaigning against the ratification of the League Covenant. The bishop in question, Thomas Benjamin Neely, was one of the best-known and most controversial Methodist leaders of the period. A traditional Wesleyan by persuasion, he had established such a reputation as an opponent of the Social Gospel and as a sympathizer with laissez-faire economics in a denomination that enthusiastically embraced the former and damned the latter that he had been forced to retire from his office in 1912.[17] He felt strongly that every Christian citizen had a duty to take an active role in political affairs but that it was no business of the church to become a partisan for any secular program. Rather, he affirmed in quintessential holiness fashion that "when each individual is saved, society and the whole world will be saved." He blamed "German biblical criticism of a destructive kind" for having unmoored Methodism from this traditional perspective, and he called for a return to "sound Wesleyan teaching."[18]

In the middle of the Senate's debate on the League Covenant, Neely published an influential book, *The League, The Nation's Danger: A Study of the So-Called "League of Nations."* The book was based on articles previously published in one of the leading anti-League newspapers, the *New York Sun*, and in it Neely surveyed all aspects of the League Covenant and all the arguments brought to support it by secular and clerical commentators. He concluded that the League resulted from false Christian teaching and that it was not the universal blessing advertised but rather "a supreme potentate," "an over-government of the Nations" that was intended "to govern the Nations of the world in practically everything." There never had been a more all-inclusive "grasping for world power" in all of human history than that institutionalized in the League of Nations, he alleged. "It out-does Ceasar, Napoleon, and even the modern kaiser, and all their kind rolled together. . . . It will be the most extensive imperialism the world has ever seen, and its yoke may prove to be the heaviest and the hardest humanity has ever borne."[19]

Neely was most of all concerned about the various ways in which he thought the League would hurt the United States. First, it would end the tradition of never entering entangling alliances and compel America into wars not of its choosing—at any time, for whatever duration, and all over the world. He feared that the binding commitment to military action abroad would destroy the economy and undermine the domestic order. Second, if the United States consented to and joined in the Covenant's provisions for mandatory great power control over some of the underdeveloped regions of the Earth, the constitutional premises of the American system would be undermined. No one asked for the consent of the underdeveloped peoples for such outside control, he pointed out, and in that omission was exposed the League's pretension to supreme sovereignty over all nations, the United States included. Third, he objected to the coequality of nations in the decision making of the League. Fourth, he feared that given the ineradicables of human nature, the League would eventually have to evolve into a one-man world autocracy. There simply was no other way of constraining the conflicting volitions of unredeemed peoples if the powers of nation-states were once removed.[20]

Fifth and most important, Neely hit upon the International Labor Organization (ILO). As the competencies, goals, and guiding philosophies of this organization were sketched in Article 427 of the League Covenant, it seemed to him to be both the controlling center of the League and "the most all-embracing socialist scheme the world has ever known." He was convinced that this organization would develop into "the soviet of bolshevism" writ large and that it would end up ruling the world "externally and internally," both in the details of social and economic policy and in the ideas underlying and legitimating all policy. Even before its charter had been finalized, he expected the ILO to start interfering in such domestic matters as the conditions of work and wages, as well as extortionate new taxes, to be levied on American citizens and to be used for the pet projects of the socialist bureaucrats at ILO headquarters.

Neely was convinced that through the ILO the League would try to incorporate a socialist system in the United States. If governments were mandated only for the physical protection that individuals needed to pursue their own salvation, as he averred, and if socialist economics ran counter to the laws of nature, this coming international imposition of socialism would not only destroy the American economy but also indeed "check the progress of humanity, and overthrow the world." That being the manifest trajectory of the League of Nations, it was clear to him that "somebody in the peace conference was swayed by pretty extreme socialist tendencies"; that the influence of labor and socialist movements on the League was "not merely academic" but central; and, finally, that by virtue of the ILO and its ideology, the whole League issued from "unearthly inspiration . . . not from above."[21]

So strongly did Bishop Neely feel about all of this that he did not even restrain himself when it came to the idealistic Christian appeals that President Wilson offered on the League's behalf. Employing sarcasm in a pointed way unusual for such a senior clergyman, Neely noted that from the ranks of those who disagreed with him "a plaintive cry arises: 'Dare we reject [the League of Nations] and break the heart of the world?'" Utterly unconvinced, he countered: "Who says it will break the heart of the world if the United States does not adopt the League of Nations? How does any one know that? That may be poetical, but is it a fact? . . . The League may itself break the heart of the world when its imperialistic machinery moves and grinds."[22]

Neely's book received considerable press attention among the evangelicals of other Protestant denominations, especially those in the dispensationalist movement;[23] it was sent to some Irreconcilable senators; and a summary of its contents was read into the *Congressional Record* (see chapter 7). However, the book's impact within the Methodist Church was negligible. No sympathetic reviews appeared in the leading Methodist journals, and Methodist bishops studiously ignored Neely's arguments. His was, as one historian called it, "a small but vocal campaign," totally unrepresentative of and at odds with the majority Methodist position.[24]

Insofar as there was a single key thread running through Neely's and his few fellow dissidents' writings, it was more nationalist and racialist than religious, more directed against Social Gospelers and secular socialists en masse than for any alternative religious program of world rearrangement. But this nationalist tone in the dissenting Methodist polemic, little as it was, should not be a surprise. Throughout the nation's history, American Methodists had tended to identify the United States with the Methodist concept of providentialism, a concept that could lend itself either to supporting the Social Gospel and the League of Nations—as an extension of "American" and "Christian" ideals—or to opposing both the Social Gospel and the League of Nations. When Neely assailed the League of Nations as a new supergovernment of the world, or Thwing attacked it as illegitimate yoke fellowship, both were continuing the tradition of celebrating the United States as a typically Methodist country with typically Methodist values, mores, and structures of governance. They were loath to suffer any diminution of its sovereignty because they had convinced themselves that it was a nation unusually attuned to the Methodist message of individual responsibility in social effort and peaceable living.

The more theological plane of the Methodists' debate was also not entirely insignificant. Even though few Methodists explicitly made the argument, the fact was that the Methodist majority's embrace of the League of Nations was highly paradoxical in view of the core theological tenets of traditional Wesleyanism. In 1919, the pro-League Methodist majority argued for the League, above all, as a social reform organization; but they failed to consider that the League was, in fact, collectivistic in nature, engaged in transferring social holiness tasks from spirit-filled individuals to a secular institution. This transfer of responsibility ran counter to the deepest traditions of the Methodist experience. It had always been an individualist experience, stressing the personal duties of the converted and the sanctified and at the same time critical of all central direction and uniformity. For Methodist Social Gospelers now to advocate international, collectivist social reform and peacekeeping by a secular legislative institution was potentially highly subversive of Wesleyan doctrine.

Had the Holiness churches still remained within the Methodist fold, they surely would have drawn attention to this crucial paradox. But those few insistently individualist Wesleyans who remained could really do very little to stem the tide of a Social Gospel that had managed to convincingly place increasingly collectivist forms of reform into the matrix of Methodist social activism, providentialism, and evolutionary hypotheses. That Neely nevertheless did try to resist the tide, and that he linked the effort with the League of Nations issue in particular, showed that American Methodism in the World War I period still had not quite entirely fallen in line behind its mainstream liberal leadership.

Episcopalian Dissenters on the League of Nations

The Episcopalians were, on the whole, just as devoted to the League of Nations as the Methodists. Their General Convention endorsed the League in October 1919, and their leading periodicals maintained a supportive editorial stance starting much earlier. In 1920 the Lambeth Conference of the worldwide Anglican Communion, of which the Episcopal Church was a part, gave a similar endorsement. The Lambeth Conference especially recommended the social reform agendas of the League's International Labor Organization.[25] Many Episcopal bishops issued their own brief statements of endorsement, most of which depicted the League as the fruit of the Christian pursuit of brotherhood and as the modern expression of a peaceful world order consecrated through joint Christian work.[26] When members of the U.S. Senate began to obstruct the ratification of the League Covenant, many Episcopalians denounced the senators as "traitors" and as "feeble, selfish, little . . . reactionaries," branding their conduct a "national disgrace."[27]

As with all other Protestant denominations, Episcopalian support for the League grew out of the Social Gospel. The Episcopalians had been among the earliest pioneers of that type of Gospel, influenced as they had been by their British brothers' and sisters' long-standing engagement with Christian socialism. British Christian socialism and the Social Gospel of the American Episcopalians were both rooted in the concept of incarnationalism, which F. D. Maurice, the influential mid-nineteenth-century British theologian, had been among the first to develop and which had then come to shape much of the Kingdom Theology of those Americans who campaigned for the League. In the Church of England and in the Protestant Episcopal Church alike, this embrace of the incarnationalist Social Gospel transected all other lines of division, so that otherwise traditionalist, respectable, and socially established Episcopalian clergy could be found among the founders and managers of some of the most socialistic Social Gospel organizations of the Progressive Era. Such, indeed, was the power of the ascendant coalition of modernist theologians and socially active traditionalists that by 1919 Episcopalian social conservatives were definitely in the minority and were increasingly being pushed out of ecclesiastical decision making.[28] When the League of Nations came to be discussed, the Episcopal Church was, therefore, driven rather irresistibly to support it.

Other lines of division further weakened the hands of those who were suspicious of the Social Gospelers' agendas. Entirely unrelated to the basic liberal/conservative divide, there existed precedent, uniquely Episcopalian divisions, that is, the three major church parties that constantly battled each other and prevented any single party from exerting full domination. In purely ecclesiastical terms, the handful of Episcopalians who dissented from the League of Nations were the theological conservatives of these various church parties, who were driven by widely diverse doctrinal emphases, were seeking different outcomes, and rarely cooperated. This additional fracturing of Epis-copalianism meant that by 1919 the Episcopalian Evangelicals, properly so called, who would have been the most likely to oppose the League of Nations, were in a definite minority, having been increasingly marginalized by the ascendant Anglo-Catholic or High Church party, which was not evangelical at all in the sense of *sola scriptura*, and by the growth of various modernist and liberal theologies among the Broad Church party, which was evangelical on occasion but certainly not conservatively evangelical.[29]

These three parties of the Episcopal Church were formed as a result of—and the strict Evangelicals departed the church because of—the ritualist controversy that had been reigning among its members since the 1860s. The introduction of sacramentalist and "Romish" rituals and the creation of the first Episcopal monastic orders in the United States had alienated the avowed Protestants in the denomination, and by the late nineteenth century its High Church or ritualist party was so firmly on the ascendant that most of the thoroughgoing Evangelicals (such as James M. Gray) had left it. Either they flocked to the new, tiny Reformed Episcopal Church or, later, to the interdenominational World Christian Fundamentals Association. In their absence, Broad Church modernists and Anglo-Catholics increasingly joined hands on the Social Gospel and chained the official ecclesiastical organs to its purposes. Resistance to this threesome did, however, linger even beyond the World War I period; yet, rather than empowering any putative opposition to the Social Gospel's domestic and international plans, the resistance only conspired to further divert the remaining Evangelicals' and other conserva-tives' attention from all nonecclesiastical concerns.

Had the Evangelicals not been so weak, things might have been different. As the historian William Katerberg and others have noted, the conservative Evangelical minority had imbibed deeply from the materials that created the Holiness churches from among the Methodists. In the worldwide Anglican Communion, the same influences found their expression in the Keswick / Victorious Life conferences. Those Anglicans who were active in these con-ferences shared the Holiness doctrine of entire sanctification, including the aversion to corporate temporal institutions that this doctrine implied.[30] Epis-copalian Evangelicals were, thus, a distinctly individualist group of people, centered on conversion and on the voluntary reform efforts that they thought holiness and sanctification automatically produced. They were unlikely to approve of large international organizations as proper instruments of world change because they were hostile to domestic collectivism in all its political and ecclesiastical forms. The bent toward a personalist concept of faith existed in some High Church circles as well, and it drove a small num-ber of High Church clergy and laity away from the Social Gospel. This took place through the Anglican mysticism that had resurged from the latter part of the nineteenth century. Although mediated by the High Church party's doctrines of the sacraments and apostolic succession, this mysticism defined faith in very individualist and experiential terms, deprecated corporate or collective social effort (as opposed to charity), and conspired against trusting nonchurch corporate institutions.[31]

A different balance of powers in the denomination might have strengthened such tendencies, given that especially among the High Church constituency there persisted another, additional dynamic that further alienated one section from accepting secular institutions as proper reform agencies: the persistent, uniquely American message of William Henry Hobart and his early-nineteenth-century followers, who had combined High Church sacramentalism and church-centeredness with a distinct aversion to taking part in political efforts. During their heyday, traditionalist High Churchmen had interpreted Hobart's strictures so literally that they even refused to exercise their voting rights in national elections. Although twentieth-century Episcopalians were almost never this consistent, the Hobartian perspective did persist to an extent, and it meant that some Episcopalians insisted on the church's supremacy over the secular state and denied the legitimacy of the church working with secular institutions on a basis of equality.[32]

Hobartian beliefs could have led to anti-League polemics much like those of the confessional Calvinists. That they did not was the result of the liberals' takeover of the main twentieth-century manifestation of the High Churchmen's church-centered political effort, the so-called Faith and Order Movement. This was the Anglican initiative for the reunion of Christian churches on the basis of the High Church position on doctrinal essentials. As championed after World War I by such Episcopal bishops as Charles H. Brent and William T. Manning, the movement's key supposition was that the world's peace and progress depended entirely on people returning to the fold of the sacramental church. Such a return would form a worldwide union of Christians, which would have at its disposal (so the argument went) all the sacramental means of grace that alone made for world betterment. Moreover, a reunion of all Christians would create a powerful supranational force, which could bring to bear on the non-Christians all its resources in a major push for conversion. Universal or near-universal conversion, in turn, would remove a major obstacle to peace and progress, namely, the persistence of heathenism and infidelity.[33]

A potentially powerful churchly alternative to the political League of Nations could have been constructed upon these suppositions, which would have resembled the notion of a Christian League, supplementary to the political League of Nations, like the one that Bishop Richard J. Cooke had suggested among the Methodists. Some Episcopalians and Anglicans did try to do this, but as the Faith and Order Movement developed, it was increasingly taken over by the Social Gospelers. Their agendas were appended to it, not the agendas of the church-centered Episcopalian conservatives.

The final factors making things difficult for Episcopalian conservatives and anti-internationalists were the denomination's social makeup and cultural self-image. Given that Episcopalians were part of a worldwide Anglican Communion with dynamics, concerns, and pretensions to power all its own, they possessed a sense of history alien to other American Christians. Having originated as an offshoot of the long-established national Church of England, the Episcopal Church tended to see itself as a fully unique *ecclesia* that had always included both Protestants and Catholics of many varieties and had, therefore, been able to act as a unifying force that weathered many a storm that would have grounded a differently constituted ecclesiastical edifice. Episcopalians were confident that in the long course of history, the Anglican model of incarnationalism and comprehensiveness would prove its worth in the American environment as well—indeed, that by its inclusive nature it would be particularly well suited to act as a de facto national church.

Doctrinal strictness obviously suffered if national influence and representativeness were what mattered. Additionally, this sense of organic history and of the Episcopalian guardianship of the nation militated against radical ruptures and preferred slow, organic, evolutionary growth. Most often, it blended with whatever was the ascendant form of respectable cultural and political effort.[34] The nationalist inclination found other expressions as well, such as the long project of building the National Cathedral in Washington—an *Episcopal* church that its founders, however, liked to portray as the leading cathedral for all American Christians.[35]

Finally, the inescapable fact was that by the twentieth century the Episcopal Church was most definitely the church of the well-off and of those with a stake in society as it existed, not an established church but certainly the church of the establishment. It had produced a disproportionate number of presidents, senators, and other policy formers, and it continued in many ways to define the perimeters of cultured discussion even in the pluralist twentieth century. The socially and politically progressive Episcopalians of the World War I period tended to define their denomination through further elaborations of an essentially noblesse oblige reform tradition, whereas for the conservatives, Episcopalianism became part of the quest to assure the stability of the existing order. Some of the most vocal and persuasive proponents of clerical laissez-faire emerged from among these latter people, and they tended to argue for American nationalism, Anglo-American racialist superiority, largely unregulated capitalism, and beneficent individualism as religious no less than political nonnegotiables.

It was, then, hardly surprising that the only member of the Protestant Episcopal Church's episcopate to publicly denounce the League of Nations represented the political right wing of the denomination. In his discourse, nationalism was more prominent than theology. He was Bishop William Lawrence of Boston, a modernist and an incarnationalist in his stance toward the Bible but otherwise a very conservative man, who had become known as one of the leading advocates of the "Gospel of Wealth." This clerical laissez-faire theory, proffered by some anti–Social Gospel clergymen of the prewar decades, held that the possession of wealth was a sign of divine favor and a testament to godly living. This philosophy of life made Lawrence in the eyes of many "a man of the world," and he certainly was not an erudite theologian or a traditional pastor. In his public teaching, there was always manifest a definite bent toward a nationalist civic religion that celebrated the American constitutional and social order. This also lent itself to a marked aversion to the Roman Catholic Church, which he tended to portray as an undemocratic and autocratic *ecclesia*.[36]

As Lawrence later recalled, he had decided against the League of Nations the very moment when he read an early copy of the League Covenant in February 1919. He had concluded that the proposed Covenant was so radically flawed that no "loyal citizen should support" it. Although in favor of closer international cooperation and a champion of a world court, he felt that it was both safer and ultimately more beneficial for the United States to retain its independence of action and to refuse binding, unchangeable commitments to defend others. Immediately upon deciding this—in minutes, it would seem—he had contacted his longtime friend, childhood playmate, and fellow graduate of the Harvard Class of 1871, the Republican Senate majority leader, Henry Cabot Lodge, who was also a fellow Episcopalian. Lawrence would not have had to use much persuasion on his friend, because Lodge was already on record as a critic of the League and was soon to spearhead the Senate Republicans' fight against its ratification.[37]

Bishop Lawrence did not limit his anti-League activities to the private exhortation of his powerful political friends. In April 1919, he also contributed a short piece to the *Churchman*, the leading Episcopalian journal, in which he expressed worry about several aspects of the original draft Covenant. The Covenant did not recognize and protect the Monroe Doctrine as it should, he alleged, nor did it preserve the right of member states to decide their own immigration policies. Its provisions for collective security were so vague and open to interpretation that they were likely to confuse, to encourage aggressive states, and to involve the United States in costly wars all over the world. Nor did the League Covenant include a clear right of withdrawal in case—and he was sure such a case would arise—later experience showed the League deficient in some area of its activities or inimical to American national interests. All these were points of danger that he hoped the Senate would redress through reservations or amendments to the Covenant. He also suggested that the majority of Americans might not actually support the League, that eminent jurists certainly did not support it, and that such jurists should know what was safe and good. Therefore, he concluded, "I believe it is my duty to oppose in any way in my power the present draft and to support the Senate, when the question comes before them, in demanding a form of league of peace so constructed and phrased that its path will be clearly pointed towards international peace."[38]

Lawrence acted upon this conviction at the Episcopal General Convention of 1919. There, a fellow bishop brought forward a resolution in support of the League of Nations, stressing that the bishops were duty-bound to define for America "what the great world issues are, and to expect them to act accordingly." Given that the League was above all a "moral" issue, this bishop insisted that Episcopalians had a "moral responsibility to endorse it." To all of this, Lawrence was "utterly opposed," and he countered his colleague by stressing that whatever others did, he himself was "not ready to take moral leadership by supporting an immoral act." The end result was that the bishops did not endorse the resolution of endorsement that had been offered. Instead, they settled on a compromise that supported not American membership in *the* League of Nations but "participation" in *a* "covenant of nations which shall effectively guarantee the authority of international law and protect the world from conditions that may menace its peace."[39]

All this must be seen in the context of a general, not theological, conservatism. Bishop Lawrence's anti-League stance cannot, in other words, be placed in any of the categories usual in dispensationalist, Calvinist, or Lutheran discourse, nor in typical Anglo-Catholicism; rather, like Bishop Neely, Lawrence was reacting to the League of Nations more as an American nationalist and political conservative than as a representative of a specific doctrinal tradition. Inasmuch as there was a religious dimension, it consisted of a fear that involvement in international organizations would hinder the free unfolding of what Lawrence regarded as the genius of an America unbound.

This kind of blending of nationalism and religion was also apparent in the League critique that flowed from the *Churchman*. In the course of 1919, this leading Episcopalian periodical switched from unquestioning support of the League Covenant to a very strong Reservationist position. It started to criticize the Covenant as soon as its full contents had become publicly known. The more vocal the anti-League senators became, the more force-fully did the *Churchman* argue against what it came to call a "travesty" of a League. The paper never deviated from its advocacy of *some* kind of a League of Nations, but it did come to take a convinced Reservationist position that insisted that with regard to *the* League of Nations, "a Christian may with propriety question both its political and its Christian merit." The journal demanded that the Covenant be extensively rewritten, especially in articles relative to collective security, before it could commend itself to those dedi-cated to the cause of Christian internationalism. The journal also began to severely criticize President Wilson for what it called his "thoroughly un-democratic" airs and aims, and once the Senate had finally defeated the League Covenant, it blamed Wilson alone, calling the defeat the result of Wilson's "sin of pride."[40]

So pervasive, indeed, were these kinds of nontheological, technical reser-vations among Episcopalians that even the *Living Church*, an otherwise con-sistently and enthusiastically pro-League publication, came to acknowledge by mid-1919 that aspects of the Covenant should be amended, that perhaps those countries that did not "accept Anglo-Saxon ideals" (like Italy and Japan) should be left out of it.[41] The *Living Church*'s position was unexcep-tional, given that by late 1919 most denominations had come to support some reservations.[42] But the *Churchman* was for reservations much earlier than others, and thereby it further testified to the existence of a real, if very small, body of Episcopalian dissent even among the High Church party.

Few Episcopalian conservatives, however, went beyond this advocacy of specific reservations and emendations. Indeed, of all the major Protestant denominations, the Episcopal Church produced by far the most dispassionate League criticism. To a large degree, this was simply the result of the fact that the denomination was not entirely Protestant and therefore did not share all the concerns typical of fully Protestant groups. The thoroughgoing Protes-tant evangelicals within its fold were a definite minority in 1919, with such principled anti-internationalists as W. H. Griffith Thomas and James M. Gray working outside its ecclesiastical fold and the remaining ones marginal-ized by powerful denominational liberals and by the (unrelated) fracturing of the denomination over ritualism. These internal schisms had redounded to the ruin of Episcopalian conservatives in many areas, and certainly so on the questions relating to modern Christian internationalism and anti-internationalism.

The simple fact was also that Episcopalians on the whole were not the kinds of Christians who insistently differentiated between the temporal and the sacral or denied the utility of secular institutions. By 1919, incarnational-ism had suffused the public theologies of all but the most marginal Episcopa-lian Evangelicals, and it made them definitely susceptible to Christian internationalist apologias for the League of Nations. This meant that the anti-League position, too, was more temporal than theological, more concerned about the effects of the League on the United States as a nation than about any religious repercussions or implications of modern internationalism. There were, of course, the generic Christian arguments about yoke fellowship and about the impossibility of legislating righteousness, but such was the composition of the Protestant Episcopal Church in 1919, and such was the dominance of incarnationalism, that these never caught on.

The Weakness of Methodist and Episcopalian Anti-Internationalism

Episcopalians and Methodists were in the vanguard of the churchly protagonists of the League of Nations. As much as any Christians, they popularized the Social Gospel view of the League's promise. That in their midst there nevertheless did exist League critics and opponents of churchly internationalism testifies to the persistence of doctrinal traditions that were opposed to the Social Gospel view of the world and of America's place in it. It is not enough to point out the starkly nationalist tone of much of the critics' discourse; it needs also to be acknowledged that behind and alongside their nationalist discourse, Episcopalians and Methodists did voice generically Christian objections to the League of Nations and sometimes even distinctly Episcopal and Methodist objections. Those few Methodists and Episcopalians who had embraced dispensationalism, and those who were Calvinist conservatives, argued their case within the categories of these two doctrinal frameworks. For the rest, the less clearly defined, traditional Episcopalian and Methodist theologies were mined for reasons to oppose the specific programs for peace, progress, and equity that the Social Gospel spawned. Opponents of these Social Gospel legitimations for a League of Nations were very few indeed among Episcopalians and the Methodists, but nothing else could have been expected from members of two denominations as profoundly in the liberal and Social Gospel camp as the Methodist and Episcopal churches. Indeed, even the few dissenting voices that were heard in these two denominations were more than most would have expected to hear.

The League controversy helped conservative Episcopalians and Methodists realize that, no matter how weak was their position in their own denomination, they were part of a broad interdenominational family of evangelicals that agreed on the menace of the Social Gospel. This realization owed to many events, but central among them was the evangelical critique of the League of Nations. Because of the very fractured terrain of their own denominations, neither could launch significant denominational challenges to the modernists, but when they joined or paralleled the anti-League polemics of the conservatives of other denominations, Methodists and Episcopalians could, in fact, contribute. They were, in fact, part of a remarkably broad coalition of Christian anti-internationalists who combined the doctrinal distinctives of various confessional traditions with an overarching aversion to the secularist trajectory of the Social Gospel to argue a case against the League of Nations.

CHAPTER SIX

Religion and the League of Nations Fight in the Senate

Ll strands of Christian anti-internationalism found their way into the political debate on the ratification of the League of Nations Covenant. Whether only nominal Christians or actual lay activists, the politicians and publicists who participated in this debate showed great interest in borrowing evangelical formulations. Most of their own critiques of the Covenant revolved around such clearly nonreligious issues as American freedom of action, European and imperialist control of League machinery, and the insufficiency and fatuity of proposed collective security arrangements. But these issues, too, came to be permeated with religion when some of the League's leading political critics addressed them. The prevalence of evangelical motifs in senatorial discourse is in fact the forgotten aspect of the political League controversy. To reconstruct the religious plane of the senators' contention is to add an important element to existing accounts not only of the League fight itself but also of the impact of conservative evangelicalism on twentieth-century American politics.

Irreconcilables and Reservationists

In purely political terms, the League of Nations' opponents fell into two distinct groups. On the one hand there were the "Irreconcilables," a collection of no more than sixteen senators, mostly Republican and Mid-western, with some Southern and maverick Western Democrats thrown in. These individuals assailed the League on a range of tracks, always vehemently and often luridly, and they were so utterly determined to prevent American membership that they approved of almost any tactic or argument as long as it appeared to further their objective. To this end, the Irreconcilables offered forty-five outright amendments to the text of the League Covenant. Partly they felt impelled to do this out of a principled opposition to certain Covenant provisions, but they also supposed that League supporters would never accept a Covenant so amended.[1]

All the Irreconcilables emphasized undiminished American national sovereignty. Some of them were left-wing anti-imperialists who objected to the League because of the great power (and especially British Empire) predominance that was built into its structures, and because of its alleged links to international financiers, whereas others were conservative nationalists who were above all interested in reserving for the United States unhindered freedom of action in all matters. These latter conservatives were particularly keen to secure American freedom of action in the affairs of the Western hemisphere, in tariff and immigration policy, and in purely domestic matters. Most of their criticism centered, however, on the League's collective security provisions, most particularly on Article X, which bound all League members to assist another member state if it came under military attack. In addition, some Irreconcilables were concerned about the coequality of races and the numerical preponderance of non-Anglo-Saxon states in the League's structures. They feared that the League formulators' decision to cede the Chinese province of Shantung to Japan and their granting of six votes to the multiracial British Empire in the League Assembly betokened a determination to empower what they regarded as the "lower races." Many of them feared, as well, that socialists and communists would come to dominate the League's International Labor Organization and would use it to subvert the free enterprise system.[2]

The other main group of League critics, the "Reservationists," was a much more mixed company and more prone to compromise. As the term itself implied, they had reservations about some specific aspects of the League Covenant, not the basic idea of an international league as such. They were willing to have the United States join the League of Nations once they were satisfied that changes had been made to certain unclear or objectionable elements in its structure and in the obligations that its Covenant imposed on America. Some in the group were, indeed, among the most consistent conservative internationalists of an earlier era, men who still stood for Theodore Roosevelt's alliance-based concept of international cooperation. Differing from these "strict" Reservationists were a group of "mild" Reservationists who supported the slightly different League to Enforce Peace program. When they came to put their demands down in writing in the fourteen so-called Lodge reservations, they did not ask for a rewriting of the Covenant but simply offered American interpretations of some of its articles and asked the other League members to accept these interpretations.[3]

In the years that followed the League fight, many in the Reservationist camp came to regret the role that they had played in defeating American League membership, and they began to search for alternative ways of securing at least American participation in the League's activities. To this end, they tried to have the United States join the World Court (or the Permanent Court of International Justice), which was part of the League of Nations, and they pushed for a redrafting of some of the Covenant articles that were objectionable to the majority of the U.S. Senate. Some Irreconcilables were not averse to such alternative forms of internationalism either, but their passionately nationalist rhetoric obscured the similarities and prevented meaningful compromises.[4]

Both the Reservationists and the Irreconcilables were, however, opposed to what they called "Mr. Wilson's League," that is, the League of Nations as it was actually offered for their acceptance—a League centered on a political institution, codifying certain universal principles, guarantees, and mechanisms that were automatic and beyond the powers of the American legislature to override or escape. Both groups appealed to ethnic and anti-imperialist prejudice, and both had frequent recourse to an anti-Semitic refrain about modern internationalism as the product and tool of "international finance." They shared concerns over the League's centralized decision-making structure and its expansive agendas for social, labor, and industrial legislation, for both groups had long been critics of socialism and the alleged tendency of the Woodrow Wilson administration to collectivism. Finally, both kinds of League critics felt that it was naive and dangerous to expect perpetual and universal peace and security from any organization, anywhere, at any time. Self-announced "realists," they preferred the traditional and supposedly proven arrangements of conflict management to the League's experimental quest for its wholesale abolition.[5]

Both of the groups fought against the League in the chamber and committee rooms of the Senate, and in the press and on the platforms of popular speaking tours, as well as through expertly organized and widely distributed pamphleteering. In all these forums, they had recourse to religious rhetoric, imagery, and appeals. Most of this rhetoric approximated the arguments of conservative evangelicals. It was more usual for the Irreconcilables than for the Reservationists to have consistent recourse to religious themes, and in some cases it is clear that the appeal to religion was made out of opportunism, or habit, while in others it was just as apparent that the politicians were actual Bible believers who shared the concerns of evangelical clergy. But according to their own contention, the anti-League stance of a surprising number of these politicians was influenced by their denominational affiliation and by what they saw as the interests and requirements of the Christian faith. Even when that was not the case, it remains a potent fact that out of the sixteen Irreconcilables, no fewer than fourteen utilized Christian arguments against the League.

Senator Sherman: Evangelical Anti-Internationalist Par Excellence

The most notable of the Irreconcilables to do so was Senator Lawrence Y. Sherman of Illinois, a sixty-one-year-old lawyer who by the time of the League controversy was almost blind, totally fed up with the arid atmosphere of the Senate, and already determined to retire from public life. His case merits detailed attention, even if this sour and cantankerous man was not a constructive senator and left no legislative achievements. His name would, indeed, deservedly have slipped into historical oblivion except for the colorful way in which he expressed some of the core conservative causes of the early twentieth century, including the cause of evangelical anti-internationalism.

Sherman's most prominent characteristic was, as Vice President Thomas Marshall recalled, "a tongue swung in the middle and as sharp as Damascus blade."[6] He had a peerless ability to coin expressions of invective and to hurl them against his chosen enemies. These enemies were always from the political left. Sherman had no denominational affiliation, and although he had been educated at the country's oldest Methodist college, McKendree College in Illinois, some have seen him as a Deist.[7] He claimed that he had never prayed in his life.[8] His religiosity was, however, real and pronounced, and it propelled him to various types of Christian and charity work (including four years as the person in charge of Illinois state charities) and to various churches and Masonic temples, to preach outspoken, traditionally pietist sermons. Acquaintances said that he was prone to unstringing his purse whenever he was told a story of personal misery or misfortune, and those who knew him best in the Senate invariably recalled that his public invective was tempered by a heart so overflowing with sympathy for the travails of his fellow men that there existed no "kindler, sweeter soul."[9]

However, this sympathy for one's neighbors did not lead Sherman to approve of the Social Gospel. He disapproved of all collective, purposive means of alleviating material grievances save those of voluntary charity. All attempts to legislate an equality of condition were, in his view, contrary to the "laws of nature," and he insisted that legislation ought to be based on those teachings of the Bible which indicated that toil and suffering were the "allwise means given by our Creator to redeem ourselves from the penalty of disobedience."[10] Before the League controversy, Sherman had translated these religiopolitical beliefs into campaigns against the organized labor movement and the wartime accumulation of executive powers, both of which he saw as aspects of a broader assault on American liberties. He had also been a prominent anticommunist polemicist.[11]

Yet it was by no means inevitable that Sherman became one of the leading opponents of the League of Nations. In wartime, he had celebrated the conflict as an American crusade for world democracy and national self-determination, and once he had even called for a postwar "commonwealth of nations."[12] He switched to a most vehement opposition of the League of Nations, partly for partisan political reasons (his hatred and distrust of President Wilson was well-nigh unbounded) and partly because the actual League Covenant, once its contents became known, assaulted his nationalist prejudices. But it appears also that his being conversant with the religious critiques of the League experiment influenced his transformation more than that of any other Irreconcilable. He was close to the Baptist anti-internationalist Richard H. Edmonds, and he corresponded with conservative, especially Southern clergymen and possessed a large collection of their anti-League writings.[13] Some of his most radical characterizations of the League were almost verbatim reproductions from these writings.

Claiming that no "more Godless document" had ever been produced than the League Covenant, Sherman actually proposed an amendment that would have introduced into its text the words "Almighty God." This amendment went down to defeat when the Senate voted on it, but it was the only attempt by an apparently secular politician to address one of the most consistently recurring evangelical reproaches against the League of Nations, the noninclusion of the name of God in its Covenant.[14] Sherman also echoed many a conservative evangelical when he branded the League as an antibiblical attempt at creating "a sinless world" that ignored human nature and the laws of God. He, like they, insisted that the liberals' enthusiasm for the League proved that they were enamored with German scientific, theological, and socialist theories, which had cost them their groundedness in true Christianity and led them to develop a purely secular "politics of morality" that tried to introduce "the millennium" through human effort. Like the dispensationalists, Sherman predicted that this secular millennialism would lead to authoritarian central control under the cover of populist social democracy. In other words, the League of Nations amounted to a modern Tower of Babel that cut Christendom loose from God and allowed it to "go our own agnostic and materialistic way." The true millennium could come only after "Satan is chained and cast in the bottomless pit," Sherman maintained, and he indignantly denied that perpetual peace was possible short of divine intervention. No written document, no matter how much influenced by the Christian goal of human solidarity, could possibly bring it about.[15]

Furthermore, Sherman branded President Wilson and supportive clergy as "traveling mesmerists" who manipulated the emotional needs of Americans and tried to produce a "self-hypnotism" in favor of the League of Nations. He suggested that this was a malicious undertaking, a deliberate decision by people who were not real Christians to appeal to the devout hopes of sincere but gullible people. Sherman claimed that these "mesmerists" tried to obscure the real message of Christ and to insinuate in its stead the false millennialist doctrines of churchly internationalists. Among them, he stressed, were men like Frank Crane, "once a minister of the Gospel" but now a "charlatan who, having left the pulpit, skulks behind it to sanctify his carnal misdeeds" and "keeps his sacerdotal robes well in the front to cover any malevolent atrocity he commits."[16] Never explicit on the motivations, Sherman sometimes claimed that the "traveling mesmerists" were only interested in monopolizing political power, but other times he granted them the sincerity of their beliefs. In both cases, however, he insisted that their undertaking was contrary to the American Constitution and subversive of its supposedly Christian polity.

To support the more conspiratorial claim, Sherman pointed out that President Wilson had seized all cable and telegraph lines *after* the Armistice (not as a war measure) and that Wilson maintained press censorship for some time after the fighting had ended in Europe. Moreover, the president had created the Committee on Public Information, a propaganda organization financed from a separate presidential fund beyond congressional oversight, and he had directed it to spread secular and churchly propaganda for the League. At the same time, his administration had placed serious obstacles in front of his critics' counterpropaganda. Convinced that the Committee on Public Information tried to manufacture popular acquiescence in the perpetuation of Wilson's wartime extensions of central authority, Sherman suggested that the League of Nations was actually meant as the ultimate global instrument of this socialistic usurpation. All of it made the Wilson administration "even under constitutional forms, a hybrid between a French revolution and an oriental despotism" and Wilson himself something like a cross between Caligula, Karl Marx, and Napoleon. There was mighty little Christian in all of that.[17]

In place of the League of Nations, Sherman proposed a traditional defensive alliance with like-minded (i.e., Christian) nations.[18] More important, he hoped that Americans would simply recognize human moral fallenness and the impossibility of perfecting the world. They should opt for the moral code of "the Nazarene carpenter's son," the "laws graven on tables of stone and delivered by Jehovah," and the values of the "self-supporting, God-fearing and industrious middle class." There should be a "return in the pulpit to preaching to the people the consequences that attend misbehavior in this world and hundred per cent sulphuric hell fire" in the next, and no one should be as attentively listened to as Billy Sunday, Sherman's favorite evangelist.[19] Sherman even told one group of Methodist petitioners that if their pro-League clergy knew the "plan of salvation" as badly as they knew the implications of the League, they had better start looking for new spiritual leaders.[20]

Sherman also launched attacks on the alleged Catholic domination of the League. He acknowledged that the Catholic Church was an important bulwark against Bolshevism and a "power for good" in other fields as well. But he also insisted that papal pretensions to temporal rule were both theologically in error and practically dangerous, and that they made the Catholic Church a "menace to just civil government."[21] The pope was bent on limiting personal liberty, Sherman alleged, and on extending Vatican influence over all predominantly Christian nations. He had been working on the latter goal when, under the cover of the war, the Vatican had sent diplomats into Protestant countries (e.g., into Britain for the first time since the Reformation), but at the same time he had made a de facto alliance with the German regime, no doubt impressed (as Sherman had it) by the similarity between German and papal authoritarianism. It was fair to conclude that both the Vatican and the Germans saw the League of Nations as yet another way of advancing their respective quests for authoritarian world rule. Because the majority of the League's original member states were Catholic, the Vatican could easily use it to expand its power and influence.[22]

Because of these oft-repeated charges, Sherman was denounced by several of his Senate colleagues, Catholics and Protestants alike. He came to be something of a bête-noir for the broader Catholic community, which censured him as a "small-bore mediocrity" and "backwoods sectarian."[23] Undisturbed by that criticism, Sherman went on to denounce the League membership of all pagan nations, only to return to the same old antipapal canard. Although he admitted that the faiths of a "primeval, barbaric" Zoroaster, a "crude" Native American, a "Mussulman," or a Jew could be valid and beneficent, Sherman stressed that a league composed of peoples not reared in the same tradition of religiopolitical values would find it impossible to meaningfully cooperate. Therefore he insisted that no League be set up before all governments and peoples "be agreed in their natures."[24]

All of this was a line of critique so congenial to conservative evangelicals that they avidly publicized Sherman's statements. No other senator received as much and as supportive churchly attention as did Sherman. A number of evangelical publications reprinted his anti-Catholic remarks in extenso and repeatedly.[25] Indeed, it was Sherman's talk about the Vatican's alleged plans for world domination through the League of Nations that prompted Theodore Graebner to make the anti-Catholic argument such a prominent part of the Missouri Synod's polemic.[26]

As even a cursory comparison with the main lines of conservative evangelical argument shows, all of Sherman's charges mirrored exactly the evangelicals' discourse. They incorporated all the usual points in that discourse, from the point about Catholic domination to the point about "yoke fellowship" with pagans and from general accusations about the false religion of internationalism to claims about the League's socialist legislative agenda. Even premillennial allusions cropped up. Not being a member of any denomination, Sherman was able to borrow freely. If taken together with the probability that Senator Henry Cabot Lodge was deliberately using Sherman as a mouthpiece and spoiler,[27] it would appear that his was a religious argument deliberately fostered and disseminated because its appeal was known to be considerable.

Evangelical Themes in Irreconcilable Discourse

Lawrence Y. Sherman was the man in whom most of the lines of the evangelical League of Nations critique converged. Yet he was by no means the only senator who employed religious-sounding rhetoric. He may have been the most extreme, but at least eight other Irreconcilable senators repeated, in more clearly secular, racialist terms, the fundamentalist argument against "yoke fellowship" with pagans. At least four of them voiced concerns over the lack of explicit guarantees in the original League Covenant for religious freedom and for Christian missionary activities. Many regularly denounced the churchly protagonists of the League for the supposedly utopian, religious dreams with which they were said to have invested the League. Almost every senator critical of the League scornfully used the word "millennium" to describe League enthusiasts. Many of them attacked the intermingling of churchly and secular campaigns for the League and detected a dilution and perversion of the churches' salvific message in that intermingling. Finally, many senators stated repeatedly that the beneficence and realism of the League enthusiasts' goals of universal and perpetual peace and of collective, globally planned social progress were disproven by a proper interpretation of the Christian scriptures.

Almost all the Irreconcilables claimed that liberal clergy and politicians were investing the League with millennial religious goals and competencies that only the churches could deliver. This was by far the most typical religious argument that they marshaled against League ratification. A rare, explicitly confessional version of this argument was offered by Asle J. Gronna, a progressive Republican senator from North Dakota, who was of Norwegian extraction and Lutheran by religious affiliation, a fact that he frequently made known to his colleagues.[28] Like Missouri Synod preachers, Gronna kept claiming that the League of Nations' churchly protagonists had lost faith in the clergy's only and abiding duty, which was the preaching of "the Gospel of Christ." Some Lutherans belonged in this class, Gronna maintained, but he insisted that his correspondence with his church's clergy showed that most of them were opposed to the League and understood that it was "worse than sacrilege" to portray the League as the beginning of the "millennium" or in any wise a proper outgrowth of Christianity. Gronna refused to accept that the clergy who did so portray the League were either true champions of peace or real believers in "the Christian faith and religion"; rather, they were beholden to "false doctrine" and God was as resistant to their prayers as He had been to the prayers of the Pharisees.[29]

Gronna also blamed the Paris peace conference for having slighted "the Trinity" and having ignored "the existence of Almighty God" when it had refused either to invoke divine assistance or include a reference to God in the League Covenant. Echoing Martin Luther's *Von weltlichen Obrigkeit*, he averred that even if the peace conference had instituted a properly Christian world league, perpetual and universal peace would have remained an impossibility, for human nature was sinful to the core and would always so remain. The Holy Alliance, which had been based on Christian sentiment, had failed for this very reason, Gronna suggested, and there had been frequent wars even between Norway, Sweden, and Denmark—three equally Lutheran nations, speaking the same tongue and apparently all dedicated to Christian unity and pacifism, yet led by inevitably "weak and selfish men." Gronna stressed that God Himself had scattered the nations after their earlier, illegitimate experiment with "the tower" had turned sour, and since then it had remained God's will that a political unity of mankind not be effected. God would punish all who attempted to forge such a unity. Gronna suggested therefore that arbitration treaties, not international political organizations, were the only biblically legitimate means of (relative) world pacification, but he seemed also to question whether it was right to negotiate such treaties with non-Christian nations.[30]

Others echoed Gronna on less confessionally rooted grounds. James A. Reed, a Democratic Irreconcilable from Missouri, faulted President Wilson and other League enthusiasts for having confused the echo of their own words with the "voice of God," and he accused the League's protagonists of all manner of millennial dreams about lions and lambs lying together under the protective canopy of their world organization. Reed kept stressing that it was not for the American people to "regenerate the earth," no matter how much the liberal politicians and churchmen had convinced themselves that it was. He said he was certain that all such attempts would fail on the rock of human depravity and would only cause more wars and other misfortunes.[31]

At one point, Reed even mocked the liberals' League as full of "heaven-born blessings that, like a celestial dove, come with healing on its wings" and supposedly "the greatest thing since Christ was born, not even excluding the passion of the crucifixion when the Savior died for all mankind." "I hope that Almighty God will paralyze my arm if I ever give my consent to so infamous a thing," he shouted, and then asserted that the true millennium was produced not by human leagues or agreements but by "the finger of the Divine Master" alone.[32]

In essential agreement with this antimillennial appeal was Pennsylvania's Republican senator Philander C. Knox. This former attorney general (1901–4) and secretary of state (1909–13) was perhaps the leading conservative Irreconcilable, certainly the most respected and internationally experienced. As secretary of state, he had pioneered the unilateral employment of U.S. military might in support of private investment and commerce, and ever since then he had been a Rooseveltian nationalist and supporter of limited, conservative international cooperation. Knox was also the grandson of a Methodist Episcopalian clergyman who acknowledged that his religious beliefs were a major reason for his opposition to the League Covenant. He claimed that this was probably the case with some 90 percent of Protestant clergy and laity in the country.[33] An avowed believer in the divine purposes of America as a nation, Knox had come in for praise from the National Reform Association for his prewar involvement in the federal legislation of morality.[34]

Knox voted for Sherman's amendment on the Deity, hit hard on the presence of pagans in the League, feared that the League would exert its powers against Christianity, and suggested that the Senate desperately needed divine guidance to realize that the United States simply had to be kept from such a League.[35] At one point, Knox even asserted that the League was "seeking to usurp the function, almost, of Almighty Providence," and that it was therefore "of wellnigh blasphemous presumption." The League aspired to "uncontrolled power," Knox felt, and he insisted that uncontrolled power was "omnipotence, an attribute of the Deity to which we bow with reverential awe. We concede it to no mere man."[36] Echoes of Methodist providentialism could be noted in his further insistence that "a higher civilization" would gradually bring about the "millennium" and that it was impossible to get it "here and now" or through a political institution not suited to the current stage of civilization.[37]

In much the same way, New Mexico's Republican senator Albert B. Fall referred to the League as "Chiliast"—that is, an organization based on a perversion of the Christian expectation of Christ's speedy return. As Fall sketched it, in the course of centuries that original expectation had been transformed into the belief that it was possible to "legislate good into man" and that enlightened human beings could determine through covenants and agreements never to go to war and always to live peaceful and prosperous lives. Such an attempt to generate "the millennium on earth" through purely human action, stressed Fall, was actually a "crime against the nations of the earth" and against Christian civilization, because it tried to enforce an artificial, formal equality and uniformity where one actually could not exist as long as peoples remained uncommitted to Christ. In Fall's view, the attempt only caused Christ to tarry further, perhaps for another thousand years.[38]

Though mentioned in the course of the only address Fall made during the League debate that had any religious content, this anti-millennial argument was almost certainly deeply believed. Fall was the grandson of a leader in the Disciples of Christ movement and had been much influenced by that movement's theology, especially as it related to questions of peace, war, and the churches' stances toward both. His grandfather, Philip Slater Fall, had been a prominent Disciples pacifist who in Civil War Tennessee had witnessed the Disciples' theology of separation from secular institutions and organized churches and focus on the "blessed hope" of Christ's return.[39]

In the case of a third conservative, Frank B. Brandegee, a senator from Connecticut, opportunism almost certainly explained the appeal to the anti-millennial theme. Even before the League Covenant had been drafted, Brandegee had lambasted those internationalist clerics who spoke of the "beauties of beating swords into plowshares and setting a good example." Possible maybe "a thousand years hence, perhaps when all the rest of the races of the world have been educated to the point of Christianity," Brandegee insisted that short of the actual, divinely wrought millennium, it would be stupendously irresponsible for nation-states to behave as if mere sentiment and a mere international agreement could produce universal peace and concord.[40]

Brandegee's own religious affiliation was indefinite, but this did not prevent him from further assailing the "hallelujah band" of "poor deluded clergymen" of all denominations and other "obsessed rainbow chasers upon their sacred ark of the covenant." These people, Brandegee suggested, were "always for virtue in the abstract, but fail to recognize vice in the concrete," and their League of Nations was nothing but an "impotent . . . mind cure." Wilson's religiously tainted appeals for the League offended Brandegee especially, and he accused Wilson and the liberal clergy of having convinced themselves that they had reached a unique "state of holiness and sanctification" and that through their League the rest of the world could also be given a new sanctifying and pacifying revelation. Brandegee objected strongly to the churches' part in what he called the "propaganda of misrepresentation" on the League's behalf, and he suggested that actually the churches were all split down the middle on the League issue. He refused to believe that the majority of "the ladies and clergymen and parishioners" who petitioned for League ratification had any idea of what they were actually asking the Senate to do.[41]

Given that Brandegee was a known alcoholic, a "cynical and morose" man who committed suicide in the early 1920s, the depth and sincerity of his personal religiosity is certainly open to question.[42] Nevertheless, he was one of the senators who were the most consistently interested in employing religious rhetoric in the Irreconcilable cause. His collaborators regarded him as "one of the keenest minds in the Senate" whose "power of analysis was amazing," and they therefore chose him as their principal parliamentary tactician whenever special acumen was needed.[43] It is, therefore, reasonable to assume Brandegee had deemed religious arguments potent ammunition serving the Irreconcilable cause particularly well.

Brandegee's reference to "poor deluded clergymen" exposed an unbroken subtheme in the Irreconcilable appeal to the anti-millennialist theme. This was the accusation that other, non-Christian forces were manipulating liberal clergy and interdenominational organizations and using their pro-League utterances in the interests of a cause that had nothing to do with Christianity. Senator Knox made that claim, as did Gronna and Sherman in slightly different ways. In his sole religious reference during the Senate debates, Miles Poindexter, Republican of Washington, a former Progressive and World War I conservative nationalist, seized upon this issue. He suggested that the mass of church petitions for ratification that the senators received in no wise indicated genuine Christian support for the League. According to Poindexter, it was rather "manufactured propaganda," paid for by international financiers, especially by Andrew Carnegie, and disseminated by a "paid official" of the Federal Council of Churches (Frank Crane) who was no real clergyman, having given up preaching the Gospel for preaching the salvific League of Nations.[44]

Likewise, Senator Joseph I. France, a progressive Republican and Presbyterian from Maryland, voiced great surprise at the Federal Council of Churches' official endorsement of a League that he saw as a culmination of "the gross materialism of our times" rather than as a product of Christian idealism. He was profoundly worried about the impact of the League's secular universalism and speculated that some "atheist influences" must have been powerfully at work in Paris for such a League to have emerged. Indeed, France asserted that it was "absolutely erroneous" to claim that most American Christians were supportive of the League of Nations. Instead the opposite was true, and whosoever supported the League would have to answer for that sin, "arraigned at the last before the eternal Power of justice."[45]

Senator Reed rendered this assertion in conspiratorial terms. He suggested that political and churchly liberals were in the throes of a revival enthusiasm, but that this revival was not for the Christian faith but for a secular political institution suffused with definitely non-Christian spiritual paradigms. Reed contradicted himself when he ascribed authorship for this secular religious revival, first accusing W. E. B. DuBois, the African American leader, and other alleged schemers for a black world despotism, then blaming British imperialists, and at another time sketching a "world-wide conspiracy" of malevolent, apparently non-Christian aliens, "international financiers," and people from the Carnegie Endowment for International Peace.[46]

Reed also made use of racialist appeals against the League of Nations. This senator did not identify himself openly with any denomination, yet he had a distinctly and profoundly Christian upbringing and background. His racist and anti-Semitic tendencies were later spectacularly exposed when he agreed to serve as Henry Ford's defense attorney after Ford was sued over the anti-Semitic calumnies of his *Dearborn Independent*.[47] In the League debates, Reed did not appeal to anti-Semitism but rather blended religious themes with more general racial prejudice and ended up with a version of the evangelical proscription against "yoke fellowship." Many Irreconcilables did this, but Reed was particularly outspoken.

Reed even quoted biblical passages against the "yoking together" of asses and oxen, of Christian and pagan nations, to make this case. Calculating from the makeup of the original League membership that "dark-skinned races" would outnumber the "white" member nations in the League's decision-making bodies by a ratio of three to one, Reed insisted that pagans would submerge the Christian civilization of the West if such a League were set up. It was impossible, he alleged, to make a "naked Hottentot," a "wild

Bedouin," or other "degenerate and dying races" understand Christian morals and American constitutional principles, and it was pointless to try to convert them, because their racial characteristics were stronger than any shared human aptitudes to ethical thought. Therefore, with just such people dominating it, the League would not only prove ineffective for any constructive or worthy purpose but would also before long repudiate both Christian morals and American constitutional principles. Race, ethnicity, and religion blended when Reed made this claim, for he stressed that many of the "dark and mixed races" engaged in "Voodoism," child sacrifice, and assorted other practices condemned by Christian morals, which facts alone made them unfit for self-government, let alone world co-government. These peoples did not share a "common destiny" with the Christian nations, and many of them could not be uplifted or reformed, even by Christian missionaries. It was therefore better to leave them alone.[48]

Reed's appeal to racialist prejudice was echoed throughout the rest of the Irreconcilable camp. In addition to his anti-millennialist arguments, Senator Fall disapproved of the League as an organization geared not toward American interests but to those of the "Buddhists of Japan and India," the "Voodoo worshippers of Africa," "the Mohammeddans [sic] of Turkey," and the "fire worshippers of Persia."[49] Senator Knox insisted that the League's "less advanced" member nations should not be given equality but that its decision making be reserved for the Americans and the British, the "proved trustees of civilization." These trustees were to use force, Knox stipulated, for it was impossible to move others with "moral suasion" only.[50] Similarly, Senator Joseph M. McCormick, Republican of Illinois, along with George H. Moses, Republican of New Hampshire, claimed that the League Covenant legitimated the persecution of Christians and missionaries when it gave equal power and rights to supposedly anti-Christian pagan nations.[51] Moses further denounced the lack of clear guarantees for religious freedom in the Covenant.[52] And Bert Fernald, Republican of Maine, insisted on the impossibility of effectual cooperation between different ethnic and religious traditions. He swore "by the Eternal" that he would never accept a League so constituted.[53]

But attempts were also made to offer reasoned, constructive, Christian solutions to the problems that had been identified. Here Senator France was pivotal. He was a German-educated physician, the son of a Presbyterian minister and a Presbyterian himself, who was especially interested in the mission field and apparently regularly read the *Missionary Review*.[54] Irreconcilable on most aspects of the League and its Covenant, he was particularly scathing about the Covenant's mandatory provisions. He regarded these provisions as a cover for the continued imperial exploitation of weaker and "less advanced" peoples, in which endeavor he did not want America to join.

Instead he called for the abandonment of the League and for American leadership in an alternative international conference that sought for other, voluntary means of world uplift. This conference, which might eventually have a permanent institutionalized form, would develop strategies for the sustainable and nonexploitative development of African and Asian societies, especially in the areas of education, health services, vocational training, and industrial development. Racialism figured in the scheme, for France supposed that American blacks might be enlisted in the effort and that in the process they themselves would be converted and "assimilated" to the legal, moral, and religious norms of white American society.[55]

Whenever France made these proposals, he referred to the beneficiaries as the "heathen" of Africa and Asia. It is quite apparent that he envisioned his new type of international cooperation as an aspect of missionary work. It should therefore come as no surprise that he was one of those senators to whom Protestant clergy turned when they lobbied for amending the Covenant to assure the freedom and safety of missionary activities.[56] But France's concept of missions was of a very modernist if not materialist kind. His missionary effort sought to spread around the world not just the "true monotheistic faith" but also what he called its "first complete manifestation" in a material civilization, that of the United States. The American system, he stressed, was based on the truths of the Bible and the historical experience of Christendom, and it yielded, as Christianity must yield, material plenty and progress. Only by exporting that system across the world could one build a universal brotherhood of rightly spiritualized human beings. Such a mission effort was geared toward material uplift as much as, if not more than, toward evangelism. But France was insistent that only such a missionary effort could bring about a peaceful and cooperative world. The League of Nations could not. "Not through the promulgation of a statute but by the regeneration of men by the spirit, must the millennium come."[57]

France, a contender for the Republican presidential nomination in 1920, was a rather radical liberal who eventually became a sympathizer and champion of the Russian Bolsheviks.[58] That later turn of events, just like much of his commentary on the League, was rooted in a pronounced modernist and postmillennial religiosity that he was wont to describe in terms of a cosmic evolution toward ever-higher stages of physical, moral, and social development, converging ultimately in a new worldwide moral civilization and but one "common mind."[59] His opposition to the League was therefore that of a distinctly leftist and theologically modernist man who could not accept the liberal clergy's contention that the League, as constituted, amounted to the attainment or furtherance of the postmillennial Kingdom of God. He did not disagree with them on the supposedly inevitable, eventual outcome, nor on the reality of those ethical processes of an incarnational and immanentist divinity that were to lead to the outcome. He just did not think that the League pertained to either.

This appraisal of the League Covenant also applied to two other left-of-center Irreconcilables who offered arguments similar to those of France. George W. Norris was a Republican from Nebraska, not a member of any denomination but applauded in any case by some Bible-believing senators as one in whom God had implanted the core ideas of Christianity and whose discourse formed a clarion call for all Christians.[60] Norris spent many hours attacking the article of the League Covenant that ceded the Chinese province of Shantung to the Japanese. Though this defense of China against Japan was a staple in most progressive anti-imperialist circles on both sides of the Atlantic, in Norris's case it took a distinctly, even passionately, Christian turn.

Claiming that the Japanese were actuated by an intense hatred of Christianity, Norris alleged that if the League Covenant was accepted with the Shantung provisions in it, the result would be that "the Christian religion is going to be blotted off the face of the earth over there." Already there was a systematic and exceedingly brutal suppression of native Christians and American missionaries going on in Korea, another territory controlled by Japan (Norris quoted from Presbyterian and Methodist reports to substantiate this charge), and it was a foregone conclusion that this was to continue if Japan's rule was not only recognized and guaranteed but actually extended. Therefore, in three passionate addresses, Norris implored all Christians to mobilize themselves to defeat ratification of the League. He even suggested that if the clergy were to actually become aware of what the League would inevitably do to the Christian faith, there would be "not a Christian minister anywhere on the face of the earth" who would support League ratification. It would be a "crime against humanity" to ratify, Norris underlined, and a "stab [to] the Christian religion in the heart," for it would mean the abandonment of all of Asia to "heathen paganism" and constitute a betrayal of God's commission to convert the world.[61]

William E. Borah, Republican progressive of Idaho and one of the most widely known and listened-to Irreconcilables, echoed Norris. Borah was no more known for consistent Christian advocacy than his progressive collaborator, but he was raised as a Presbyterian and was a Bible class teacher while a senator.[62] His familiarity with biblical turns of phrases was thus both considerable and assiduously resorted to. Borah repeated many of Norris's arguments on Shantung and Christian missionaries, and he tried to show from his own correspondence how Christian opinion was actually opposed to the League. He branded as "sacrilegious" all attempts to insert into a document as oppressive as the League Covenant the name, or ask for the blessing, of the Deity.[63] Furthermore, Borah refused to accept that Christian and pagan nations—actuated by entirely different notions of right and wrong, as he put it—could meaningfully cooperate in a joint political organization. He stressed that basic human depravity made it unlikely that even professedly Christian nations could do so.[64] In addition, the League tried to extinguish all national and individual differences and "standardize the human family," which Borah thought was contrary to God's will and the manifest teachings of history, and he suggested that the project would inevitably degenerate into an unprecedented global exercise in coercive despotism.[65]

So strongly did Borah feel about all this that at one point he even promised—in a statement denounced by the clergy of many denominations—that he would not vote for the League Covenant, as it stood, even if the "Saviour of mankind" appeared to campaign for it.[66] That may have been a curious promise from a Bible class teacher, but he meant it to underline that the League of Nations in fact had very little of the Christian about it and that no amount of modernist clerical appeal to high moral authority could change that.

Most progressive Irreconcilables agreed. It is notable that of the seven progressive Irreconcilables, only two—Hiram W. Johnson, Republican of California, and Robert M. La Follette, Republican of Wisconsin—failed to make any noticeable appeal to religious themes, and one—Charles S. Thomas, Democrat of Colorado—attacked nearly all forms of political religion. All the others followed Borah and France's general line of argument. Thomas's case was unique and unrepresentative, because he was not a member of any church or a believer in a personal Deity. Indeed, he thought that religion was itself a major cause of intolerance and war. Therefore, as far as Thomas was concerned, the less religion was mentioned or thought about, the better for all concerned.[67]

All the progressive Irreconcilables were, however, dedicated to the causes of peace, anti-imperialism, and progressive social reform. They tended to support Wilson's Fourteen Points and hoped that this clarion call would pave the way to substituting traditional power politics with a new era of purposive international reform. After League ratification failed, these men pioneered a distinct "peace progressive" foreign policy agenda, which they tried to thrust upon the Republican administrations of the 1920s, an agenda predicated on the nonuse of military might and other coercive means, seeking cooperation and social reform on the basis of supposedly universally shared ethical values and aspirations.[68] These proposals had definite Christian roots; they were attuned to the immanentist ethical theologies of the Social Gospel but refused to accept that an international political institution was the best means of carrying out the Social Gospel program.

The conservative Irreconcilables, conversely, did not develop any single or uniformly recurring lines of religious critique. Sherman was an exception, but the rest of the conservative Irreconcilables simply tended to repeat religious arguments derived from many different theological and denominational sources. The incidentals of the conservatives' religious argument did not materially differ from those of the progressives; only, the theologies that underlay the conservatives' argument were always less optimistic about ethical progress, more heedful of original sin and human depravity, and consequently more traditionally evangelical.

Reservationists and Evangelical Anti-Internationalism

Whether of a conservative or a leftist type, the borrowing of religion to make the anti-League case remained a predominantly Irreconcilable phenomenon. Few Reservationists employed religion in the same way. This may be explained by the rather technical nature of the Reservationists' effort, or it may have been a commentary on the lack of conservative religious faith in men who were in other areas prone to pragmatism and compromise. Though it was clear that the racialist sentiments of James A. Reed or the missionary concerns of Joseph I. France rather easily lent themselves to religious appeals, it certainly would have required some ingenuity to see how religion was relevant to amending specific sections of the League Covenant by way of interpretive resolutions. Whatever the reason, the Reservationists' use of religion was muted, dispassionate, and definitely secondary to other concerns.

Thus, Henry Cabot Lodge, the Republican majority leader and chairman of the Senate Foreign Relations Committee, the leading strong Reservationist and a rather lax Episcopalian, only once portrayed the League as a human attempt "to reach the millennium of universal and eternal peace."[69] He opposed Senator Sherman's proposed insertion of the name of the Deity into the League Covenant and also refused to ask for divine blessing on the Covenant—because, as he put it, such a request would have made him "irreverent."[70] Lodge also identified liberal professors and "preachers of sermons" as the League's most vociferous and most mistaken supporters, and he called their whole project "the evil thing with the holy name."[71] As has been seen, his close friend William Lawrence, the Episcopal bishop of Massachusetts, encouraged his fight against ratification.

Another strong Reservationist, New Jersey's Republican Joseph Frelinghuysen, of illustrious Dutch Reformed lineage, took the peace conference to task for not having prayed or acknowledged God as the ruler of all the earth,[72] but he said nothing else about religion. Warren G. Harding, a Republican senator from Ohio and Wilson's successor as president, who was Baptist by church affiliation, blamed League enthusiasts for having appropriated goals that could be reached only on "the millennial day that marks the beginning of heaven on earth."[73] He further denounced the League Covenant as a venture that would "destroy the soul" of the United States in that it would have transferred the nation's duty to make its own moral judgments onto a foreign institution. Such a transference, Harding felt, could only have silenced America's Christian conscience.[74]

The leading Republican mild Reservationist, Senator Porter J. McCumber of North Dakota, reached the opposite conclusion. He opined that since "the God of international justice" had "in His special favors" given the United States incomparable power and resources, America was divinely called to join the League and lead it on Christian and humanitarian paths.[75] Senator Irvine L. Lenroot, a Congregationalist and Republican mild Reservationist from Wisconsin, ventured that inasmuch as human nature was "imperfect" but not "condemned," the organism of nations was also likely, in time, to develop toward such "perfection . . . where shines unmolested the light of the justice of God." Only slight alterations in its Covenant were needed for this process to begin.[76]

McCumber's and Lenroot's appeals to religion in support of League ratification were both noticeably muted and rare among even the mildest Reservationists, of whom these two men were the leaders. For whatever reason, most Reservationists were prone to compromise and search for a pragmatic middle ground, and they shied away from expansive future hopes of any kind. This bent for compromise caused frequent friction between them and the Irreconcilables, and especially so in January 1920, when a group of mild Reservationists induced Senator Lodge to begin several rounds of bipartisan negotiations with League supporters.[77] It was a fruitless exercise, but one markedly free of any investment of the League, either amended with reservations or not, with expansive spiritual goals and competencies. This underlined the reality that, apart from the Irreconcilables and the liberal Christian enthusiasts for the League, no one in the Senate seemed to have cared strongly enough about the possible religious dimensions of the League to have made these the crux of his argument.

There was, however, one dimension in the League Covenant that united the Reservationists and the Irreconcilables and called forth religiously colored denunciations from both. This was the question of the International Labor Organization (ILO), which was one of the permanent institutions of the League of Nations and which President Wilson and the Social Gospelers tended to depict as the principal international fruit of the Social Gospel. Conservative critics, conversely, presented this organization as proof beyond all doubt that the League of Nations was in fact a socialist enterprise.

Circumstantial evidence suggests that Bishop Thomas Neely's *The League: The Nation's Danger* was crucial for this argument to have taken hold of Irreconcilable and Reservationist discourse. This book predated the rise of the political anti-ILO argument, was widely publicized by conservative evangelicals, and was the only one of its kind. A summary of the book was read into the *Congressional Record* immediately after its publication in early August 1919, and several rounds of debate on the ILO followed immediately afterward.[78] When both the Irreconcilables and the Reservationists began to attack the ILO, they more often than not borrowed Neely's arguments. Most often they did this by alleging that the ILO's permanent Labor Office constituted a world socialist propaganda center that eventually would start to disseminate atheist and anti-Christian notions under the guise of some liberal and humanitarian ideals.

Senator William H. King, Democrat of Utah, who supported the League in principle, warned that the ILO was a portent of a "communism of nations" and that as an institution was likely to give international protection to the Bolshevik Third Internationale and subsidize its "poisonous" propaganda. King was especially concerned about the "imperium in imperio" of the permanent Labor Office, which was (actually) led by European socialists and had already (or so King supposed) started to "provide a nursery for the germination, sprouting and dissemination of socialistic and bolshevistic doctrines." King implicated liberal Christian clergy in this germination and sprouting process, and he attacked all in that category that showed sympathies for such doctrines or the upholders of such doctrines. Instead, he asked the clergy to concentrate on preaching the doctrine of Christ alone, not the doctrines of the socialists.[79]

These latter doctrines, according to another senator, were nothing but "hell in the hearts of men," and they could only be effaced through "an act of God . . . a great revival of religion." No states or international association of states could produce such a revival, continued this senator, Henry L. Myers, Democrat of Montana, a mild Reservationist from a long family line of Presbyterians. Conversely, states and Leagues of Nations most definitely could further the false materialist religion of socialism. Insofar as the ILO created an internationally recognized and financed center for collectivist propaganda, it was therefore "fraught with great danger," and Myers was convinced that it would turn out to be one of the institutions that would undermine Christianity the most. He regarded as a particularly "grave sign" the support that the modernist ex-clergyman George D. Herron, who was a well-known leader in the Socialist Party, had given to the ILO.[80]

The Irreconcilable senators Knox, Thomas, Reed, Sherman, McCormick, Fall, Poindexter, and Fernald denounced the ILO on much the same grounds, as did the Reservationists Lodge, Frelinghuysen, and Thomas Sterling. Even the sole Republican champion of the League as presented, Senator McCumber, stated that he could not vote for a League that contained such an "obnoxious and abhorrent" agency as the socialist ILO.[81] So widespread were these kinds of sentiments that practically all those in the Senate who opposed the ratification of the League Covenant gave the ILO as a major cause of their stance. Indeed, the reservation that was offered against American adherence to the ILO passed by a clear margin, and many a senator otherwise supportive of the League joined in the vote.[82]

The interpollination of evangelical and conservative political argument had significantly paved the way to that outcome. In all likelihood it would have come in any case, for at that time conservative fears about communism were so deeply entrenched that an international agency as manifestly compromised by the socialist support that it enjoyed as the ILO hardly had a chance. Still, the constant evangelical complaints about the danger that the ILO posed to the Christian faith played a role in all this. It was a retired bishop of the Methodist Episcopal Church who first brought the ILO to the attention of the senators, and it was the constant pamphleteering by evangelical laity and clergy that helped keep this agency at the center of controversy. Evangelicals imbued with clerical laissez-faire notions and with an overriding aversion to the Social Gospel invested the ILO with profound anti-Christian meanings in ways that got the attention of conservative senators. If nothing else, the evangelical polemic suggested to them that there was a large religious constituency in the nation to which they could appeal on this matter.

Reed Smoot and Mormon Anti-Internationalism

The last originally Reservationist senator who did not accept the League of Nations' beneficence was Reed Smoot, a Republican from Utah. Smoot's case was unique, because he was an apostle in the Church of Jesus Christ of Latter-day Saints, a member of the very highest Mormon priesthood. He made religious arguments against the League from early on, and eventually, as he stated in a much publicized open letter in August 1919, he came to regard Irreconcilable opposition to the League as his "duty to my church, to my country and my God."[83]

Smoot appealed to the *Book of Mormon* and to the prophecies of Joseph Smith, the founder of Mormonism, in support of his contention that God had deliberately preserved the United States from entanglements with the rest of the world. God had reserved an apocalyptic mission for America, and America had to be kept pure from European and Asiatic influences if it was to fulfill that mission. Any American adherence to the League of Nations, Smoot therefore insisted, would mean that the nation had "turned away from God" and would be punished. He was sure, also, that the League enthusiasts' promises about world peace and progress neither could nor should be fulfilled through a world political institution, "the Lord Himself having declared that such a thing cannot come until His Second Coming." Smoot stressed that peace could be achieved only by following "the teachings of our Lord and Savior," as interpreted by "the rock of Mormonism"; all secular means to that end, be they "peace-keeping alliances" or compacts with infidel nations for other purposes, were proscribed by the Word of God. Smoot could not understand, therefore, why in the face of clear and long-taught Mormon doctrine so many fellow Mormons still "take it for granted that the League of Nations will do more for the world than the teachings of the Savior." He was convinced that God was "not pleased" with the League.[84]

These Smoot statements came after lengthy personal questionings and amid a general Mormon sympathy for the League of Nations. In September 1919, the Mormons' presiding bishop had announced that the League conformed to the Mormon understanding of redemptive history. The president of the church, Heber J. Grant, had also spoken favorably of the League and prayed for its ratification in the Senate. Other leading Mormons even claimed that all who opposed the manifestly divinely inspired organization were engaged in a "fight against God."[85] Faced with these dictates, the other Mormon senator, William H. King, a onetime missionary to Great Britain, who had had reservations about the original draft Covenant, became supportive of the League, apart from the ILO.[86]

However, Smoot through his membership in the highest Mormon priesthood was in a unique position. It was a tenet of the faith that although the presiding bishop (who was appointed by the highest priesthood) oversaw all the temporal activities of the church, binding doctrine for the church as a whole was enunciated by the highest priesthood and especially those of the Quorum of Twelve Apostles, of whom Smoot was one. Moreover, every member of this group could receive private divine revelations. Smoot seems to have regarded his religious case against the League of Nations as one such revelation.[87] Nor was he the only prominent Mormon who thus interpreted his religious duty. There were Mormon mass meetings arranged against the League in the Tabernacle at Salt Lake City; many letters supportive of his stance reached Smoot; his writings on the League were printed and disseminated in pamphlet form by California Mormons; and the important Mormon leaders Bishop David W. Nibley and laymen David O. McKay and Joseph Fielding Smith Jr., two future presidents, gave Smoot strong support.[88] The debate on the religious implications of the League of Nations was thus just as lively in the one major church that many regarded as non-Christian that had representatives in the U.S. Senate as it was among the evangelicals. For the Mormons, too, the religious debate spilled over into politics.

Politicians' Co-optation of Evangelical Anti-Internationalism

What does it all signify? Many of the Senate critics of the League probably used religious rhetoric for a political, secular purpose. None of them made the religious argument the foundation of their anti-League case, and most seem not to have been driven by any specific creedal or confessional conviction either in their politics in general or in the League debate in particular. According to his own contention, Senator Knox was so driven, and Senator Smoot clearly was so driven, and probably Gronna, too; but even Senator Sherman, the most avid borrower of religious rhetoric, was not in fact a member of any Protestant denomination. This was illustrative of the blending of general conservative prejudices and inclinations with religious rhetoric, as opposed to deep theological conviction or exegesis, that characterized the role of religion in the Senate's debate.

Undoubtedly, some of this blending took place either out of unconscious habit or as a result of an opportunistic gauging of the appeal that religious rhetoric still had in the population at large. It is therefore important to separate the reasons for senatorial employment of the religious argument from the argument itself. Yet it remains a potent and significant fact that of the sixteen Irreconcilable opponents of the League of Nations, at least fourteen used religious arguments of one or another kind when they stated their case against ratification. Quite apart from their motivations, it was this use of religion that mattered, for it contributed a distinctly religious character to the political League controversy.

All the senators' religious arguments against the ratification of the League Covenant both mirrored and gratified the conservative evangelicals. These arguments showed that many of the leading conservative politicians of both parties in 1919–20 were still attuned to religious rhetoric and, in some cases, also to religious categories of thought and explicitly Christian goals. Such saturation of the secular League debate with religious rhetoric highlighted the fact that in 1919–20 America still regarded itself as a Christian nation where clergy were men of importance and clout. What the clergy had to say about the religious implications of such secular projects as the League of Nations was still appreciated and even heeded by conservative politicians, who were at least nominal Christians and just as interested as the conservative, fundamentalist clergy in perpetuating traditional religious legitimations of the sociopolitical and international status quo. Many of these men, too, saw the League issue as inherently and unavoidably religious. To them, just as much as to conservative clergy, it was not just a novel international attempt to prevent wars or assure social justice but also an attempt to inculcate particular secular valuations and goals in all of humankind.

Many of these senators may have preferred traditional religiopolitical valuations to newer secular valuations for reasons other than a personal Christian affirmation, but they did nevertheless endorse in their speech and action the Christian-ness of those traditional valuations. This is what mattered, because it was this public political endorsement that helped make Christian anti-internationalism not just a persuasion indigenous to, and compartmentalized in, the various conservative evangelical church groups. No matter what their motivations, the senators' use of evangelical arguments popularized Christian anti-internationalism and helped carve a place for it in the political arena. In subsequent decades, this intermingling of religion and international politics was only to grow in importance.

These facts suggest that existing interpretations of the political League fight have overlooked a significant aspect of that fight. No major reconstruction or scholarly analysis of the senators' fight has given any attention to the religion of the combatants. It is true that the religious promptings of the League's political supporters—with the partial exception of Wilson himself—have not been extensively addressed either. But at least the importance of religion is implicitly recognized in the frequent criticism of Wilson's supposed "messianic" fixation that many have leveled against his League of Nations project.[89] The conservative evangelical promptings of many of the League's most important senatorial opponents have not received even this kind of attention.

Instead, the typical explanations of Irreconcilable and (some) Reservationist stances have dwelt on the isolationist, anti-intellectual, or outright racist beliefs of the Irreconcilable minority. The concentration of the Irreconcilables in areas with significant Anglophobe and anti-imperialist immigrant populations has also been emphasized. Older interpretations in particular have stressed the personal animosity toward President Wilson of many of the anti-League activists.[90] This was undoubtedly a factor in many cases, for Wilson was notorious for his propensity for fighting a man rather than just a man's opinions, and many rebelled against that.

All these points are valid and nothing contradicts them in the re-creation of the senators' religious beliefs and arguments. However, without a clear understanding of such religious beliefs, all reconstructions of the political League fight remain incomplete and ultimately misleading. It remains a fact that many of the League's most consistent and vocal senatorial opponents were also evangelical laymen of one or another Protestant denomination (and one of them of the Mormon Church). This was not without significance when these individuals chose to take up the anti-League cause. Even if it can only be instanced, not qualified or weighed, the conservative evangelical beliefs of these individuals must have had a central impact on their decision to contest the League of Nations. Even more centrally, such beliefs must have figured in the utter persistence and uncompromising nature of the Irreconcilables' efforts.

In other words, some Irreconcilables were clearly irreconcilable to the League of Nations because the particularly powerful force of *their religion* told them to be so. Even on the less charitable supposition that the Irreconcilables were largely opportunistic and not sincere in their appeals to religion, their avid use of religious arguments surely must have influenced those in their audience who were more genuinely attuned to religion. These people were already being fed a diet of Christian anti-internationalism by conservative evangelical clergy in most major denominations; and when they then turned to the Senate, the same arguments assailed them from there. The combined effects of these two appeals to religion would have been quite significant.

Whether a given senator intended so or not—and many may well have intended—the rehearsing of Christian arguments in the course of League debates was, in fact, a great boon to all who wished to reassert more traditional theologies in national discourse. The Senate's apparently purely political League of Nations controversy appears therefore not only as an episode in the early-twentieth-century making of public theology but also as an episode in the continuing effort of conservative Christian politicians to Christianize the politics of the United States in their chosen image and to keep it from being dominated by nonconservative Christians and non-Christians. Thus, much more was involved in the controversy than secular politics.

CHAPTER SEVEN

Religion and the League for the Preservation of American Independence

The Irreconcilable and Reservationist senators were not the only politicians who resorted to religious arguments when they campaigned against the League of Nations. Concurrently with their debates, there was afoot in the country a number of other anti-League publicity, propaganda, and persuasion campaigns, some of them coordinated with or by these senators, some of them independent and pursuing manifestly different goals. Of the former type, by far the most important was the campaign undertaken by the cumbersomely named League for the Preservation of American Independence, which here will be called the Independence League. Though the Independence League proffered the whole range of anti–League of Nations arguments, and relatively few specifically religious ones, between the overt lines of its principal propaganda there persisted a distinct subtheme of Christian anti-internationalism. It would have been picked up only by those already attuned to conservative religiopolitical argument, but that limited circulation did not make it any less important for the development and perpetuation of the conservative evangelical tradition of anti-internationalism.

Most of the Independence League's leaders and most of its important publicists were evangelical laymen. Many of them were theologically and culturally conservative, and all of them were insistent on forwarding their alternative religiopolitical solutions for the pressing problems of the moment. Even when they did not do this explicitly, for those who knew of their evangelical grounding, the religious implications of their message were immanent in the whole of their public conversation, in its tacit assumptions, its categories and expectations, and much of its tenor. Even when the actual genuineness of such a publicist's evangelical faith was open to reasonable suspicion, their many evangelical listeners and readers would have read reinforcing messages into the arguments that these men delivered in Christian terms.

The journalist Henry Watterson, the Independence League's president, was a member of the Disciples of Christ;[1] and its executive secretary, the lawyer George Wharton Pepper, and its treasurer, the banker and railroad executive Stuyvesant Fish, were both conservative Episcopalians.[2] Board member Thomas W. Hardwick, a former Democratic senator from Georgia, was also an Episcopalian, whereas the inventor and industrialist Henry A. Wise Wood, another board member and instigator of the whole organization, came from a long line of Quakers.[3] As has been seen, the onetime board member Albert J. Beveridge was a conservative Methodist of some renown. Finally, the Independence League's most important publicist, the professor David Jayne Hill, also a board member, was a former clergyman in the Northern Baptist Convention, a man with his own, unique twist to the religious anti–League of Nations argument.[4]

In different ways, many of these men believed (or claimed) that goals of the ultimate kind that liberal clergy and politicians associated with the League of Nations could only be reached by the Christian churches and only if these churches maintained a traditional evangelical witness to the Christian faith. Most of them were just as committed to the Christianization of the United States and the world as were the clerical League of Nations enthusiasts, and just as dedicated to the goals of peace and social progress. But they maintained that a political international organization not only could not assist in reaching these goals but would in fact hurt, hinder, and retard their achievement.

These men did not create the Independence League to spread a specifically Christian anti-internationalism. Their activities in the Independence League should not be read reductively so that all roads lead back to their religious beliefs. But it is equally true that many of the Independence League's leaders viewed the world through confessional Christian prisms and revealed their religious groundedness in much of their commentary related to the League of Nations. It is clear that many of them were opposed to the League of Nations not least because they saw it as a challenge and substitute to the Christian faith and ecclesia. How this came to be requires an analysis both of the Independence League's activities and types of argument and of the biographical trajectories of its leading propagandists.

The Independence League: Structure, Aims, Activities

The Independence League was set up in the spring of 1919, at about the time when the first draft League of Nations Covenant had become public. It was in theory a bipartisan organization, but most of its activists came from the ranks of Republicans, and from the ranks of the most conservative, traditional, and partisan Republicans at that. With funds supplied by two millionaires, Andrew Mellon and Henry Clay Frick, among others, it conducted extensive nationwide propaganda campaigns against the League of Nations. These campaigns consisted of pamphleteering and of the lobbying of individual, wavering senators, as well as of a separate speaking tour that trailed the two other tours of late 1919 that addressed questions of internationalism, those of President Woodrow Wilson and the World Christian Fundamentals Association. The Independence League printed and disseminated the Irreconcilable senators' speeches, and sympathetic senators helped it by reading into the *Congressional Record* some of the pamphlets that it produced. Many of these were then printed and mailed around the country under senatorial franking privileges.[5]

The Independence League was well poised to disseminate the senators' utterances, because it had not just two separate headquarters (New York and Washington) but also eight district offices and chapters all across the country. The local chapters received instructions from a national board of directors and from an advisory board that included many a leading Irreconcilable senator. Others—including some leading Reservationists—expressed their support for the organization's aims without actually joining in. Senators Miles Poindexter, George Moses, Joseph France, and Harry New of Indiana were on the advisory board, whereas Senators William Borah, James Reed, and Hiram Johnson also took an active part, including as traveling propagandists. Senators Philander Knox and Henry Cabot Lodge sympathized with the group, supported it, and sometimes cooperated in its campaigns. It proved very difficult, however, to coordinate efforts between senators, all of whom seemed to have very high opinions of their own input and very low opinions of all other senators' input. Consequently, the Independence League let the senatorial advisory board fall into relative desuetude.[6]

Even though many Irreconcilables belonged to it, the Independence League's aims did not mimic those of the Irreconcilables. Rather, the Independence League insisted that ad hoc alliances and adjudication of international disagreements were better and safer than a permanent political institution that in certain circumstances bound all member states to make war. Its Declaration of Principles simply stated that it was "opposed to the covenant of the League as reported from Paris." If the League of Nations Covenant could be modified in the direction of adjudication and case-specific alliances, the Independence League would in principle have been willing to have the United States join it.[7]

This willingness did not mean, however, that the Independence League was ready to countenance any merely minor tinkering with the proposed League of Nations Covenant. It wanted a wholesale rewriting of most of the contentious articles. Above all, the Independence League disapproved of those articles that placed decision making on justiciable international disputes not in an independent judiciary but in a political assembly (the League of Nations Council) and that stipulated that all member states were bound by the political majority decisions of this assembly. As others had done, the Independence League, too, rehearsed all the racialist, nationalist, and pacifist arguments against such a concentration of power in foreign hands, and it suggested that only a new world despotism could come from such hands. Compelling taxes from American taxpayers for its upkeep, forcing Americans to fight in whatever foreign wars suited the interests of the League of Nations' directorate, and intruding into a range of domestic affairs, the new world despotism would inevitably destroy American national sovereignty and individual freedom alike.[8]

In addition, the Independence League spent much of its effort on combating the social reform aspects of the League of Nations structure. Many of its publications alleged that only socialists of one or another variety could really be interested in these aspects of the League of Nations Covenant, which meant that the League of Nations should be seen as an attempt to substitute for the democratic institutions of America a socialist world government. The Independence League therefore accused President Wilson and the conservative internationalists of the League to Enforce Peace of having entered a gigantic conspiracy with professed socialists, international financiers, and various churchly and pacifist internationalists, all of whom were supposedly interested in socialistic world rule. In this context, the League of Nations Covenant's provisions for international labor legislation came in for specific criticism.[9] All commentary of this kind equated Wilsonian social reformism, wartime collectivism, and Germanic autocracy. The resulting compound was then thrown back at all League of Nations supporters as the true, secret content of their internationalist vision.

As this summary of its message implies, the Independence League tried to appropriate most strands of the League of Nations critique. Although its leadership was predominantly of the Republican right, it tried hard to tap into every conceivable kind of resentment, grievance, and fear that World War I had tossed to the surface of popular thought and to spread all manner of arguments, many of them contradictory and not actually accepted by its leaders, so that it could influence all conceivable anti–League of Nations constituencies. Much of the Independence League's propaganda, in fact, constituted a regurgitation of the long-standing antisocialist and antiliberal concerns of its leading members. Another part of its propaganda centered on just as ancient nativist fears about foreign peoples, influences, and entanglements, and yet another on an essentially leftist critique of the League of Nations as an imperialist and capitalist block of power. Much of this argument was far from sincere, none less so than the track that appealed to anti-British prejudice. This appeal figured prominently in Independence League propaganda despite the well-known Anglophile convictions of many of its leaders (indeed, someone in the Independence League gave prior warning to British authorities that such anti-British talk would come from the organization but that it should be disregarded as it was necessary for domestic reasons).[10]

All in all, then, the League for the Preservation of American Independence aspired to be the single most authoritative and audible voice for the League of Nations critique outside the Senate, and to this end it tried to meld both anti-internationalist and internationalist voices into a singular, comprehensive barrage timed to coincide with that of the League of Nations' senatorial critics.

Relatively little of the organization's pamphlet matter was explicitly geared to religion. There were very occasional references to the liberal clergy's alliance with suspect socialists and other dangerous visionaries, and sometimes the allegedly unrealistic, millennial nature of some of the League of Nations' provisions was noted, as was the impossibility of Christian nations cooperating successfully with non-Christian nations.[11] But this is not what made the Independence League important from the point of view of evangelical anti-internationalism. The organization was important because it gathered together some of the most articulate conservative laity of several crucial denominations and because, being devout Christians, these individuals could not but infuse their commentary on U.S. foreign policy with their conservative Christian presuppositions. These presuppositions colored their whole approach to the League of Nations question and informed the alternatives that they offered. The three men who best exemplified this approach to religion, politics, and the League of Nations were also the three best known and most widely read of all those who worked with the Independence League: Henry Watterson, George Wharton Pepper, and David Jayne Hill.

⌐━━━○ Henry Watterson, Restorationism, and the League of Nations

The largely ceremonial president of the Independence League, the octogenarian Louisville newspaper publisher "Marse" Henry Watterson, was a Democrat of a particularly old-fashioned Southern variety, a former Confederate officer and onetime Democratic congressman. He had made his reputation as the long-serving editor and proprietor of the *Louisville Courier-Journal*, which was an important mouthpiece of Southern Democrats in the Gilded Age and the Progressive Era. An impassioned Democratic partisan and opponent of all things Republican, Watterson had taken a central part in the 1876 efforts to have Samuel Tilden, not Rutherford B. Hayes, confirmed as president in the uniquely contested elections of that year. Later he had been a prominent critic of President Theodore Roosevelt's supposedly imperial and autocratic aspirations, as well as an opponent of protectionism, Dollar Diplomacy, and the plutocratic power of trusts and other major corporations. In the early stages of the 1912 electoral process, Watterson had become a prominent supporter and publicist for Wilson's presidential candidacy, and although his relations with Wilson were broken before Wilson was elected president, in the 1916 elections Watterson again endorsed Wilson. In the van of this endorsement went an apparently passionate portrayal of the president's Republican challengers as pro-German, imperialist, plutocratic, and altogether un-American.[12]

None of this, however, prevented Watterson from joining ranks with a largely Republican group of anti-internationalists, for by 1919 he had become sorely disillusioned with President Wilson. He felt that Wilson was both an unprincipled, ambitious, and unscrupulous turncoat and a "namby-pamby . . . schoolteacher" with a "half-baked overtrained mind." In the latter guise, Wilson struck Watterson as a man congenitally incapable of resisting abstractions and varied New Liberal enthusiasms, and Watterson therefore concluded that Wilson was not the conservative Democrat that he himself had assumed Wilson to be. Once Wilson had started on his ambitious legislative reforms, Watterson became convinced that the president's agenda would collectivize the government and economy of United States and undermine the whole American way of life. He started to refer to the various attempts of Social Gospelers to legislate their social ethics, of which he gave Wilson as a prime example, as attempts "to compel virtue by act of conventicle." By 1919, Watterson feared that if Wilson were ever to be reelected, he would establish "a veritable autocracy in Washington—the White House converted to a fortress of the one man power."[13]

It was this anticollectivism that initially prompted Watterson to castigate the League of Nations Covenant. The League of Nations' social reform aspirations and its open-ended call for worldwide American military activity seemed to Watterson to establish the true nature of the League of Nations as a "fad" and an "iridescent dream" that would dangerously overextend American responsibilities and tie the nation into entangling alliances not in the national interest and in breach of national sovereignty and freedom of action. In essence, Watterson depicted the League of Nations as but the latest reformulation of imperial and militarist aggrandizement, and he alleged that it would entail military and financial outlays that would undermine American civil liberties and economic prosperity. Occasionally, he claimed that Wilson was bent on instituting the League of Nations as a supranational government that would perpetuate his autocratic governance.[14] Most of the time, Watterson therefore assailed the League of Nations as a rather old-fashioned isolationist and nationalist. His critique mirrored that of the peace progressive Irreconcilables and that of subsequent generations of libertarian conservative opponents of a national-security state.

At the same time, however, Watterson was prompted by his conservative Christian faith. It does not matter whether his politics were primarily fashioned by his religion or whether his many other prejudices incorporated religious rhetoric. The end result of whatever combination of promptings and motivations was a man who *did* speak in very conservative Christian terms and whose conversation during the League of Nations controversy would have been understood in those terms by men and women who did not know whether in his heart of hearts he was a fully fledged evangelical. This part of Watterson's conversation formed, in fact, a major contribution to the political dimension of the emerging Christian anti-internationalism of which evangelical clerical discourses formed the theological dimension.

Watterson was born a Presbyterian, baptized a Catholic, taken to Methodist revival meetings when a child, raised as an Episcopalian, and converted in adult life to the Disciples of Christ.[15] From the point of view of his religious commentary on public affairs, this last was of great significance, for it grounded his conversation in a uniquely American form of Protestantism that yielded many a skeptic of modern internationalism. Though it seems that he was not officially a member of the First Christian Church of Louisville, to which his wife belonged, he regularly worshipped there, maintained very close relations with the congregation's preacher, and was regarded by the congregation as one of their own. He had known many of the luminous antebellum leaders of the Disciples movement, and frequently in the course of his public career he had given voice to a distinctly Disciples form of religious sentiment. He had also published Disciples sermons in his newspaper and had written religious editorials that had been so popular that they had been widely republished in the evangelical press.[16]

Watterson's apparent acceptance of key Disciples of Christ concepts was of crucial significance for his anti–League of Nations rhetoric, because it meant that his statements often came to be couched in terms of the particularly eclectic form of Christian anti-internationalism that the Disciples had championed since their emergence in the early nineteenth century. The Disciples and their predominantly Southern breakaway, the Churches of Christ, both of which were strong in Watterson's Kentucky, were denominations with a sizable pacifist witness that was distinctly susceptible to many of the liberal arguments offered on behalf of the League of Nations. However, they had traditionally stressed that a warless world could only result from the gradual adherence of all peoples to the primitive Christianity for which they stood.[17]

There were two distinct and eventually conflicting theological strands to this argument—the highly optimistic postmillennialism commonly associated with the early-nineteenth-century preacher Alexander Campbell, and the pessimistic apocalypticism of Campbell's colleague Barton W. Stone. Both of them agreed that it was futile and possibly sinful for Christians to place their hopes for world peace and progress in secular organizations, for theirs was a radically biblicist view of the world that refused to accept any ordinance, practice, or institution that was not specifically mentioned in the Bible. Both Campbell and Stone insisted that only Christian Restorationism—the calling of all Christians out of their organized, creedal churches and into the fold of the Disciples—could reach the goals that God had set for the church. The Stoneites interpreted this in apocalyptic terms; that is, they maintained that only such a Christian union could convince the unbelieving world of the truth of Christianity and pave the way to that apocalyptic intervention of Christ that would perfect the world. In the meantime, the Stoneites wanted to separate from the world and all its preoccupations and live in their own biblicist communities. Campbellite Restorationists, conversely, stressed proactive temporal reform and supposed that it was particularly up to the Americans—a new people, relatively unencumbered by a creedal and ecclesiastical past—to effect the apocalyptic regathering of all peoples to primitive, apostolic community.[18]

By the early twentieth century, traditional Restorationists of both strands were increasingly under pressure from those in the Campbellite tradition, who started to redefine their postmillennial vision in terms of leftist political internationalism. Partly due to this pressure, by 1906 many Stoneites had left the Disciples of Christ to form the Churches of Christ. Neither the new group nor the remaining Disciples managed, however, to solve the persistent denominational struggles over self-definition and control in favor of either eschatological interpretation.[19] Given the traditions of pacifism and church-centeredness that animated the whole Reconstructionist community, much of their internal conflict came in one way or another to revolve around the internationalist debate.

On that plane, conservative members of the Disciples of Christ were challenged by the ascendant leftist ecumenical and internationalist vision of which the two nationally best-known Disciples ministers were the powerful pioneers and popularizers. These two men—Charles Clayton Morrison, the editor of *Christian Century*, and Kirby Page, a long-standing activist belonging to the Fellowship of Reconciliation and the Fellowship for Christian Social Order—were rare liberal clerical critics of the League of Nations who objected to all use of force and coercion and refused to accept the League of Nations' collective security and sanctions provisions. They did volunteer that the League of Nations "is the thing all Christians pray for when they say, 'Thy Kingdom come,'" but they insisted that it did not go far enough and was not "liberal, humane and Christian" enough. According to them, the best hope of peace and social justice lay in a worldwide, ecumenically produced, essentially socialist reorganization of society.[20]

Page's and Morison's prescriptions were rooted in the traditional pacifism of Christian Restorationism, and in Campbellite postmillennialism. But they incorporated the Social Gospel in ways that conservative Restorationists could not accept. It was partly as a function of the resultant denominational schism and struggle that conservatives like Watterson came forcefully to engage the liberals. To a degree, the same applied to Senator Albert Fall, another conservative Restorationist. In both men's cases, the League of Nations debate appeared as an occasion for rehearsing and disseminating a conservative Christian Restorationist message that juxtaposed strict primitivist evangelicalism to all forms of sacralization of political institutions.

Distinct echoes of an unreconstructed Christian Restorationism could be heard in many of Watterson's wartime editorials. He often referred to World War I as "the most momentous moral crisis since the Crucifixion of Christ" and claimed that it had been caused not just by great power aggrandizement and pursuit of commercial gain but, more important, by a division among Christians that had led to a grave diminution in their aggregate moral power. This division, in turn, was traceable to the sway of creedalism and ecclesiasticalism that had unmoored the organized churches from apostolic faith. Christendom, Watterson underlined in November 1914, was only nominally Christian, and it was in actuality "a vainglorious egotist, deluding itself with virtuous homilies and displays of fashionable piety" while being led by men and women really only interested in power and dominion. Therefore, the world war might be an ultimate means by which God tried to teach such nominal Christians that no creeds or ecclesia and no kinds of human civilizations could save.[21]

After the war, Watterson insisted that the world could be saved from spiritual and physical destruction only by "the Christian religion" and only if this religion was understood rightly, as "the source and resource of all that is worth having in the world that is, that gives promise in the world to come; not as an abstraction; not as a huddle of sects and factions; but as the mighty force and principle of being." Against this simple religion, "Satan has been turned loose for one last, final struggle," Watterson claimed; in the ensuing struggle, "democracy is but a side issue" and surrender to the "religion of Christ and Him crucified" all that the world really needed.[22] It followed that Wilson's and the Social Gospelers' redefinition of Christianity as international social reform was but another form of "human conceit," an effort to "re-create the Universe" by methods of coercion "'that knew not of God.'"[23]

"I cannot too often repeat that the world we inhabit is a world of sin, disease and death," Watterson wrote as soon as he had read the League of Nations Covenant. "Men will fight whenever they want to fight, and no artificial scheme or process is likely to restrain them." The strength of "national and racial ambitions" still canceled out whatever moral promptings resided in unredeemed mankind and proved that "perfectibility is not designed for mortal man." It was, indeed, incumbent on all Christians to preach the doctrine of love for one's fellows and to work for peaceful solutions. But Watterson stressed that even as clergy went about that task, they should not lose sight of the fact that "eternal peace, universal peace was not the purpose of the Deity in the creation of the universe." The doctrine that the clergy should preach, therefore, was simply "the regeneration of man through the grace of God." If they did that, they would be true to real Christianity as opposed to the "churchism" of the "rank material" denominations, and in the process they would perpetuate the pulpit as the "moral hope of the universe and the spiritual light of mankind." However, only a humanity that worshipped at the "shrine of Christ and him risen" could have any hope of peace; no secular institution of any kind could provide it.[24]

In Watterson's whole line of argument, distinct Disciples of Christ emphases were clearly to be seen. His deprecation of churchism and of clerical essaying into secular politics echoed the Stoneite Restorationists' opposition to all secular institutions, among which they classed the Protestant denominations. His denunciation of the liberal clergy's sacralization of the League of Nations likewise underlined the supposedly apostate nature of existing churches. At the same time, it witnessed to definite millennialist, even if not dispensational, views of the future where Christ, not men and women, would redeem the world.

All of Watterson's discussion cohered with an understanding of progress and redemption in which all or most political institutions were part of the problem and the churches alone were the solution. As has been seen, this was an argument shared by a range of conservative evangelical clergy. In Watterson's case, it may have been based on a unique theological interpretation (which actually excluded most Protestant churches from the solution), but it was nevertheless broadly congruent with the conservative evangelicals' principal argument. Understood in this, its proper context, Watterson's writings during World War I and then during the League of Nations controversy were most definitely part of the conservative evangelical assault upon modern internationalism.

George Wharton Pepper's Episcopalian Anti-Internationalism

Sentiments broadly similar to Watterson's, but even more rooted in a specific and different confessional tradition, were voiced by the man in charge of the Independence League's day-to-day organizing: George Wharton Pepper. Throughout his long public career as a law professor, corporation lawyer, and publicist—and eventually as a Republican senator and opponent of the New Deal—Pepper had been interested in the role that the churches could play in building up a citizenry cohered by traditional values and worldviews. To him, evangelical-pietistic religion was the primary value-transmitting and -enforcing mechanism available, and he was intent both on contributing to its advancement and on combating all its challengers and substitutes. He believed that "without Christianity, our civilization cannot long endure. Without the Church, Christianity will cease to be a force and will become a mere theory."[25]

Consequently, Pepper became more intensely involved in ecclesiastical activities than any other political critic of the League of Nations. For twenty years, he served as a lay member of the Protestant Episcopal Church's Board of Missions, for forty years as a lay delegate to diocese conventions, and from 1901 to 1934 as a lay delegate to most Episcopal General Conventions. He knew many of the important leaders of Anglicanism, including some of those who on the other side of the Atlantic championed churchly opposition to the League of Nations. He was also an active Bible class and mission study teacher, a writer of devotional manuals, president of the Church Club of Philadelphia, and the first layman to deliver the Lyman Beecher Lectures on Preaching at Yale University.[26]

Pepper was neither an Anglo-Catholic nor exactly a fully confirmed Calvinist. Certainly a High Churchman, he had been influenced by the evangelical trends of early-twentieth-century Anglican theology and piety.

Consequently, his personal faith was grounded in a sacramentalism that would have seemed out of place to Presbyterians and Baptists, but this sacramentalism was tempered by a pronounced bent for mysticism and for a very personal, emotional religion that stressed the evangelical and proselytizing aspects of faith. To Pepper, the essence of the Protestant faith was in the supposition that "man's fundamental interest is his relationship with the Unseen," and he saw mystical communion with Christ as the only means of establishing such a relationship. He recognized the importance of social service and regarded works of charity as inherent to Christianity, yet always stressed that the believer who tried to reduce Christianity to the "brotherhood of man," to "social service," or to "ethical culture" fell short of the demands of faith.[27] The overwhelming Episcopalian embrace of the Social Gospel, which coincided with Pepper's activity as a layman, thus left him cold, and he stood squarely in the continuity of those Episcopalians who affirmed clerical laissez-faire instead of purposive, collectivist social change. This combination had very definite religiopolitical implications, which Pepper transposed onto the League of Nations as well.

The direction of Pepper's religiopolitical effort was exposed first of all by his participation in the so-called Plattsburg movement. This movement was an early-twentieth-century effort by some in the upper echelons of fashionable society to produce a stable, spiritually aware populace through bodily exercise and discipline applied at special military-style camps. Those involved in this movement supposed that modern conditions of leisure enfeebled body and soul and had produced a population that was increasingly out of touch with the nobler, more altruistic qualities of human nature. Convinced that the Plattsburg model of self-discipline was an important conduit to a higher, purer type of the Christian life for society at large, they insisted on transferring it to other spheres of life, and on witnessing for personal spiritual transformation as the root and prompter of all meaningful change in the world.[28]

As he involved himself in these activities, Pepper stressed that the multiethnic United States was bound to implode unless it re-cohered in the character building that only the Plattsburg movement and the churches could provide. To him, all the nation's problems were "fundamentally religious question[s]" and even the Constitution provided but the barest, outward framework within which they were to be solved; the solving itself could come about only after Judeo-Christian beliefs invested the constitutional framework with meaning and instilled in every citizen the habit of continual "squaring yourself with the will of God." In a public religion so understood, churches and temporal government alike became agencies "through which divine purposes are carried out among men."[29]

Only the Christian religion, however, could provide lasting solutions to all the personal and interpersonal problems that the individual faced, and by the time of World War I, Pepper supposed that "an entirely new world" could indeed be built, but only through the agency of the church. He stressed that such a new world order had to be based on a prior change in the nature of humanity and that such a change could never come about through any secular institution no matter how nobly legitimated. A new world could arrive only through the conversion of individuals to the Christian faith. To that end, Pepper regarded it as absolutely necessary that the Christian churches unite and thus both manifest and practice en masse the only power—the spiritual power—that could transform the world.[30]

The last-mentioned belief was the most important. It was impressed upon Pepper with terrible force when he contemplated how the professedly Christian nations of Europe had disregarded Pope Pius X's 1914 peace appeal and had rushed to war against each other. This development had convinced Pepper that the peoples of the world would never really convert to the Christian Gospel unless the churches were first to prove to the world that they really did stand for that Gospel and not just for their own separate ecclesiastical powers and privileges.[31] To achieve this, Pepper became an early activist of the Faith and Order Movement and, for a while, a sympathizer of the Federal Council of Churches. But as soon as these organizations began to devise extra-ecclesiastical schemes for the attainment of a new world order, Pepper felt compelled to distance himself from them, and he began to stress that no social reform schemes and certainly no world political institutions could reach the ends that he envisioned.[32]

When he came to discuss the League of Nations, Pepper first of all noted that many Episcopal priests and other clergymen were to be found among its most passionate protagonists. He implied that these clergymen had misunderstood the function and promise of the church when they had so attached themselves to the cause of the League of Nations. Inasmuch as they offered a secular political institution as the solution of individual and social problems, they were doing a disservice to the American people, who so needed their guidance, because in the process of advocating a political institution, they were devaluing and ignoring the public means of grace that had been reserved for the church. Consequently, both before and after the Episcopal endorsement of the League of Nations, Pepper insisted that clergy should not involve themselves in politics and should not invest secular contention or organizations with moral or salvific content.[33]

Pepper did not take the churchly League of Nations enthusiasts to task only for having confused salvific instruments with temporal agencies. As far as he was concerned, clerical endorsement of the League of Nations' specific provisions and structures was wrong also on the merits. On this level, too, he regarded modernist clergymen's League of Nations campaigns as mistaken and counterproductive. These clergymen had apparently unbounded confidence in the political means of world pacification and progress; but peace, as Pepper had stressed in his Beecher lectures of 1915, could never come through international conferences or other political means. Because the participants in such conferences had been either nominal Christians or not Christians at all, dedicated to national aggrandizement and essentially German notions of national deification, it had been a forgone conclusion that they could not agree on the essential moral bases of peace. Pepper stressed that whenever international conferences were convened between nations, some of which were truly Christian and some of which had deified their own nation, the political means of change were always bound to transpire into an exercise of national "selfishness."[34]

Only "a sense of oneness in Jesus Christ" could save nations from such selfishness and pave the way to meaningful international cooperation, because only a universalized Christian religion could provide a shared international moral code and a shared sense of allegiance to something higher than the conflicting volitions of nation-states. Therefore, a powerful world association of churches (the Faith and Order Movement) was needed first of all, and this Christian confederacy had to convert the nations of nominal Christendom and to instill in them the Christian tenets of internationalism.[35]

When the Anglican bishop Charles Gore of Oxford, the leading British clerical apologist for a socially reformist League of Nations, arrived in the United States to propagate his vision among Episcopalians, and it fell on Pepper to introduce him, Pepper seized on the occasion to reassert his church-centered alternative. He insisted that "we are not going to accomplish that for which we are fighting merely by the adoption of systems or by the making of international compacts. It will stand and continue to stand as the only hope for the uplift of the world, that there shall be a process of transformation and uplift in the individual man," a transformation that could only be achieved by conversion to Christ.[36] No political world association of (unredeemed) nations could ever produce the needed transformation.

Given this frame of reference, it was understandable that Pepper made short shrift of the liberals' concept of collective security. The theory of collective security of course violated that core Christian tenet that differentiated between a change of conduct wrought by outside compulsion and conduct freely entered into. Few anti–League of Nations people drew explicit attention to this conflict, and Pepper certainly was not one who did, but he did nevertheless attack collective security in just that way one could have expected from someone dedicated to the doctrine of free will. It was hardly a moral proposition to bind nations to attack each other, Pepper stressed, if they had not been able to reach a settlement by other means. According to him, collective security indeed did equal "coercion" and was but a new rendition of "force so applied as to attain a righteous end"—conceptions that he deemed contrary to all moral civilization and far inferior to conferences of like-minded peoples called to settle specific disputes.[37]

The same applied to the League of Nations' social reform agenda. As Pepper saw it, this agenda was based on the pursuit of material progress through an essentially socialist, always coercive, use of collective powers. Pepper therefore accused President Wilson of trying to subvert the Constitution in order to set up in its stead a world supergovernment under one single man—himself—and imbued with a socialistic gospel of envy and class strife.[38] The League of Nations, claimed Pepper as so many others had done before, provided the ultimate, because international, instrument for making the world socialist.

It was not that Pepper opposed all organized political cooperation between nation-states. Politically, he was no Irreconcilable on the League of Nations. In purely political terms, he was a nationalist, an Anglophile, a believer in an Anglo-American alliance, and an upholder of international law, arbitration, and the Hague Court of International Justice. Indeed, when he joined the U.S. Senate in 1922, he became one of that body's leading campaigners for a new World Court.[39] But throughout, he argued that international law, not political organization, was the hope of the world and, more important, that international law itself, if it was to last and be effective, had to be based on and to flow from an antecedent international moral unity of mind. This moral unity could come only from a shared acquiescence in Christ.

There was no single text of Pepper's where this entire argument was set out in clear terms. The argument underpinned all his thinking and sometimes broke through into an explicit statement related to the League of Nations. But it was absolutely central. This reality was powerfully underlined when, in 1931, Pepper finally decided no longer to serve as a lay delegate at the Episcopal General Convention. The reason he gave for his resignation was his opposition to the continued campaigns by liberal Episcopal clergy for the League of Nations. Because of pressing legal work, he had not been able to take part in the crucial 1919, 1922, and 1925 General Conventions— where official Episcopalian endorsement for the League of Nations had been enjoined—but in the later 1920s, he took it upon himself to have this endorsement reversed. Losing that fight, and regarding churchly advocacy of a secular world institution as a violation of the Christian faith, he disassociated himself from official ecclesiastical business.[40] It was the ultimate that could be done by a man as intensely active as a layman as he was. The decision—coming as it did after League of Nations membership had already been defeated—powerfully underlined the strength of his Christian anti-internationalism.

By the time he had disassociated himself from the liberal-dominated Episcopal General Convention, Pepper had already affiliated with a newly created interdenominational conservative evangelical group. This was the so-called Moral Re-Armament Movement, and it was as emphatically geared toward the Christianization of the world as the only road to peace as the liberal mainstream denominations were dedicated to the League of Nations. Also known as the Oxford Group, the Moral Re-Armament Movement was a transatlantic propaganda, proselytizing, and Christian fellowship group that had been initiated in the 1920s by the American Lutheran clergyman Frank N. D. Buchman. This group was primarily oriented toward political elites and decision makers, because it saw itself as a movement that was to Christianize the governments of the world by converting the leaders of the world. Most of its members in the United States were well-off Episcopalians, many of them old Plattsburgers who were intrigued by Buchman's other emphasis, his pursuit of group cohesion through intimate fellowship and therapeutic, emotional means of character building.[41]

Most important of all, Moral Re-Armament saw itself as the only truly "supernational" means to what it called the "God-control" of national policies and the international community. Its leader, Buchman, constantly stressed that the League of Nations had failed, as expected, and that all political efforts at peace and progress would likewise fail. The only road to peace lay in the Christian conversion of each nation's leadership and in the resultant supernational brotherhood of "new men" unencumbered by old nationalist and power-political pursuits.[42]

Pepper's membership in the Moral Re-Armament Movement highlighted that single most important constant of his religiopolitical worldview, which, as much as anything, characterized his public case against the League of Nations. As a High Church Episcopalian, he reserved the means of grace and world betterment for the church alone and denied them to any secular organization. He did not regard the Social Gospel, which by early twentieth century had conquered official Episcopalian thinking, as the proper use of the church's means of grace. Therefore, he could not accept a League of Nations that pretended to have salvific functions yet employed coercion and force to reach ends reserved for personal, voluntary religion. His alternative—voluntary arbitration of international differences—was based on his concept of self-control, but even this arrangement he regarded as temporary and insufficient as long as the arbitrating nations were not equally rooted in and guided by the Christian religion. It was a Christian world church that Pepper regarded as the only hope of the world, but only such a Christian world church that actually saw to it that all significant people in all lands were reborn in Jesus Christ and put away their old natures for good.

David Jayne Hill's Modernist Anti-Internationalism

David Jayne Hill's case was unique in another sense. Alone among the major Independence League publicists, he showed how modernist theology, too, could yield a politically very conservative opposition to the League of Nations. He was a renowned international lawyer and legal theorist, former ambassador, and assistant secretary of state, as well as a prolific writer of antisocialist articles and books, and a onetime professor of rhetoric and president of Rochester University. His institutional affiliations included not only the American Society for International Law and the Carnegie Endowment for International Peace but also the American Defense Society and the National Security League, two major preparedness, military training, and patriotic propaganda organizations. He had also been one of the American delegates at the Second Hague Peace Conference of 1907, and he had written the instructions that guided the American delegation at the first conference. He always remained deeply committed to the conservative form of internationalism, the arbitral regime of voluntarily cooperating nation-states engaged in the further codification of international law.[43]

Because Hill brought to his League of Nations commentary the unusually weighty credentials of an international lawyer and diplomat, the religious dimension of what he had to say tended to get obscured. But he was also the born-again son of a Baptist minister and a onetime Baptist minister himself. In the latter part of the nineteenth century, he had been converted to theological modernism and had as a result been forced to resign his presidency of Rochester University, then a Baptist institution, and to leave the Genesee Baptist Association in 1894. His case had been a minor, since then largely forgotten, episode in the early Baptist struggle over denominational control. Those very issues of incarnationalism, ethical evolution, and postmillennialist Kingdom theology that were soon to propel most of his fellow modernists into the internationalist cause had then been rehearsed, and he had forcefully argued the modernist case on all points.[44] He did not lose his faith afterward, but on the issue of modern internationalism he drew conclusions very different from other modernists. During the League of Nations debates, by drawing both on his complex theology and on his international experience, and by eclectically blending modernist theology, conservative politics, and clerical laissez-faire, he developed a unique case against international political organizations.

The full implications of Hill's anti–League of Nations arguments would have been lost on all who were not aware of his radically incarnationalist theology and his reservations about the divine authorship of the Christian Bible. He so worded his post-1894 religious commentary as to obscure his modernist theological presuppositions and he apparently did this deliberately, courting political support from among political and theological conservatives who would not have wanted to associate with a radically modernist theologian. This circumstance suggests that he had learned from the loss of his university presidency and therefore no longer made his theology explicit. This did not mean, however, that his League of Nations commentary was devoid of profoundly and uniquely religious content.

Ever since his conversion to theological modernism, Hill had argued for science and reason as forms of divine revelation coequal with the Christian Bible. He doubted the divine authorship of the Old Testament and the existence of Satan, denied the theories of plenary inspiration and biblical infallibility, and admitted to having "real intellectual difficulties" with theism as a doctrine. "All my life I have not been so much devoted to religion as opposed to irreligion," he even wrote in one private memorandum. In what he came to call the "Genetic Philosophy," he suggested instead that God was immanent in every individual and that this fact made for a gradual process of ethical evolution that produced an ever-fuller human approximation to the divine reason. In his view, Jesus' originality consisted in his having been able to possess this immanent divinity most fully, but he affirmed that it was a "work in which all men may participate." However, he averred that neither special revelation nor human reason alone was capable of exposing ultimate truth; only when both were used in conjunction could humanity grasp the essentials of divine natural law and start to consciously approximate the development demands that these imposed.[45]

In this context, temporal law and legislation were primary media for actualizing evolutionary insights; in the end, religion was nothing but "self-subordination to a reign of law," and law was nothing but the "system of rules for the regulation of will derived from the authority of reason." According to Hill, law was, in other words, the means by which evolution actualized itself in social practice, and both religion and reason were its components. Religion and reason were the two coequal means used by an immanent divinity both to actualize a given stage of evolutionary insight and to curb residual passions that belonged to a lower stage of development.[46]

These core assumptions led to a radically personalist and anthropomorphic theology that fully accommodated the Baptist distinctives of soul liberty and individual freedom. They meant also that Hill had no sympathy with any collective, purposive efforts of speeding up the evolution of which he spoke. In domestic politics, he was led to champion the cause of laissez-faire as the natural process through which human evolution would reach its higher stages, and he distinguished himself as a prominent clerical critic of all forms or approximations of socialism and other collective dictation. Socialism was, as he wrote in 1885, "a revolt against development," a reversion to a lower stage of social organization where an overpowering state would dictate all activity. The processes of diversification, trial, and rational experiment that created evolution could not operate in a socialist system, he stressed; they could operate only in an American-style constitutionalist system that was geared to assuring their freedom.[47]

Hill's evolutionary, laissez-faire modernism always had an international dimension. Already as a Baptist clergyman he had written of his profound distaste for what he regarded as the antitype of modern internationalism— the papal presumption to wield universal power and to act as the mediator between humanity and divinity. He regarded this notion as a residue of that pre-Christian divinization of emperors whereby Roman rulers had legitimated their autocratic powers. When Constantine had Christianized the state, Hill suggested, he had not abandoned this presumptuous principle, which gradually came to be known as the divine right of kings. Ethical and political evolution had managed to eradicate the principle from most Western countries in his lifetime, but Hill insisted that the papacy still retained it.[48] All socialist systems of governance and thought also retained the ancient autocratic presumption, he claimed, and the League of Nations was of this order.

Reworking the papal theme in the course of World War I, Hill came to stress that there was nothing to distinguish the new "imperium" of a socialistic League of Nations, which "assumes the right to govern," from earlier forms of authoritarian and dictatorial rule, except the rhetoric used to legitimate it and the explicit addition of the social and industrial sphere to its areas of presumed supremacy. He suggested that socialist and New Liberal theory had by then renamed the old "divine right of kings" as the "will of the people" and then further configured the "will of the people" into "making the world safe for democracy" through a League of Nations. Dependence on unaccountable absolutist power had not, however, been relinquished, he wrote in May 1914, but "in the passage from monarchy to democracy this conception of sovereign omnipotence has merely been transferred." Socialism and New Liberalism alike were grounded in this renaming, he averred, and both of them violated the purpose of constitutional government—which existed "to end forever the idea that there is no rightful depository of unlimited power."[49]

The League of Nations was a logical result of the process that Hill was sketching. He concluded that the League of Nations contained the germination of a new international "despotism" that would destroy all the protections of property and individual liberty that had been torturously effected through the long history of Anglophone constitutionalism. He denounced the League of Nations, and its International Labor Organization in particular, as an autocratic usurpation of authority that was essentially socialist in nature and tended irresistibly to subvert personal and national freedom. According to him, this "imperium" was likely to evolve into an agency for "unlimited social reconstruction, . . . and even absolutism under omnipotent government control," that would dictate the conditions and rewards of labor and standards of economic and industrial life the world over. It was thus part and parcel of the more general global upsurge of "the Socialized State," begun before the war, which the war and the attendant risen expectations had caused to unfold in measure never seen before. Hill regarded it as a major menace because it unfolded both nationally and internationally, by way of the domestic reform policies of the liberals as well as through their new international organizations. This unprecedented international interference in the affairs of free individuals would retard development and hinder progress by rendering all human activity and the human mind itself into "iron shackles."[50]

As far as automatic collective security was concerned, Hill regarded it as a violation of a *Jus Gentium*, which persisted in the very nature of things, was rooted in natural law and the law of God, and could not be abjured without resulting in disaster. Reason and social science, he suggested, could unearth the forever-valid principles of natural law, and only those nation-states (they happened to be Anglophone and Francophone) that had reached the higher stages of ethical and scientific development could be trusted to codify and maintain these principles. Therefore, collective security was sustainable only among nations rooted in the same presuppositions, and even then it had to rest on voluntary decisions to cooperate. The only workable system of international cooperation was "a system arrived at by the voluntary consent and maintained by the voluntary support of those who [form] a community of purpose."[51]

This meant also that inasmuch as Article X of the League of Nations Covenant fixed existing borders and systems of governance, it condemned the right of revolution and thus prevented a people from implementing any possible developments in its moral and social sense that necessitated a new order of existence. According to Hill, this last point alone made the liberal, enforced, universal, and automatic concept of collective security a profoundly immoral and counter-evolutionary proposition. In other words, he insisted that national diversity was of primary importance, that development came through freedom of action, and that only voluntary and evolving systems of international cooperation could safeguard the essential building blocks of progress.[52]

As those knew who were conversant with Hill's eclectic religious and political philosophy, even this apparently purely secular argument on collective security and international social reform was actually religious. For Hill had always predicated his religiosity on a typically Baptist emphasis on individual freedom and social, political, and economic autonomy. In his modernist rendition, individual freedom was the prerequisite for intellectual and moral growth, unfettered by creeds or other ecclesiastical authorities; and in his political rendition, it precluded all international organizations engaged in collectivism and central direction. Even his portrayal of socialism as but the renaming of the divine right of absolutist kings resembled his earlier strictures against the pope's pretensions to universal rule.

Hill may have couched his argument in legalistic and philosophic terms, and those terms may have had validity and meaning on their own. But the fact was that every point in his line of reasoning was rooted in a modernist evolutionary theology that celebrated the free interaction of individuals and nation-states. And this nexus of freedom and diversity was to him not just a practically beneficent arrangement; it was also a theological sine qua non directly grounded in his "Genetic Philosophy" of religion.

Hill's relatively few overtly religious comments on the League of Nations also exposed his modernist presuppositions. These explicitly religious statements centered on a denunciation of what he regarded as President Wilson's attempt to infuse the League of Nations effort and machinery with religious content. He insisted that the League of Nations was condemned by the basic commands of "individual conscience" and that Wilson had tried to silence such commands by attempting, with federal funds, to generate a secular "religious revival" for internationalism. "Mr. Wilson's gospel was a creed regarding a world to come," he claimed, and an attempt to "vote in the millennium"; it contained not only all the stirring emotional appeal of a false religion but, more important, also "all the perils of a religious revival." For a modernist believer in rationality, religious enthusiasm was ipso facto suspicious, for it silenced reason and reduced individuals to a lower, less discerning and evaluative level. Hill therefore insisted that the Wilsonian attempt to "vote in the millennium" was theologically false and dangerous, for the fact was that "the Kingdom of God is within ourselves, and that its fullness of time must come by our own inner growth" and not by outside secular authority. This stipulation led Hill to suggest that Americans should listen to "the voice of individual conscience" and not bow to the president's will on the League of Nations question.[53]

This series of religious reasoning was actually a radically immanentist, evolutionary, and experiential argument. In terms of its theological locus, it was not unlike that of the most expansive clerical proponents of the League of Nations, but Hill put forth the argument in a context where it nevertheless combated the internationalist plans of his fellow modernists.

All in all, then, David Jayne Hill exposed his religious presuppositions in each of the several tracks of his League of Nations critique. Unlike Pepper and Watterson, he did not argue that the established Christian churches could or should direct the world toward a more ethical, cooperative, and peaceable future. Ever since Hill's ejection from the University of Rochester, his theology had been radically modernist to such an extent that he had little regard for organized religion as such. What he did argue, however, was that organized political institutions were unsuited to the tasks with which liberal clergy and politicians invested the League of Nations. He affirmed evolutionary theory and laissez-faire to an extreme degree, and he was willing to regulate these two supposed instruments of progress and redemption only to the extent that independent nations were voluntarily willing to codify international law. Yet even this codification of law was regarded by him as only a means toward the regulation of the volitions of those not yet sufficiently evolved, and he always emphasized that the immanent divinity that was ethical and material evolution was the only real influence that could make a better world, by and by. Political, coercive institutions could not help in this regard; they could only hurt the unfolding of an immanent divine purpose. Though Hill approached the question of the League of Nations from very different theological premises than Watterson and Pepper, he thus arrived at the very same practical conclusion.

The Ubiquity of Conservative Evangelical Anti-Internationalism

Whereas the Irreconcilable senators showed themselves avid borrowers of religious anti-internationalist arguments but often of questionable personal religiosity, the case with the Independence League was the reverse. Most of the Independence League's leaders were known evangelical laymen of a conservative variety; and some of them, like George Wharton Pepper, had very definite theological convictions that shaped their whole public doctrine. Yet the incidence of overtly religious arguments was significantly lower in official Independence League propaganda than among the Irreconcilable senators. This was because the Independence League aspired to be the voice of all kinds of anti–League of Nations sentiment and to appeal to broad sections of the populace, in each specific constituency with the arguments deemed the most appealing.

This should not, however, be taken as proof that the Independence League's leaders failed to regard religion as one aspect of the fight over the League of Nations. It is noteworthy that those of its leaders who had the most frequent recourse to religious appeals were rooted in denominations in which the ecclesiastical contention between those for and against the League of Nations reflected a stark imbalance of power between a liberal majority and a conservative minority. These individuals felt their own religiopolitical affirmation to have been under attack, and consequently they utilized the League of Nations controversy as an opportunity to rehearse and disseminate their own, often very conservative theologies. These men were nationalists and unilateralists in their foreign policy preference, and they had powerful partisan instincts and a deep personal distrust of President Wilson and his party. But they were also Christians, conservative ones at that, who recoiled from the religious and spiritual aspirations that liberal clergy attached to modern internationalism. They were in fact impelled to critique and contest these aspirations even regardless of the League of Nations. Given that these aspirations formed part of the League of Nations project's core, the religious countercase also had to be immanent in the anti–League of Nations effort.

Did it have an impact? This question—more than the rather moot question about the balance between Watterson's, Hill's, and Pepper's evangelicalism and their nationalism—is what is important from the point of view of Christian anti-internationalism. It is an inescapable fact that those Christians who followed the League of Nations discourse of 1919–20 were assaulted by a constant if uncoordinated barrage of religious arguments against the League of Nations and the liberal ideals encoded in its Covenant. These arguments assailed them from conservative Christian newspapers, from pulpits, and from the camp tents and assembly halls filled by the traveling World Christian Fundamentals Association. They assailed them from the Senate. And they also assailed them from the platforms of the Independence League's roving campaign, from the Independence League's pamphlets, and from the great number of books and articles of the Independence League's most important publicist, David Jayne Hill.

The evangelical Christian argument may not have been the principal argument that the Independence League broadcast, but it was nevertheless present. It may not have been as explicit in the majority of the Independence League's materials as it was in the Senate, and it certainly came nowhere near the conservative clergy's argument in its explicitly Christian anti-internationalism. But the Independence League's religious appeals were part of a larger whole, an element in an exceptionally broad, secular, and political array of arguments offered against the League of Nations over a sustained period of time and in all conceivable forms and media. Taken together with the multitude of religious arguments emanating from elsewhere, the Independence League's effort could not but have had an impact. Its argument was, in fact, a key part in that construction of a distinct Christian anti-internationalism that took place at the time of, and was not unrelated to, the political debates about the League of Nations.

CHAPTER EIGHT

The Persistence of Christian Anti-Internationalism

The League of Nations controversy set the parameters for all sub-sequent conservative evangelical commentary on modern internationalism. Some contextual modifications were later effected, but these changes were minor and did not materially unsettle any core parts of the corpus of interpretations that had been devised in 1919 and 1920. All the themes in the evangelical critique of the League of Nations survived throughout the interwar years and were carried over, largely in toto, into the cold war experiment with the United Nations. They survived beyond the cold war, too, and resurfaced in the early-twenty-first-century debates about the international community's response to modern Islamic terrorism. Throughout, Christian anti-internationalism continued to provide a reso-nant background to public policy debates, and its several motifs were bor-rowed as avidly as ever by secular conservatives, whether they were isolationist or unilateralist. In the process, an increasingly close collaborative relationship emerged between the secular and the evangelical.

The Struggle Continued: The Interwar Years

Conservative evangelicals were buoyed by the Senate's final rejection of the League of Nations Covenant in May 1920. It showed that a significant num-ber of conservative politicians were attuned to their concerns and could be trusted, more or less, to serve the evangelical agenda. At the same time, evangelicals were painfully aware that all nationwide interdenominational organizations except the World Christian Fundamentals Association (WCFA) had become devoted supporters of the League of Nations and that the conventions of all but two denominations had officially bound their members to the League project. The fight to defeat the League had, in other words, been won on the political and legislative plane but lost on the ecclesiastical level.

Religious conservatives had not managed to purge their denominations of those modernist notions of immanentist progress that had spawned modern internationalism. Instead, the League controversy had shown how firmly liberal Protestants had come to control the interdenominational organizations, how strong they were inside the denominations, and how profound was their influence on secular thinking. Moreover, the League controversy had exposed a nexus between political and ecclesiastical liberals, which, if it were to continue, would create a preponderance of power inimical to conservative evangelical influence and to the perpetuation of the hitherto existing religio-political order.

For these reasons, evangelicals insisted on continuing the struggle against the modernists and the liberals, inside and outside the churches, with undiminished vigor. In the immediate aftermath of the League Covenant's rejection, however, they felt that the chances of U.S. membership would for some time remain quite remote and thought that the antimodernist fight should now be transferred to the domestic arena. There followed the so-called fundamentalist/modernist controversy of the middle to late 1920s. At first it was fought over control of denominational mission and education agencies, and it culminated in the political efforts to ban the teaching of evolution that yielded the so-called Scopes Monkey Trial of 1925. Former secretary of state William Jennings Bryan, an erstwhile opponent of the League Covenant, led that fight together with the leaders of the WCFA.[1] This controversy was a continuation of the evangelical critique of the League of Nations, or, put differently, both were aspects of the overriding evangelical urge to expose, fight, and defeat all manifestations of modernist theological apostasy.

Technically, the fundamentalists and their allies won the Scopes trial and the teaching of evolution continued to be banned in most states. But popular opinion turned against them, and further political victories proved impossible. The incipient politicization of conservative evangelicalism was arrested, and for the next twenty-plus years the fundamentalists lived in their alternative parachurch communities, largely separated from the rest of society, engaged in countercultural and increasingly conspiracist discourse, unable to influence American politics and international relations. This started changing only in the late 1940s when a group of thus-far-separatist fundamentalists, now calling themselves the "New Evangelicals," emerged from their isolation and reengaged in the political conversation of their time. Thus was born the modern evangelical movement, out of which eventually emerged the new Christian Right.[2]

Throughout the long separatist interlude, Christian anti-internationalism had, however, continued to wax strong. It was kept alive by the modernist-leaning denominations' continued witness for the League of Nations and for the internationalists' three successor causes: the disarmament campaigns of the 1920s and the movements for the World Court and to outlaw war of the 1920s and the 1930s. Conservative evangelicals knew, too, that their churchly enemies were still dreaming of American membership in the League itself, so they deemed continued anti-internationalist polemics essential.[3] Eventually, a number of conservative clergy (and some Irreconcilable politicians) did lend their support to disarmament and the World Court, and some even to outlawing war; but many more became mainstays on the isolationist right, insistent on American separation from the corruptions of the wider world.[4]

More often than not, interwar conservative evangelicals depicted disarmament conferences and the World Court as "contrary to God's plan" because, as William Riley put it, "not once has the Word of God been considered as providing a basis for [their] procedure" and "not once has the leadership of Christ been recognized." These attempts at world pacification continued to be seen as steeped in apostate theologies that were part and parcel of that deification of humanity whereby "presumptuous man [was] forever trying to turn the tables instead of taking God at His Word."[5] So strongly, in fact, did the evangelicals continue to feel about this that in the late 1920s the WCFA even took an official position on "man-made programs" for "universal" and "lasting peace" in which it condemned all of them as "contrary to the Word of God." When so stating, the WCFA denounced all the "atheistic, bolshevistic and modernist ecclesiastics" whom it claimed to be campaigning for such programs. The labor of such people would yield the Antichrist's world empire and much misery in the meantime, but nothing else.[6]

Throughout the interwar period, conservative evangelicals expected that the Social Gospelers and their political allies would eventually try to replace the League of Nations with a stronger organization and cause America to join it. Nor were they proved wrong. When World War II erupted, modernist Protestants were again the leading champions of international organization, and such had been their triumphal march in the meanwhile that almost all denominations endorsed the project.

As outlined by the Federal Council of Churches' Commission on a Just and Durable Peace, the churchly case for a United Nations was remarkably similar to that offered in 1914 to 1920. This was ensured by the theologically liberal Presbyterian lawyer and later Republican secretary of state, John Foster Dulles, who led the commission (and its National Mission on World Order lecture tour). Dulles had represented Presbyterian modernists in some of their 1920s' legal battles against the fundamentalists, and before that he had been a member of President Woodrow Wilson's delegation to the Paris peace conference. Now he argued that it was up to the churches to make sure that the postwar order that was to be created really did perpetuate peace and did not repeat the mistakes of Versailles. He insisted that the coming United Nations be based squarely on the "broad moral principles" that all modernist Protestants agreed upon and that the "national sovereignty system" be recognized as "no longer consonant with peace or with justice." The worldwide "resumption of political evolution" was necessary, he further insisted, and at times he got carried away into fully millennialist promises about the Kingdom of God on Earth being attainable through international ethical action.[7]

Largely similar arguments arose out of most Protestant denominations, and many of them undertook systematic publicity and education campaigns to spread the message. Even the United Lutheran Church, which had once been so suspicious of the League of Nations, changed positions, joined the Federal Council of Churches, and enthusiastically cooperated with Dulles. Its representatives even attended the UN's founding conference.[8] Just as active were the Methodist bishops, still the leaders of Protestant internationalism in the United States. In 1943–44, they unleashed a concerted and prolonged "Crusade for a New World Order" that was pegged on the goal of a world assembly and legislature. Determined to avoid the mistakes of the earlier 1919 crusade, this time the Methodist leadership set out to convert the American people long before the covenant of a new world league was likely to come up for acceptance.[9]

In these and other denominations, most of the resultant agitation centered on the so-called Six Pillars of Peace, which Dulles's commission had enunciated. In large part, these were eventually incorporated into the structures of the United Nations. Some of the League of Nations' arbitral and collective security procedures were revised in favor of more great power say-so (like the inclusion of a veto power), but the religious rationale for the organization and its social reform agenda remained unchanged. The UN's clerical protagonists still predicted that world unity and peace would flow from the supposedly shared ethical values of all the world's peoples once these were institutionalized in a world association. This incarnationalist presupposition was literally set in stone, for the UN's founders chose to engrave on their headquarters building words from the Old Testament book of Micah that promised a millennium of peace and contentment through their institution.[10] The International Labor Organization (ILO) remained at the very core of the United Nations, the sole agency of the League of Nations that was not only carried over but also invested with a reform agenda that was even more radical than the original. As the ILO's Charter was revised in the so-called Philadelphia Declaration of 1944, it came to incorporate much of the socialists' agenda at the 1919 Berne Conference.[11]

Dulles, for one, applauded the final UN structure for having incorporated these social reform dimensions that in 1919 had been so contentious.[12] His stance, given that he was ostensibly a conservative politician, powerfully highlighted the extent to which the core assumptions of the modernist Social Gospel had, by 1945, taken over mainstream American Protestantism. This may partly have explained why so few mainline Protestants assailed Dulles's plan during the war. Even few conservative politicians assailed it. Only the octogenarian veteran from the Irreconcilable fight of 1919, Senator Hiram Johnson, cast his vote against ratification of the UN Charter.[13] But moulds had irreversibly hardened, and once the UN was up and running, there was to be no escaping from a portrayal of that organization, too, as somehow inextricably linked with Antichristian empire building and with the sacralization of secular institutions.

Evangelicals against the United Nations

Evangelicals started by denouncing the absence of a reference to Almighty God in the UN Charter. They bemoaned the fact that an attempt to insert such a reference had been defeated by the supposedly Christian delegates from the United States and other Western countries, and they complained about these delegates' pointed refusal to ask for divine guidance for their work through public prayer.[14] Then the evangelicals swiftly proceeded to subject the specific structures, goals, and rationalizations for the new UN to the same critique as in 1919–20. These lines of critique were perpetuated throughout the cold war era and remained in force at the beginning of the twenty-first century, practically unchanged from what they had been when they were first enunciated. Relatively little would now be heard about the anti-Catholic argument, and the overtly anti-Semitic argument, too, became latent, but in other ways Christian anti-internationalism remained just what it had been in 1919.

Some organizers of the fundamentalists' anti-League fight actually survived to see the early stages of the construction of the United Nations. They were aghast, but not surprised, at the resurgence of all those aspirations that they had hoped had died in 1919–20. Riley himself died in 1947, but he was an active commentator on international issues until the very end and he left a noteworthy set of writings on the United Nations. In 1919 he had not, as he put it, been one to "fall into the folly of promising my auditors, 'an approaching world peace'"; therefore, the swiftly ensuing second world conflagration had not embarrassed him, and now he felt confident to reassert his old position with even more assurance. He insisted that all the "suave speeches of President Roosevelt" notwithstanding, humanity had not found the way to solve the problems of a "wrecked world," nor could it ever succeed in "redeeming the globe," for it was a fallen and sinning humanity, out of touch with God, whose only hope was in the Second Coming of Christ.[15]

To the end of his life, Riley maintained that the United Nations constituted the "present popular plan of taking the world over, church included, placing all in the hands of a few mortals, for remaking." It was just as condemned by a literal reading of the Bible as had been the League of Nations, for it was but "another term for the unification of ideals and thrones that must pave the way for the coming of the Antichrist," and no less an "idle dream" than the earlier "promise of a millennium without the fulfillment of prophecy."[16]

Of special concern to men like Riley was the UN's Universal Declaration of Human Rights. This 1948 declaration was drafted by various modernist Christians acting together with Muslims, Hindus, and Confucians; well-known atheist philosophers; and socialist politicians. This panoply of internationalists saw in the declaration an authoritative, universal moral code that would at last give legal voice to the long-standing belief of the left that international security and justice were bound up with assuring a catholicity of human rights and not just with collective security or the arbitration of conflicts. This human rights agenda could be understood as the universalization of a given modernist set of Western values, but it could also be seen as the approximation of a more inclusive, multicultural synthesis culled from the world's varied ethical and cultural traditions. Modernist Christian theology, having always believed in the immanence of divine revelation in all cultures, certainly could endorse the latter interpretation. Whatever the interpretation, the declaration did form the first legally binding, codified set of human rights principles.[17]

Conservative evangelicals saw the Universal Declaration of Human Rights (and similar pronouncements by the UN's educational agency,

UNESCO) as the denouement at length brought about from all that syncretist mixing of Christian and pagan faiths to which they had drawn attention at the time of the League of Nations' founding. The framers of the declaration, noted *Our Hope*, not unpredictably "decided to leave God out."[18] They created the first-ever group of global agencies, funded partly by the so-called Christian nations, that was tasked with developing and spreading propaganda for a set of ethical principles synthesized from the core teachings of the great world religions. These principles were presented as universal and superior to the teachings of any one religion. According to Wilbur Smith, a key early cold war dispensationalist, it was only to be expected that a growing number of people would be taken in by "this satanic serpent" that was using the UN's "vast program for world education" to "mock God and deify man" under the seemingly innocuous cover of humanitarianism.[19] Even the supposedly moderate *Christianity Today*, the New Evangelicals' flagship, thought that this was the road to the "totalitarian superstate" that presumed to be the "origin of all rights."[20]

The believed import of the Universal Declaration of Human Rights worried the dispensationalists more than anyone else. They had always pegged their predictions about the future on the supposition that a worldwide apostate faith would emerge before long. The League of Nation's "yoke fellowship" had prefigured this, and the UN's new declaration seemed to be fulfilling the prediction. From Riley's message in his last years to the cold war popularizers of dispensationalism and beyond, the dispensationalists' argument had, in fact, remained unchanged. They engaged in just as much international commentary as before, and in just as much searching for the "signs of the times." They still saw liberal Christianity, political liberalism, and Soviet communism as interwoven dimensions of the gradually emerging antichristian world empire that they thought was prefigured and anticipated by the United Nations.

Thus we find Louis A. Bauman, a leading Church of the Brethren evangelist, writing a series of articles in 1950 on the "impending world state," stressing how there was just then afoot the construction of that "great godless organization, ostensibly to obtain 'international peace and security' just preceding Armageddon." The UN was, quite simply, "man's supreme attempt to bring 'on earth peace, good will among men,' without the partnership of Him whom Almighty God has ordained as 'The Prince of Peace.'" It would fail on the rock of its godlessness.[21] Eight years later, the leading journal of militant fundamentalism, the *Christian Beacon* of Carl McIntire, insisted that the UN was "organized in hell for the sole purpose of aiding and abetting the destruction of the free world."[22] McIntire even wrote two books on the topic—strident premillennarian tracts against the Antichrist, the communists, and all manner of liberal Protestants.[23] Thirty years later, some of the stridency had vanished but the core message remained the same when the newest dispensational luminary, Hal Lindsey, denounced the UN in his *The Late Great Planet Earth* for its false promises of peace and plenty and for the way in which "Jesus has been excluded from the premises."[24]

The Soviet Union played a central role in such cold war dispensational discourse, and many evangelicals started to recover their respect for America because of its leadership in the fight against communism. Increasingly, dispensationalists conflated America's anticommunist mission with their own work, and through outlets such as McIntire's Twentieth-Century Reformation, Fred Schwarz's Christian Anti-Communism Crusade, and the New Evangelicals' *Christianity Today*, they started again to lend their support to American nationalism and to become politically active.[25] This activism, which was further accentuated in the 1960s when liberal politicians and the Supreme Court started assailing the availability of school prayer and other religious freedoms that evangelicals prized, was geared just as much against the UN as it was against international communism and its supposed domestic approximations.[26] Indeed, some of them supported the proposed Bricker Amendment of the mid-1950s, a secular conservative proposal that would have given the U.S. Congress the power to override international treaties enjoined by the UN.[27]

Nondispensational conservatives agreed entirely. America could be safe and secure, insisted the influential Lutheran Church–Missouri Synod broadcaster Walter A. Maier in the late 1940s, only if it rejected all "anti-Scripture programs," whether these were by "atheist Communism" or by the "godless politicians" who believed in "world control" by a "world organization" that refused to take guidance from God. How, asked he, "can you expect anything God-pleasing from international leaders who hate our Savior?" Only Christian civilization was capable of making the world better, he emphasized, but there could be no universal Christian civilization—no matter how much churchly internationalists tried—until the non-Christian and anti-Christian leaders of the UN were converted out of their evil ways. In the meantime, all efforts at reform through evolution, education, force, or international legislation were but so many different ways of willfully abandoning God.[28]

Among the nondispensationalist evangelicals, the school of apologetics known as presuppositionalism especially provided doctrinal underpinnings for such fears. It was this apologetics, more than any other single influence except dispensationalism, that helped perpetuate Christian anti-internationalism beyond the cold war, when the so-called culture wars seized the imagination of many on the political right who until then had fought communists and their alleged UN allies. Presuppositionalism owed to the work of several Calvinist theologians and philosophers, but most important, to J. Gresham Machen's disciple Cornelius Van Til, a professor at Westminster Theological Seminary.

Basing his argument on the Kuyperian tradition in Calvinist theology, Van Til suggested the impossibility of mutual understanding across the bridge of fundamentally different premises (or presuppositions) of the Christians and the nonbelievers. He stressed that as God was the ultimate reference point for a Christian's thought, so was humankind the ultimate reference point for the nonbelievers and the rationalists, and that from these premises two different epistemologies followed, both with their intrinsic beliefs about every process observable in the world. One led to utter dependence on God in everything, including politics, and to a demotion of human competency, whereas the other led to just those kinds of anthropocentric assumptions of human self-sufficiency and potency that underlay all efforts at world reform through political institutions. Only a "head-on collision" between the two could result if both stayed true to their presuppositions.[29]

This type of Christian anti-internationalism influenced the editors of *Christianity Today* and many a Christian anticommunist during the cold war, but it reached its clearest expression in the so-called Christian Reconstructionist (or Dominionist) movement—above all in the writings of its late cold war theological spearhead, Rousas John Rushdoony. Though he was a figure little known to the general public, Rushdoony was very influential across a range of conservative Christian opinion, and he was to inspire a late-twentieth-century resurgence of the Calvinist pursuit of Christian dominion in American law and government.[30] He was also a sworn enemy of the UN who insisted that "any discussion of the United Nations is inevitably a religious discussion, for the principles which that organization embodies are not merely political or economic but inevitably religious."[31]

According to Rushdoony, the United Nations had developed a new "religion of humanity." It had combined the Enlightenment beliefs in rationalism, egalitarianism, and pure democracy with the modernist Christian supposition that all world religions shared a moral core but were, also, all devoid of uniquely salvific insight. It was up to the UN to translate into international legislation these supposedly shared moral values, and in this it had the right to use coercive means—"socialistic as well as totalitarian." The project, he stressed, was entirely acceptable to Western nations because it was legitimated in terms of global democracy and high ethical endeavor. The end result, however, could only be "faith in humanity as such, not in a transcendental moral or spiritual order," a moral egalitarianism that had lost all linkage with the Christian God, and was, as long as traditional Christians did still persist, enforceable only by a despotic world state.[32]

To Rushdoony and those like him, the United Nations was, therefore, "a new humanistic culture aimed at destroying all others by means of the imperialism of world law and world police," a "crusading missionary organization" imbued with a "false and deadly faith," an "Antichristian faith" bent on using the state and legislation to "save man." It could not be reconciled with historic Christianity on any level. In fact, concluded Rushdoony in 1978, the UN was "anathema to all real Christians" and had to be checked through "religious warfare."[33]

A pronounced conspiracism accompanied this rendition. According to Rushdoony and his disciples, the universal moral principles that the UN and its Universal Declaration of Human Rights proffered were actually rooted in the ancient decision of man to "join with Satan in an attempt to set up a new world instead of the one that God created." Therefore, whether they realized it or not, the internationalists were ultimately in rebellion against God Himself. Put differently, history was littered with a number of specific conspiracies (like the Illuminati, on which Rushdoony dwelt a lot, and secular Zionism and communism), each with specific, contextualized aims. But all these were invested with meaning by the broader, spiritual conspiracy of all those who placed their faith in humanity and in worldly progress. In the twentieth century, Rushdoony went on, such people had latched on to the power of international organizations, to "the imperialism of world law and world police," because in it they had perceived the mightiest and the most likely victorious instrument for the attainment of the goals of both their spiritual-existential and incidental-historical conspiracy.[34]

"The UN, by placing total power within man's grasp, has heightened accordingly the potentialities for a vast inter-play of forces that use the façade of the UN as camouflage for unrelenting drives of power," Rushdoony summarized in his book *The Nature of the American System* (1978). "Great and total stakes are at issue below the surface of publicized events. Total war is under way, and hence total conspiracy."[35]

The New World Order

Such suppositions were especially important after the ending of the cold war. It was then that conspiracist fears over the ultimate ambitions of existing international organizations truly burst their banks. Some evangelicals did silently break ranks and, now that the Soviet Union was no longer part of the UN, chose to start working from inside its specialized agencies, trying to steer them toward the evangelical agenda.[36] But many more concluded that all justification for suffering *any* secular international organizations—grudgingly accepted in some form as a part of the anticommunist struggle—was truly gone.

The reorganized and increasingly political Christian Right of the late twentieth century started to claim that the United Nations, the ILO, and other similar organizations were in fact just that remnant of the old communist, modernist, and apostate conspiracy, of which the West's cold war victory had destroyed most recognizable outward forms. In many a commentary, these international organizations again appeared as the very core of the conspiracy, adapting to changed circumstances, throwing off track their communist affiliates, and resuming their evil work replenished and stronger. That the communist enemy had been vanquished had supposedly generated a false sense of security in the West, which it was easy for the conspirators to use as a cover as they went on to complete their work.

Now all manner of additional conspirators were detected, ranging from feminist theologians and gay activists to members of such semiprivate assemblages of politicians and financiers as the World Economic Forum, the Trilateral Commission, the Council on Foreign Relations, and the Bilderbergs. All these were still, however, seen as cohered by the apostate theologies that had allegedly characterized modern internationalism from the first. Some commentators traced these so-called globalists to the worship of Mother Earth (Gaia) that characterized some New Age religions; others traced them to Theosophy, Spiritualism, and related occult movements; and still others claimed that the Dalai Lama or Pope John Paul II was in ultimate charge. The end result, in any case, would be a "final ecumenical union of all the world religions"—"the dream of the UN" and the goal of the Antichrist.[37]

Many an evangelical saw the Kyoto Protocol (1997) and the expensive projects agreed to at the UN Conferences on the environment (1992), on population and development (1994), on women (1994), and on biological diversity (1993) as that many attempts by the apostate "globalists" to bankrupt the chief obstacle to their plans for world conquest. This was the United States, a country not exactly "Christian" any longer but still with a powerful evangelical leaven. The "idolatrous, satanic and atheist" servants of the UN conspiracy had to destroy this leaven, suggested a typical dispensationalist, the Texas pastor John Hagee in 1996, because "as long as you believe in the Word of God, you are loyal to the kingdom of God . . . [and] represent a government within a government and you are a hindrance to the New World Order."[38]

Conservative politicians eagerly latched onto these notions after the cold war. From its beginnings in the 1960s, the neoconservative movement had been a passionate critic of the UN; now it incorporated clearly religious themes into its discourse and started to systematically cooperate with evangelical anti-internationalists in jointly created and jointly led organizations.[39] More traditional conservatives such as the onetime Republican presidential hopeful Pat Buchanan borrowed avidly from the evangelicals' conspiracy theory in their equally passionate denunciations of the "new world order,"[40] whereas others—including George W. Bush in his 2000 presidential campaign—promised never again to place American soldiers under the command of the UN. As president, Bush eagerly opened his UN delegation to varied conservative evangelical activists and co-opted their opposition to established UN population, environmental, and education policies and to the International Criminal Court.[41]

After the cold war, evangelically anti-internationalist notions spread widely into popular American culture as well, not least because of the persuasiveness of several evangelical fiction writers. Foremost among them were the Southern Baptist Convention pastor Tim LaHaye and his writing colleague Jerry Jenkins, who in the 1990s began to churn out their phenomenally popular *Left Behind* series of dispensational novels. These novels depicted the fictional UN secretary-general, Nicolae Carpathia, a native of formerly communist Romania, as the Antichrist. These novels—twelve volumes of explicit description of the horrors that the unraptured would have to go through during the Great Tribulation, when the Antichrist would use his world organization to prescribe a false religion, control all aspects of private as well as public life, and kill all who dissented—popularized the old dispensationalist thesis for the increasingly secular audiences of post–cold war America. By 2005, some 70 million copies had been sold.[42]

The popularization of dispensationalist anti-internationalism owed also to the Republican Party presidential hopeful of 1988, the television preacher and Christian media entrepreneur Pat Robertson. As president (until 2001) of the Christian Coalition and of his own Christian Broadcasting Network, Robertson had at his disposal an enormous media empire that could be chained to new, saturation methods of spreading the message worldwide. For those so minded, there were also available a range of Robertson's popular fictional and nonfiction books. Many of these were specifically geared toward addressing internationalism from a conservative Christian perspective, and all belied a profoundly conspiracist approach.

This was singularly clear in Robertson's best-selling 1995 novel *The End of the Age*, in which a demon-possessed dictator takes charge of the entire United States (except for a few hidden Christian satellite television and radio stations) and conspires with foreign New Age believers to set up the Antichrist's world empire.[43] Earlier, Robertson came out with *The New World*

Order, the most important of his explorations into post–cold war international organizations, which was written from the vantage point of dispensationalism but tempered with pretensions to culturalist custodianship. This book was also shot through with Illuminati theories about the secret conclave of (Jewish) international financiers that supposedly led international organizations. To Robertson, the post–cold war "New World Order" was but the latest stage and configuration of these people's pursuit of "one-world government under a centralized authority." They aspired to an "occult-inspired world socialist dictatorship" complete with its "world police force, world courts, world banking and currency, and a world elite in charge of it" and, finally, its "new, universal religion." Robertson was convinced that all this was "from the depth of something that is evil" and "under the domination of Lucifer."[44]

Robertson (and others) worried deeply about the Persian Gulf War of 1991 because it was fought under the auspices of this "satanic" United Nations. Robertson feared that by combining the military might of practically all the world's nations in the single war alliance that was then constructed, the UN was establishing the end-times military force that would soon start persecuting Christians and Jews. A consistent premillennialist would have stopped here, but Robertson, a believer in *post*-tribulation rapture, went on to sketch ways of retaking America from the "globalists" in the time that remained. These included the domestic campaigns of the Christian Coalition, including the goal of electing a Christian conservative as president. But they also included a marked strain of Christian nationalism and a call for a new "Community of Democratic Nations" that was to supplant the UN. This putative community would be structured around national sovereignty and voluntary cooperation between nations that accepted core Christian values.[45]

The continuity between this rendition of Christian anti-internationalism and that offered in 1919 and 1920 was palpable. The one apparent major change was brought into focus when Robertson was subjected to severe criticism for having cited the writings of the anti-Semitic Illuminati theorist Nesta Webster. No matter how commonplace in the conversation of a William Bell Riley eighty years earlier, by the late twentieth century it simply was not acceptable for evangelicals to converse in terms that appeared anti-Semitic.[46] As Robertson's case showed, the old aversion to secular Jews (whom the fundamentalists used to call "apostate Jewry") did, however, remain part of the evangelical anti-internationalist worldview. Having been code-named "international finance" and still transposed onto international organizations, it continued to inform the Christian Right's view of Jews just as much as the more openly expressed Christian Zionism.

Christian Zionism, too, was related to anti-internationalism. The crucial moment in its emergence was the Six-Day War of 1967, during which Israel reconquered Jerusalem and the biblical lands of Samaria and Judea, thus convincing the dispensationalists that the prophesized restoration of the Jews to their land had finally been achieved. But of course, that restoration had always been thought more or less coterminous with the rise of the Antichrist's world empire. Dispensationally minded evangelicals became (as one historian put it) "Israel's best friend" because they expected the Antichrist's organization—the UN—soon to start persecuting the Jews on a massive scale and because they saw it as their religious duty to stand with God's chosen people in the run-up to that end-times catastrophe. Evangelicals—more influential as a foreign policy lobby in the late twentieth and early twenty-first centuries than ever before—insisted on defending Israel not only against its Arab Muslim enemies but also against United Nations demands for a peace settlement that would have splintered the lands, as they believed, that God had given to the Jews forever.[47]

In the early twenty-first century, along with the Christian Right's sometimes incongruous blending of premillennialist separatism and Christian Reconstructionist pretensions to political and cultural dominion, another persistent theme in Christian anti-internationalism was brought to crystallization. More latent than active in the eighty years after the League debates, this was the tendency toward Christian nationalism and American unilateralism that many League critics had sketched as their alternative to multilateralist, secular international organization. Evangelical support for America's cold war struggle against international communism had exposed elements of this tendency, but it was really only with the Iraq war of 2004 that its full import became manifest.

Robertson and other Christian Right leaders could enthusiastically support the Iraq war, not least because it was not fought under the auspices of an international organization. This was a war by a unilateralist United States consenting to a "coalition of the willing" that it led itself, a coalition that did include some non-Christian members but was so completely under American direction that one could hardly speak of a "yoke fellowship." Moreover, the war was directed by a born-again president who in his public statements took care to advertise his evangelical worldview and understanding of history and who did not offer to export a Social Gospel–style democracy but always emphasized the spiritual aspects and requirements of right living and governance. He spoke of the power of intercessory prayer, referred to the "angel that rides and directs the storm," and studded his public statements with conservative evangelical motifs (including unattributed Bible quotations with well-established anti-internationalist meanings for evangelicals). In the wake of this president's war, conservative evangelicals flocked to the areas conquered to do traditional missionary conversion work.[48] This was the kind of Christian nationalism and American unilateralism that even the League of Nations' most passionate evangelical critics could easily have supported.

Conclusion

From Riley to Robertson and from the dispensationalist specter of the Antichrist to the presuppositionalist quest for Christian dominion, the evangelical discourse on modern internationalism remained essentially unchanged. This was because in these first eighty or so years of the Christian encounter with modern internationalism, the liberal Protestant case for existing international organizations also remained the same. In the years during and after the cold war, the liberal case was as firmly rooted in the assumptions of an incarnationalist and immanentist Social Gospel that had seized secular means of forwarding the cause as it had been in the World War I period, and the liberal Protestants were just as interested in welcoming the ethical insights and practical cooperation of non-Christian religions and peoples into what was supposedly a shared quest for peace and progress. Conversely, the conservative evangelicals' anti-internationalism, once it was established from what they saw as a literal interpretation of the Bible in the World War I period, could not change as long as they wished to remain biblical literalists in the sense that they understood that designation. In any case, it did not change.

CONCLUSION

Christian Anti-Internationalism in Historical Context

Two crucial consequences of the religious League of Nations controversy stand out. First, it had an important proximate result in that it helped conservative evangelicals of very different denominational traditions acknowledge each other as allies in a struggle against shared churchly and secular enemies. This realization assisted in paving the way to the cultural and political agitation that started during the League fight and culminated a few years later in the fundamentalist/modernist controversy.

Before the League controversy, conservative evangelicals and churchly modernists had combated each other over purely theological and clearly ecclesiastical issues in the areas of missionary work, denominational control, and creedal contention. From the early 1920s, they continued to battle each other on all these issues, but in addition they more clearly tackled political matters and embraced explicitly political means of influencing national affairs. In between stood the major crossroads of the League of Nations controversy. This fight prefigured subsequent political battles during which evangelicals of all kinds came to conclusions about natural allies, the opposite forces, and the methods of combat most likely to be successful.

The League controversy's second, longer-term result—the creation and perpetuation of a distinct Christian form of anti-internationalism—was even more significant, because it helped shape the worldviews of many Americans for generations to come and had to be taken into account by democratically elected makers of foreign policy. Especially important in this regard was the conservative politicians' co-opting of the evangelical argument. This did not, on the whole, lead conservative evangelicals into direct political work—not yet—but it did make them aware of conservative politicians' interest in combating the liberal and modernist ascendancy.

In 1919 and 1920, conservative evangelical newspapers and periodicals assiduously publicized the use of religious arguments against modern internationalism by men like Senator Lawrence Sherman, and this reporting helped many evangelicals to conclude that among the political class of the nation they could still find allies for their own religiopolitical fights. Some of the Irreconcilables genuinely believed that as Christians it was their religious duty to oppose the League of Nations, and they were utterly uncompromising for that reason. For others, the appeal to religion was a useful tool with which to whip up the nationalist and ethnic prejudice that they considered useful to their cause. But whichever the motivation, the Irreconcilables showed themselves to be available to conservative evangelicals.

This is not to say that the evangelicals of 1919 and 1920 engaged in a concerted effort to influence politicians with a view to defeating the ratification of the League of Nations Covenant. On the whole, no such direct forays into partisan politics took place at this time. Rather, the churchly discourse on modern internationalism helped shape U.S. foreign policy in an altogether more diffuse and indirect way—that is, by contributing to public opinion a religious strand of some importance, which the Irreconcilables and other anti-League politicians picked up and used. Evangelical critics of the League did not set out to thus influence the politicians, but through their sustained and passionate polemics they did, in fact, arrive at that outcome.

The Christian anti-internationalism that was thus created was a clearly argued and widely believed-in set of attitudes that objected to multilateral cooperation in international organizations that were multiethnic, secular, and political; that contained members from many different religious traditions; and that pretended to worldwide supranational authority. Each evangelical group fashioned its own confessional types of League critique; yet all shared the chief characteristics common to a generic Christian anti-internationalism, which itself was an aspect of the wider fight against modernist theology and the Social Gospel. Christian anti-internationalism was a subtheme of anti-modernism, because conservative evangelicals regarded the modernist embrace of the League of Nations as an aspect of an apostate deviation from that divine truth that had been given once and for all.

To the dispensationalists, the prevention of increasing apostasy and of the eventual emergence of the Antichrist's expected world empire—prefigured in the League—was doctrinally impossible. Nevertheless, they were intent on using the League controversy to assail and to weaken the liberal forces that they regarded as apostate on that and all other issues. The same applied to the Pentecostals. The Calvinists did not view the matter from the same pessimistic and resigned millennialist angle, but they also felt that the League controversy constituted one of the important spaces for their continuing antimodernist fight. Both kinds of fundamentalists saw the League as a purely secular instrument for the attainment of modernist spiritual ends, and both—as much as they approached the associated issues from differing theological positions with regard to history and eschatology and the functions of the church—were utterly dedicated in their opposition.

The Lutherans entered the debate over the League of Nations convinced that their confessions alone amounted to the true doctrine of God. They were therefore passionately opposed to all mixing of secular and religious aspirations or competencies, and they worried that such a mixing was taking place in the League of Nations, to the detriment of the Christian Zion. For the Baptists, the stress was on soul liberty and the threat thereto posed by all forms of collectivism; for the conservative Methodists, the emphasis was on the individual's direct social responsibility, which no far-off institution should be allowed to supersede; and for the Christian Restorationists, the stress was on the need to return to primitive, noncreedal, and nonhierarchical Christianity as the only means to a warless world. Additional theological grounds applied for those critiques of the League of Nations that (more rarely) issued from the ranks of conservative Episcopalians, Mormons, Catholics, and others. But all were equally anti-internationalist.

All these very dissimilar groups profoundly disagreed on a number of key theological issues, and for that reason, they could not combine in any actual coalition against modern internationalism in 1914–20 any more than they could act as a single force in the fundamentalist/modernist controversy of the 1920s. But separate though their contention remained, they were all united in the basic contention that secular world organizations that were so legitimated and so tasked as was the League of Nations by its modernist Social Gospel apologists and their Wilsonian liberal allies were at best hindrances and impediments to a true Christian witness and at worst its overt enemies. All these groups agreed that it was wrong and dangerous to sacralize such organizations, that it was wrong and dangerous to seek material progress or expect perpetual peace from such organizations, and that it was wrong and dangerous to subject such a predominantly Christian country as the United States to a system of decision making that was predicated on the coequality of nations with different religions and different ethical insights. That conservative evangelicals of all confessional traditions continued to broadcast this set of claims and grievances more than eighty years after the original League fight confirms that Christian anti-internationalism was indeed able to be perpetuated on the basis that was sketched in 1919 and 1920.

The one major change that did take place during these eighty years was the ever-clearer coupling of Christian anti-internationalism and American nationalism. As Richard M. Gamble has shown, in the historical circumstances of the World War I period, Christian nationalism in America was the preserve of those modernist Social Gospelers who regarded America as a nation as the closest approximation to, and therefore the instrument of, socially aware Christianity. Their "messianic nationalism" consisted of an attempt to forward modernist Social Gospel practices under a League of Nations that was led by America as the "Christ-Nation."[1] No conservative evangelical grouping embraced such a view of America during the League controversy. Many of them were just as critical of America as they were of other nations—for they believed that, to the extent America was approximating the Social Gospel vision, it was actually diverging from true Christianity.

That said, even the fundamentalists of 1919 regarded the United States as a uniquely Christian nation, specially blessed by God and with a special role to play in the world. Before the ascendancy of the Social Gospel, many of them had been passionate supporters of American imperialism because they had seen the U.S. government as a usable instrument in spreading the Christian faith. Although this dimension of their public conversation largely disappeared during the League of Nations debates, it lived on in presuppositions and unstated assumptions. In those debates, the anti-internationalist evangelicals could easily imagine circumstances where evangelical anti-internationalism might again be transformed into Christian nationalism. With the exception of the consistent dispensationalists and the strict Lutherans, all the evangelical opponents of liberal internationalism did maintain that if America—or its leaders—ever was to embrace their doctrinal distinctives, the churches, too, should play a key role in supporting the Christianized state's worldwide activities. If such an America were to emerge, the conservative evangelicals could easily become, once again, Christian nationalists who championed a unilateral American foreign policy.

Put another way, by the time of World War I, Social Gospel internationalists had concluded that world public opinion was already sufficiently infused with Christian thought forms for a system of mutual and equal cooperation to be sustainable. And they thought that America, as the nation that was the most suffused with their Social Gospel view of Christianity, should lead such an international system through the League of Nations. The conservative evangelicals did not then, nor would they for the next eighty or so years, believe that the world had been thus Christianized; nor did they think that America had been thus Christianized; nor yet did they accept that Christianization meant what the Social Gospelers said it meant. But if America or its leaders were to meet the several confessional criteria that the different conservative evangelical groups put forth, then it would be entirely conceivable that they would again become American nationalists qua American Christians. Already in 1919, a conservative Episcopalian like Bishop William Lawrence and a Methodist conservative like Bishop Thomas Benjamin Neely were near that denouement, and even some of the statements of the dispensationalists John Roach Straton and J. C. Massee approached it. A missionary evangelical could hardly stay an isolationist for long.

Arguably, the shift from Christian anti-internationalism to Christian nationalism began to occur during the cold war, when many on the Christian Right conflated America's anticommunist world mission and their own religious mission. In the post–cold war campaign against Islamic terrorism, in the defense of Israel and a "Christian" America, they did the same again. In both cases, however, Christian anti-internationalism remained, the opposition to "yoke fellowship" remained, and the denial of unredeemed human potentiality remained. American world leadership was acceptable precisely because it was unilateral, unfettered by international organizations that contained pagans and not predicated on Social Gospel presuppositions about temporal progress and human potentiality apart from God.

Whatever else it was, then, the League of Nations controversy was thus also a pivotal moment in a long-sustained, remarkably successful attempt by conservative evangelical clergy and laity to assure that the United States, in its international affiliations, would continue to deny that secular international organizations were valid agencies for world transformation. This demotion of international organizations also applied to organizations that were following America's lead, for the evangelicals did not believe that America, as constituted in 1919, was truly Christian.

Conversely, it was during the League of Nations controversy that conservative Christians first put in systematic terms their doctrinal insistence that the nation's faith should be placed only in the instrumentality of those Christian churches that were engaged in traditional evangelism and that trusted God, not humanity, to perfect the world in due time. They taught that America could play a special role in the world only after it had reposed its faith in Christ and had thereby been transformed. Whether that had taken place or not, they further insisted that America must not be tied to non-Christian nations but must remain a free agent in the world's affairs. Such beliefs—precisely because they were based on religious doctrine shared by great numbers of ordinary Americans, including not a few practicing politicians—would have a profound impact on American foreign policy for the eighty or so years after the original debates over the League of Nations. In all likelihood, Christian anti-internationalism in its doctrinal and popular forms would last for a long time to come.

Notes

Introduction

1. See Miller, *American Protestantism*, 322–23; Lancaster, "The Protestant Churches"; Kuehl and Dunn, *Keeping the Covenant*, 49–51, 61; and Margulies, *The Mild Reservationists*, 145, 147.

2. *Congressional Record*, 66th Cong., 1st sess., vol. 58, 2068–69. The *Christian Century* claimed that "scarcely a denominational journal in America can be found on the opposing side" ("The League and the Nation's Mood," *Christian Century*, November 11, 1920, 6), whereas the bishops of the Methodist Episcopal Church claimed in 1919 that not a single Methodist clergyman was opposed to the League (Miller, *American Protestantism*, 320).

3. Each of the major studies of fundamentalism mention but none analyzes the role of religion in the League controversy. See Carpenter, *Revive Us Again*, 89–93; Marsden, *Fundamentalism and American Culture*, 141–68; Weber, *Living in the Shadow of the Second Coming*, 125–27; and Weber, *On the Road to Armageddon*, 87–88.

4. This, too, can be called internationalism, as in Nicholas Kristof's "Following God Abroad," *New York Times*, May 21, 2002, and "Hope Is on the Right," *Kansas City Star*, December 23, 2004, where twenty-first-century evangelicals are called the "newest internationalists, increasingly engaged in humanitarian causes abroad." Their passionate opposition to international political organizations as presently constituted, however, remains unchanged.

5. This definition is indebted to Marsden, *Understanding Fundamentalism and Evangelicalism*, 4–6.

6. See Ambrosius, *Woodrow Wilson and the American Diplomatic Tradition*; Cooper, *Breaking the Heart of the World*; Bailey, *Woodrow Wilson and the Great Betrayal*; Fleming, *The United States and the League of Nations*; and Stone, *The Irreconcilables*.

7. For rare explorations of these issues by historians, see Weber, *On the Road to Armageddon*; Gamble, *The War for Righteousness*; and Vintz, *Pulpit Politics*.

8. See Ambrosius, *Wilsonianism*; Ninkovich, *The Wilsonian Century*; and Hunt, *Ideology and U.S. Foreign Policy*.

9. For a rare call to do this, see Kirby, "Religion and the Cold War: An Introduction."

Chapter 1

1. Matthew, *Gladstone*, 183–84, 271–75, 374–77.
2. See Sykes, *The Rise and Fall of British Liberalism*, 87–91, 101–4, 133–42; also see Bentley, *The Climax of Liberal Politics*.
3. Sotirovich, *Grotius' Universe*, 51–59.
4. Brock, *Freedom from War*, 21–35, 43–57, 100–114, 175–84, 289–98.
5. Hutchison, *The Modernist Impulse*, 2.
6. Quoted by McBeth, *The Baptist Heritage*, 599.
7. Hutchison, *The Modernist Impulse*, 2–16, 24–48, 76–98.
8. Hutchison, *The Modernist Impulse*, 76–98, 122–44.
9. Herron, *The Menace of Peace*, 16–17, 60–61; Herron, *Woodrow Wilson*, 44–45, 105.
10. Coe is quoted by Gamble, *The War for Righteousness*, 204.
11. Abbott is quoted in ibid., 30.
12. Herron, *The Menace of Peace*, 14–17.
13. Mathews, *The Gospel and the Modern Man*, 169.
14. Carter, *The Decline and Revival of the Social Gospel*, 4–15, 23–26; May, *Protestant Churches and Industrial America*, 170–81, 235–62.
15. William Newton Clarke quoted by Gamble, *The War for Righteousness*, 38.
16. Gamble, *The War for Righteousness*, 70–81.
17. Quoted by Freeden, *The New Liberalism*, 85.
18. Freeden, *The New Liberalism*, 78–116.
19. Quoted by Link et al., *The Papers of Woodrow Wilson* (henceforth *PWW*), vol. 19, 221; *PWW* 24, 207.
20. *PWW* 16, 227–29; *PWW* 22, 385–86.
21. Thompson, *Woodrow Wilson*, 18–20.
22. Woodrow Wilson to Randall Davidson, December 20, 1918, Randall Davidson Papers, vol. 410, Lambeth Palace Library, London.
23. Shannon, *The Socialist Party of America*, 58–61.
24. Spargo, "Christian Socialism in America," 16–20; Spargo, *Marxian Socialism and Religion*, 77, 80, 100, 125–26; Spargo, "Socialism and Internationalism."
25. See Kloppenberg, *Uncertain Victory*, 233–56.
26. Quoted by Ruotsila, *John Spargo and American Socialism*, 64.
27. See Tuveson, *Redeemer Nation*; McDougall, *Promised Land, Crusader State*; Higham, "Ethnicity and American Protestants, 246–55.
28. See Knock, *To End All Wars*, vii–ix, 50–58, 66–83, 265–67; and Ninkovich, *The Wilsonian Century*, 12, 24–25.
29. For the evolutionary presuppositions of early-twentieth-century conservatism, see McCloskey, *American Conservatism in the Age of Enterprise*; and Rossiter, *Conservatism in America*, chap. 5.
30. See Ambrosius, *Woodrow Wilson*, x–xiii, 1–13, 21–32, 40–42; and Kuehl and Dunne, *Keeping the Covenant*, 8–19, 21–32, 59–89.
31. Taft, *Why is League of Nations Necessary?* 8–13; Taft, *The Obligations of Victory*, 5–6.
32. Root, *Letters of the Hon. Elihu Root*, 10–11, 19.
33. Cooper, *Breaking the Heart of the World*, 10–15.

34. See Bartlett, *The League to Enforce Peace.*

35. See Knock, *To End All Wars*, vii–ix, 50–58, 66–83, 265–67.

36. "Reconstruction," *Independent*, December 4, 1918, 304.

37. Gannett, "The Third Internationale."

38. Addams, "Feed the World and Save the League."

39. "Labor in the Treaty of Peace," *New Statesman*, October 12, 1918, 24–25.

40. Knock, *To End All Wars*, 35–39, 75–78, 95–119, 206–11, 220–24.

41. Ibid., vii–ix, 50–58, 66–83, 265–67.

42. Ambrosius, *Woodrow Wilson*, x–xiii, 1–6. The quotations are from Ross's *Social Control*, 63–64, 411, 429.

43. See Helbich, "American Liberals"; Gamble, *The War for Righteousness*, 85, 94, 135, 205; Kuehl and Dunn, *Keeping the Covenant*, 39–61, 94–96; and Mayer, *Political Origins of the New Diplomacy*, 55–96, 182–88.

44. "Notes from the Conference Notebook," *Intercollegiate Socialist* 4 (October–November 1915): 15; Spargo, *The Spiritual Significance of Modern Socialism*, 36–39.

45. Ruotsila, "'The Great Charter'"; Winkler, *Paths Not Taken*, 26–58.

46. Henderson, *The League of Nations and Labour*, 9–13; Shotwell, *The Origins of the International Labor Organization*, vol. 2, 336–37.

47. Shotwell, *The Origins of the International Labor Organization*, vol. 2, 23–26, 44–49, 336–40.

48. Ruotsila, "'The Great Charter,'" 30–35, 38–41.

49. Ibid., 36–37.

50. Croly, "The Obstacle to Peace," 403–7; "A Silent Revolution," *Independent*, July 21, 1917, 84.

51. "President Wilson and Labor," *American Federationist* 24 (June 1917): 454.

52. *PWW* 53, 618; *PWW* 63, 110–15; *PWW* 63, 127–28.

53. *PWW* 45, 202; *PWW* 51, 128; *PWW* 63, 33–36, 184–90.

54. Walling, "Comparison of Wilsonian Peace Terms"; Sinclair, "Explaining President Wilson."

55. Rauschenbusch, *A Theology for the Social Gospel*, 4, 107–10, 142–43, 164–65.

56. Vintz, *Pulpit Politics*, 19–26, 31–37.

57. Gore, *The League of Nations*, 3–12, 16–24; Skevington, "A Great War and Peace Meeting."

58. Bridgman, "A World-Unity Conference"; Ranck, "Christianizing International Relations," 430–52; Strong, "My Views of the Universe in General."

59. Jefferson, "The League of Nations and Religion"; Faunce, "The Church and Social Reconstruction."

60. Burton, "Ought the United States to Be a Missionary Nation?"; Snape, "'On Earth Peace.'"

61. Snape, "'On Earth Peace'"; Crane, "The Cement of the League of Nations."

62. See Hutchinson, *Errand to the World*; Carpenter, *Earthen Vessels.*

63. Herron, "Labor and the New Order"; Herron, *Woodrow Wilson*, 10, 41–42, 44–45, 77.

64. Ambrosius, *Woodrow Wilson*, 13.

65. Benedetti, *Origins of the Modern American Peace Movement*, 98–105; Meyer, *The Protestant Search for Political Realism*, 8–25, 40–58, 153–58.

66. Carter, *The Decline and Revival*, 23–26; Eighmy, *Churches in Cultural Captivity*, 98–99; Kuehl and Dunn, *Keeping the Covenant*, 50–51; Lancaster, "The Protestant Churches," 598–600, 606–10; Miller, *American Protestantism*, 317–23.

67. Lancaster, "The Protestant Churches," 598–600, 606–10.

Chapter 2

1. See Marsden, *Fundamentalism and American Culture*, 50–71; Sandeen, *The Roots of Fundamentalism*, 3–14, 18–50, 60–70, 76–95; Flegg, "*Gathered under the Apostles*," 292–441.

2. This and the following paragraphs are based on Clouse, *The Meaning of Millennium*.

3. Cohn, *The Pursuit of the Millennium*, 30–36, 89–98, 119–26.

4. Sandeen, *The Roots of Fundamentalism*, 36–39, 60–70.

5. Ibid., esp. 29–38, 55–65, 76–80, 188–232.

6. "Demon Possessed Women Continue Their Crimes," *Our Hope*, August 1914, 109; Gaebelein, *Current Events*, 98–144, 153–54; Riley, *Reasons for the King's Delay*, 6–13; Riley, "The Fall of Mystical Babylon."

7. "The United States of Europe," *Our Hope*, July 1914, 41–42; Gaebelein, *Current Events*, 10–11, 31–35, 47–49, 54; Riley, "The Significant Signs of the Times," 100; Torrey, *The Return of the Lord Jesus*, 89–91.

8. See Marsden, *Fundamentalism and American Culture*, 141–53; Sandeen, *The Roots of Fundamentalism*, 224–39; Weber, *On the Road to Armageddon*, 68–88.

9. Bebbington, *Evangelicalism in Modern Britain*, 223–24.

10. "Statement of Belief," *Monthly Bulletin of the Advent Preparation Prayer Union*, June 1919, 1; Gray, "The English Manifesto on the Second Advent."

11. *Advent Testimony Messages*, 21, 41, 72–79; "Advent Testimony Meetings," *Monthly Bulletin of the Advent Preparation Bible Union*, March 1920, 75–77.

12. William B. Riley to J. D. Adams, December 14 and 21, 1918, William B. Riley Papers, folder 1, Northwestern College, Roseville, Minn.; Gaebelein, *Half a Century*, 110–11.

13. "A Call for a Confederacy in the Faith," n.d. [c. Sept. 1918], Riley Papers, folder 1; Riley, "The World Premillennial Conference."

14. Riley, *The Gospel for War Times*, 8–11; Riley, "A Study in Revelation."

15. Torrey, "The Blessed Hope," 22.

16. Riley, "The Last Day"; Riley, "When Will the Lord Come?"

17. Riley, "A Study in Revelation." Also see Myers, *Christ Is Coming Back*; Massee, *The Second Coming*, 161–66.

18. Gaebelein, *The League of Nations*, 4–8, 15–30; "Why Won't the World Reform?" *Our Hope*, September 1919, 171–72.

19. Gaebelein offered the most complete description of this thesis in *The Conflict of the Ages*, 78–87, 93–100, 111–19, 138–41.

20. Gaebelein, "The Pre-Eminence of the Lord Jesus Christ"; Gaebelein, *The League of Nations*, 23–30, 36–38.

21. "Current Events and Signs of the Times in the Light of the Bible," *Our Hope*, July 1920, 40.

22. Riley, "The Fall of Mystical Babylon," 82–85; Riley, "The Significant Signs of the Times," 103–5.

23. Fereday, "After the Great War," 37–38.

24. See Ruotsila, *British and American Anticommunism.*

25. May, *Protestant Churches and Industrial America*, 13–16, 44–45, 136–38; Marsden, *Fundamentalism and American Culture*, 80–93.

26. Marsden, *Fundamentalism and American Culture*, 145–48.

27. Thomas, "German Moral Abnormality"; Thomas, "The German Attitude to the Bible."

28. Gray, "The Age and Its Apostasy"; Myers, "War on German Theology."

29. "The League of Nations," *Our Hope*, July 1919, 49–50; Massee, *The Second Coming*, 161–64, 203–4; *Baptist Fundamentals*, 153–54; Thwing, *The League of Nations*, 3–4.

30. Sermon notes, "The Holy Spirit and the Race Problem," n.d. [c. 1920], and May 5, 1918, J. C. Massee Papers, boxes 12 and 4, American Baptist Historical Society, Rochester. Courtesy of the American Baptist Historical Society.

31. Gaebelein, *The League of Nations*, 18–19.

32. Gray, "The League of Nations," 7.

33. Sermon notes, October 31, 1920, John Roach Straton Papers, box 30, American Baptist Historical Society, Rochester. Courtesy of the American Baptist Historical Society.

34. Sermon notes, May 12, 1918, Massee Papers, box 12; Massee, *The Second Coming*, 175–77.

35. Hankins, *God's Rascal*, 82–84; Gaebelein, *The League of Nations*, 28–29, 37–38; "The Vatican to Be Approved as a Member of the League," *Our Hope*, February 1920, 479–80.

36. Riley, "The Eclipse of Faith"; Riley, "The Interchurch World Movement"; Gray, "The League of Nations."

37. See Cohn, *Warrant for Genocide.*

38. Rausch, *Fundamentalist-Evangelicals*; Weber, *On the Road to Armageddon.*

39. Gaebelein, *The League of Nations*, 39–45; Gaebelein, "The Capture of Jerusalem"; "Coming Together," *Our Hope*, July 1920, 12–13; Gray, *Prophecy and the Lord's Return*, 26–27, 110–19.

40. Gordon, "Predictions About the Peace Table."

41. Trollinger, *God's Empire*, 62–82; Ribuffo, *The Old Christian Right*, 57–74, 146–57, 167–77, 113–18.

42. Riley, *Wanted: A World Leader!* esp. 41–50, 71–80.

43. Fereday, "The Present Crisis"; Russell, "The Earthly Destiny of Israel," 363–66; Gaebelein, *The League of Nations*, 31–38, 45–49; Gray, "Prophecy Changing the Map of Europe."

44. "The United States and Prophecy," *Our Hope*, February 1915, 489; "Preparedness for War," *Christian Workers Magazine*, February 1916, 430. For an exception, see Gray, "The League of Nations," 7.

45. "What We May Expect," *Our Hope*, November 1913, 266–67; "The United States and Prophecy," *Our Hope*, February 1915, 489; Gray, *Prophecy and the Lord's Return*, 22–23, 35–39; Fereday, "After the Great War," 38.

46. For an in-depth examination of the role that prophecy thought has played in American popular culture, see Boyer, *When Time Shall Be No More.*

47. Riley, "The Great Divide."

48. *God Hath Spoken*, 211–27, 329–44, 405–25.

49. Dates and places for Riley's appearances are derived from "Dr. W. B. Riley: Places & Subjects," n.d., Riley Papers, folder 1; "A Group of Conference Speakers," *School and Church*, October–December 1919, 216; "Continent Wide Conferences," *School and Church*, January–March 1920, 282. For Wilson's itinerary, see Link et al., *The Papers of Woodrow Wilson* (henceforth *PWW*), vol. 63, 11–502; for Wilson's plans for a separate Eastern tour, see Cooper, *Breaking the Heart of the World*, 187–91.

50. "Continent Wide Conferences"; "The Great Northwestern Series of Correlated Conferences," n.d., Riley Papers, folder 1.

51. *PWW* 63, 15–16, 33–42, 190, 351–56.

52. Ruotsila, " 'The Great Charter.' "

53. Riley's undated sermon notes, "Christ and the Present Crisis," "Consummation of the Ages," "Christ, the Church and the Kingdom," and "The Usurper's Short Reign," Riley Papers, folders Sermon Texts A–Co and Sermon Texts Sh–Z. That these were among the sermons that Riley gave on the tour is clear from his list in "Dr. W. B. Riley: Places & Subjects," Riley Papers, Folder 1.

54. Riley's undated sermon notes, "Christ and the Present Crisis," "Consummation of the Ages," "Christ, the Church and the Kingdom," and "The Usurper's Short Reign."

55. See Welch, *Response to Imperialism*, 88–99; Hunt, *The Making of a Special Relationship*, 154–68, 286–88. The quotation is from Massee, *The Second Coming*, 199.

56. "Preparedness for War," *Christian Workers Magazine*, February 1916, 40; Gray, "The League of Nations," 787–88; "The President's Power," *Christian Workers Magazine*, April 1920, 613.

57. Gaebelein, "The Pre-Eminence of the Lord Jesus Christ," 19; "The Threatening Revolution," *Our Hope*, October 1919, 312–13; "The Appeal to the Wrong Party," *Our Hope*, September 1919, 173–74.

58. Gaebelein, *The League of Nations*, 3–4, 32–38.

59. Sermon notes, July 13 and August 3, 1919, Massee Papers, box 12.

60. Massee, *The Second Coming*, 202–6.

61. Myers, "Things Not Shaken"; "The Conference on Fundamentals," *Baptist*, July 3, 1920, 800.

62. Sermon notes, October 31, 1920, Straton Papers, box 30. Courtesy of the American Baptist Historical Society.

63. Erdman, "The Prophetic Mold of the Present Dispensation"; "The League of Nations," *Our Hope*, January 1921, 393; Riley, "The Challenge of Orthodoxy," 368–71.

64. See Anderson, *Vision of the Disinherited*, 205–8, 214–19; Blumhofer, *Restoring the Faith*, 143–49; Wacker, *Heaven Below*, 194–96, 220–24, 240–50.

Chapter 3

1. Smith, *The Seeds of Secularization*, 15–19.

2. Kuyper, *Calvinism*, 55–59, 186–93; Warfield, *Biblical Doctrines*, 112–18, 125–29, 623–37.

3. Vos, "Eschatology of the New Testament"; Sproul, *The Last Days According to Jesus*, 113–27.

4. Warfield, *Biblical Doctrines*, 643–64.

5. Warfield, *Biblical Doctrines*, 662–63.

6. McBeth, *The Baptist Heritage*, 66–85, 371–80, 440–47, 623–56; George, "The Future of Baptist Theology"; George, "James Petigru Boyce."

7. See Glass, *Strangers in Zion*, 185–213; Eighmy, *Churches in Cultural Captivity*, 43–48, 74–78, 102–3; Harvey, *Redeeming the South*, 200–26.

8. See Foster, *Moral Reconstruction*, 19–30, 107–10.

9. See Noll, *The Princeton Theology*.

10. See Bratt, "The Dutch Schools"; Smith, *The Seeds of Secularization*, 42–58; Zwaanstra, *Reformed Thought and Experience*.

11. See Smith, "The Southern Tradition"; Thompson, *The Spirituality of the Church*.

12. Kuyper, *Calvinism*, 28–42, 63, 73, 135–39, 258–68, 283–98.

13. Ibid., 127–32, 135–42, 145–54.

14. "President Wilson's Peace Terms," *Presbyterian*, January 17, 1918, 4–5; "Why We Must Win This War," *Presbyterian*, April 18, 1918, 4; Gimmell, "The League of Nations," 9–10; "An After View," *Presbyterian*, March 6, 1919, 3; "The Versailles Treaty," *Presbyterian*, May 15, 1919, 2.

15. "The Nation's Danger," *Presbyterian*, August 21, 1919, 6.

16. "The League of Nations," *Presbyterian*, December 26, 1918, 7; "The New Year's Problems," *Presbyterian*, December 26, 1918, 3; "A Republic of Nations," *Presbyterian*, January 9, 1919, 3.

17. "A Republic of Nations," *Presbyterian*, January 9, 1919, 3.

18. "A Sinning, Suffering World," *Presbyterian*, November 4, 1920, 3.

19. "A Republic of Nations," *Presbyterian*, January 9, 1919, 3; "Christian Internationalism," *Presbyterian*, May 8, 1919, 3; "Kingdom and the Law," *Presbyterian*, August 21, 1919, 3; "A Sinning, Suffering World," *Presbyterian*, November 4, 1920, 3.

20. "Editorial Notes and Comment," *Presbyterian of the South*, January 8, 1919, 1; "A Question for the Peace Conference," *Presbyterian of the South*, January 15, 1919, 2.

21. "Three Cogent Reasons Why the 'League of Nations' Is Doomed to Failure," *Presbyterian of the South*, September 3, 1919, 14–15.

22. Gage, "Problems of Peace."

23. For a summary, see Ruotsila, "American Baptists and the League of Nations."

24. "T. R. on the League of Nations," *Standard*, January 25, 1919, 532; "The Defeat of the Treaty," *Standard*, November 29, 1919, 308.

25. "A War-Time 'Peace Conference,'" *Watchman-Examiner*, April 25, 1918, 532; Ames, "What Shall We Do with Victory?"

26. "Editorial Comment," *Journal and Messenger*, January 23, 1919, 3–4; "All Sorts and Sizes," *Religious Herald*, February 6, 1919, 3; "The League of Nations," *Religious Herald*, July 17, 1919, 10–11; Nevins, "Unfair to Roosevelt"; "Two Reflections Regarding the League of Nations," *Baptist World*, March 20, 1919, 7.

27. Dixon, "The League of Nations"; "An Interview with A. C. Dixon," *Watchman-Examiner*, July 31, 1919, 1118.

28. Moore, "The League of Nations"; 'Seeing What Is Not There," *Missions*, April 1919, 253–54; "The Defeat of the Treaty," *Standard*, November 29, 1919, 308.

29. "Will America Fail the World?" *Standard*, March 8, 1919, 676; "We Should Keep the Vision," *Standard*, May 1, 1920, 470; "The League of Nations," *Watchman-Examiner*, April 3, 1919, 415.

30. Quoted by Vintz, *Pulpit Politics*, 50–52.

31. "The Baptists and World Democracy," *Watchman-Examiner*, January 31, 1918, 134; "Foreign Missions and World Peace," *Watchman-Examiner*, March 7, 1918, 295–96.

32. "Regeneration and Reconstruction," *Standard*, March 1, 1919, 651; "A Disappointing Outcome," *Missions*, June 1919, 438; Stalker, "Kant on Perpetual Peace"; "The Baptists and World Democracy," *Watchman-Examiner*, June 31, 1918, 133–34.

33. "Northern Baptist Convention, Denver, May 21–27, 1919," *Journal and Messenger*, June 5, 1919, 12.

34. "Regeneration and Reconstruction," *Standard*, March 1, 1919, 651.

35. See Gaffin, *Redemptive History*, ix–xiii; Hamstra, "Geerhardus Vos," 409.

36. See Vos, "Hebrews, the Epistle of the Diatheke"; Vos, "The Kingdom of God." See also Vos, *Biblical Theology*, 374–402; Olinger, "The Writings of Geerhardus Vos."

37. Vos, *Grace and Glory*, 15–16, 64–65, 163–66, 240–41, 256.

38. Vos, "The Second Coming and the Millennium"; Vos, "Eschatology of the New Testament."

39. Vos, "The Second Coming and the Millennium"; Vos, "Eschatology of the New Testament."

40. Vos, "The Second Coming and the Millennium."

41. Vos, "The Eschatology of the Psalter," 1–43.

42. Bratt, "The Dutch Schools"; Gaffin, *Redemptive History*, ix.

43. Foster, "Rome, the Antagonist of the Nation," 113–26.

44. Foster, *Reformation Principles*, 58–65, 271–76, 222–32.

45. Foster, *The Covenant Treaty*, 2–8.

46. Ibid.

47. Ibid.

48. Wadsworth, *Nebuchadnezzar's Image*, 3–7, 11–15.

49. Ibid., 1, 17–22.

50. See Hart, *Defending the Faith*; Stonehouse, *J. Gresham Machen*.

51. J. Gresham Machen to Horace J. Bridges, May 17, 1924, J. Gresham Machen Papers, Montgomery Library, Westminster Theological Seminary, Philadelphia.

52. Hart, *Defending the Faith*, 23–25, 45–46; Stonehouse, *J. Gresham Machen*, 240–50, 299–300.

53. Machen, "The Church in the War," 10–11; Machen, *God Transcendent*, 23–27.

54. J. Gresham Machen to Ralph Easley, October 10, 1923, Machen Papers; J. Gresham Machen, "Does Fundamentalism Obstruct Social Progress?"; Machen, *Christianity and Liberalism*, 49–50.

55. J. Gresham Machen to Mary Gresham Machen, October 12, 1919, Machen Papers.

56. Sentinels of the Republic executive committee minutes, May 8, 1925, Machen Papers, box 1924–25; E. M. Dilley to J. Gresham Machen, March 2, 1925, Machen Papers, box 1924–25; Hart, *Defending the Faith*, 137–41; Stonehouse, *J. Gresham Machen*, 464.

57. Hart, *Defending the Faith*, 135–45.

58. Machen, "Does Fundamentalism Obstruct Social Progress?"; Machen, *Christianity and Liberalism*, 9–14, 62–68, 136–44, 154–58.

59. Stonehouse, *J. Gresham Machen*, 406.

60. Lancaster, "The Protestant Churches," 606–7.

61. "General Assembly," *Presbyterian of the South*, May 28, 1919, 24; "The Federal Council," *Presbyterian of the South*, August 6, 1919, 2; "Editorial Comment and Notes," *Presbyterian of the South*, November 5, 1919, 1.

62. Richard H. Edmonds to Henry Watterson, February 28, March 6, and March 7, 1919, Henry Watterson Papers, box 4, Library of Congress, Manuscripts Division, Washington.

63. Kelsey, *Social Ethics among Southern Baptists*, 118–20.

64. Edmonds, "Against the League of Nations."

65. "Editorial Comment," *Journal and Messenger*, January 16, 1919, 3–4, and February 13, 1919, 3; "Editorial Review of the Week," *Journal and Messenger*, March 13, 1919, 4; (no title), *Journal and Messenger*, May 1, 1919, 4; "Concerning Centralization: A Caveat," *Journal and Messenger*, June 19, 1919, 8–9.

66. "Editorial Comment," *Journal and Messenger*, August 14, 1919, 3, and September 4, 1919, 5; "Editorial Review of the Week," *Journal and Messenger*, November 20, 1919, 18.

67. Mullins, "Recent Phases of Democracy"; "President Mullins and the League of Nations," *Religious Herald*, July 3, 1919, 3; Lancaster, "The Protestant Churches," 606–7.

68. Carver, "The Effect of the War on Foreign Missions"; Carver, "'The Church and World Peace'"; Carver, "'Some Aspects of International Christianity.'"

69. Eighmy, *Churches in Cultural Captivity*, 98–99.

Chapter 4

1. See Noll, "American Lutherans Yesterday and Today"; and Waltz, Montreal, and Hoffering, "Pastors in the Two Kingdoms."

2. See Moellering, "Some Lutheran Reactions to War and Pacifism"; Luebke, *Bonds of Loyalty*.

3. Wentz, *Lutherans in Concert*, 6–9, 12–22, 32–33.

4. Fevold, "Coming of Age, 1875–1900"; Meyer, *Moving Frontiers*, 372–73.

5. Wentz, *A Basic History*, 177.

6. Gritsch and Jenson, *Lutheranism*, 180–81, 184–90, 191–207.

7. Schoenfeld, "Old Truths for a New Age"; Fischer, "Christ's Return to Judgement."

8. Fevold, "Coming of Age"; Graebner, "Lutherans and Politics"; Meyer, *Moving Frontiers*, 344–53, 364–73, 379–83; Reichley, *Religion in American Public Life*, 199–200.

9. Marty, *Modern American Religion, Volume I*, 150–52, 169–78.

10. Fevold, "Coming of Age," 305–7, 354–56; Meuser, "Facing the Twentieth Century," 377–89; Meyer, *Moving Frontiers*, 365; Wentz, *A Basic History*, 317–23.

11. Rudnick, *Fundamentalism and the Missouri Synod*, 49–50, 67–102. On Machen's support, J. Gresham Machen to J. Searles Runyon, June 30, 1925, Machen Papers, box 1924–25.

12. Keyser, *The Conflict of Fundamentalism and Modernism*, 9–18, 19–30; Keyser, *Contending for the Faith*, 263–64, 281–95, 307–8; Keyser, "Handling the Word of Truth Aright."

13. "A Confession of Faith," *Lutheran Witness*, August 9, 1914, 58.

14. See Bachmann, *The United Lutheran Church in America*.

15. Nelson, *The Lutherans*, 290–92, 305–10, 373–77. On the smaller synods, see Arden, *Augustana Heritage*; Nelson and Fevold, *The Lutheran Church among the Norwegian-Americans*.

16. See Meyer, *Moving Frontiers*; Baepler, *A Century of Grace*; Jordahl, *The History of the Wisconsin Synod*; Ottersberg, "The Evangelical Lutheran Synod of Iowa."

17. "Moral Aims of the War," *Lutheran Church Work and Observer*, April 25, 1918, 3; "Christian Internationalism," *Lutheran Church Work and Observer*, September 12, 1918, 3 n. 4; Roehner, "Let the Churches Speak Out"; Mottern, "Blessings of the War."

18. Hall, "Fundamental Factors in World Peace"; Pfatteicher, "'Christian Internationalism'"; Peercy, "The World's Unfinished Task."

19. Meuser, "Facing the Twentieth Century," 381–84; Lueker, *Lutheran Cyclopedia*, 440.

20. Haas, "The Present Problems of Political Philosophy," 183; Haas, *The Problem of the Christian State*, 172–73.

21. *Minutes of the First Convention of the United Lutheran Church*, 9–10.

22. *Minutes of the Second Biennial Convention of the United Lutheran Church*, 40.

23. *Minutes of the Sixteenth Biennial Convention of the United Synod of the Evangelical Lutheran Church in the South*, 11–12, 103; *Proceedings of the Forty-eighth Convention of the General Synod of the Evangelical Lutheran Church*, 92–93.

24. Lancaster, "The Protestant Churches," 612–13; Meuser, "Facing the Twentieth Century," 418–19; "'A Message from the National Lutheran Council,'" *Lutheran Church Review*, January 6, 1920, 9–11.

25. Haas, "The Present Problems," 179–83, 188–89.

26. See ibid., 179–94; Kistler, "No New World as Yet"; and Schmauk, "Politics and the Church." Also see Haas, *Freedom and Christian Conduct*, 307–9.

27. Baushlin, "The Collapse of a Bad Theory," 193–95; Schmauk, "National Will and World Tragedy"; Schmauk, "Politics and the Church," 41–42; Taylor, "The World Movement"; "An Economic and Ethical Religion," *Lutheran*, May 13, 1920, 24.

28. Hall, "Fundamental Factors in World Peace," 70–71.

29. "The League of Nations," *Lutheran Church Work and Observer*, March 27, 1919, 4.

30. Meyer, *Moving Frontiers*, esp. 61–70, 73–89, 90–102, 125–27, 139–44, 149–61, 282–90.

31. Leith, *Creeds of the Churches*, 64–107.

32. "Vom weltlichen Regiment," *Der Lutheraner*, April 20, May 4 and 18, 1920, 129–30, 146–47, 163–64; "Peace Plans," *Lutheran Witness*, January 26, 1915, 26–28; Graebner, "Moral Issues and Religious Aspects of the Great War: III."

33. "The League of Nations," *Lutheran Witness*, May 13, 1919, 157; "There Is Much Joy," *Lutheran Witness*, June 24, 1919, 201; "The Churches and the League of Nations," *Lutheran Witness*, October 14, 1919, 328–29; "The Lure of Politics," *Lutheran Witness*, November 25, 1919, 378–79.

34. "Mangel an Selbstkenntnis in den reformierten Kreisen unseres Landes," *Lehre und Wehre*, April 1919, 190–91; "Über Rekonstruktion," *Lehre und Wehre*, July 1919, 329; "Im Anschluss an die erwächten falschen Missionziele," *Lehre und Wehre*, July 1919, 335–36; "Weissagungen über das Ergeben des lutherischen Kirche in Amerika," *Lehre und Wehre*, August 1919, 375–76.

35. "Eine traurige Äusserung der National Lutheran Commission for Soldiers and Sailors' Welfare," *Lehre und Wehre*, September 1919, 428–29. Italics added.

36. Luther, "Temporal Authority: To What Extent It Should Be Obeyed," 90–92. The editors of *Der Lutheraner* quoted, in German, from the Weimar edition of Luther's works.

37. "Luther über einer Völkerbund," *Der Lutheraner*, June 15, 1920, 200–201.

38. Reu, "Homiletical Sketches"; Johnston, *Anthology of the Sermons of J. Michael Reu*, vol. 1, 21–22, 41–43; vol. 2, 232, 248–49. Also see "Der Trost der Kinder Gottes im Zusammenbruch der Welt," *Kirchliche Zeitschrift*, March–April 1919, 181–83; italics added.

39. Johnston, *Anthology of the Sermons of J. Michael Reu*, vol. 1, 116–18.

40. "Ernste, böse Zeit," *Der Lutheraner*, April 23, 1918, 141–42; "Die neue Zeit mit ihrer Aufgaben," *Der Lutheraner*, January 28, 1919, 17–18; "Die herrliche Gemeinschaft der Kinder Gottes," *Der Lutheraner*, June 17, 1919, 181; "Der Name Jesu Soll in die Landeskonstitution," *Der Lutheraner*, February 24, 1920, 60.

41. "Materials for the Catechist," *Theological Quarterly*, January 1919, 31–41, 45; "Pacifism and the League of Nations," *Lutheran Witness*, September 16, 1919, 300.

42. "Law and Hate," *Lutheran Witness*, August 11, 1914, 129; "Preachers and the Treaty of Peace," *Lutheran Witness*, March 2, 1920, 71.

43. "Fruits of Political Preaching," *Lutheran Witness*, January 6, 1920, 7; "Preachers and the Treaty of Peace." See also Johnston, *Anthology of the Sermons of J. Michael Reu*, vol. 1, 116–18. The senator in question was William E. Borah. See McKenna, *Borah*, 153.

44. Schoenfeld, "Old Truths for a New Age," 65–68.

45. Hertzberger, "Perverted Democracy and Religious Education"; Behnken, "Testimonials to Old-Fashioned Faith," 71; Baushlin, "The Collapse of a Bad Theory"; "An Economic and Ethical Religion," *Lutheran*, May 13, 1920, 24.

46. "The Lure of Politics"; "Fruits of Political Preaching"; "Politicians and Preachers," *Lutheran Witness*, February 3, 1920, 40; "Preachers and the Treaty of Peace."

47. See Hennesey, *American Catholics*, 223–36.

48. Bishop John Glennon took the most uncompromising public stance against the League of Nations; see Meriwether, *Jim Reed*, 78–80.

49. McShane, *"Sufficiently Radical,"* 136–68, 177–86, 209–31; Piper, *The American Churches in World War I*, 23–31, 69–106, 146–58, 186–98.

50. *Triglot Concordia*, 471–77; Edwards, *Luther's Last Battles*, 97.

51. Meier, *Moving Frontiers*, 66, 284, 300, 364–65; Wentz, *A Basic History*, 203–4.

52. "Roman Catholic Designs," *Lutheran Witness*, January 15, 1914, 19; Graebner, "The Vatican and Diplomatic Relationships," 233–34.

53. Theodore Graebner to D. H. Steffens, August 8, 1919, Theodore Graebner Papers, Concordia Historical Institute, Saint Louis, box 101.

54. Graebner, "The Vatican and Diplomatic Relationships."

55. "Autocracy in the Saddle," *Lutheran Witness*, March 30, 1920, 100–101; "The Powers Behind the Curtain," *Lutheran Witness*, May 25, 1920, 169.

56. "Roman Catholic Designs," *Lutheran Witness*, January 15, 1914, 19.

57. "Papal Claims," *Lutheran Witness*, December 28, 1915, 409.

58. Graebner, "Moral Issues and Religious Aspects of the War: IV"; Lillegard, "What Should Be the Contribution of the Lutheran Church to the Religious Life of America?"

59. Janssen, "The Roman Catholic Ideal of a League of Nations."

60. Taylor, "The World Movement"; Schmauk, "National Will and World Tragedy," 288; Schmauk, "Politics and the Church," 41–42; "Luther über einer Völkerbund," *Der*

Lutheraner, June 15, 1920, 200–201; Johnston, *Anthology of the Sermons of J. Michael Reu*, vol. 1, 92.

61. Pollard, "Religious Liberty and World Peace"; "Foreign Missions and the Peace Conference," *Missions*, July 1920, 413; Federal Council of the Churches of Christ circular, May 23, 1919, *Congressional Record*, 66th Cong., 1st sess., vol. 58, 6614. The Missouri Synod did not belong to the National Lutheran Council, which conducted the bulk of this pressuring, but it did cooperate with it; see Meyer, *Moving Frontiers*, 411–14.

62. "Lutherische nationalkonzil und die Lutheraner im Ausland," *Lehre und Wehre*, June 1919, 281–82; "Die Konferenz für lutherische Heidenmission in Chicago," *Kirchliche Zeitschrift*, September 1919, 447–52; D. H. Steffens to Theodore Graebner, July 28, 1919, Graebner Papers, box 101.

63. Taylor, "The World Movement," 474–78; "Religious Liberty," *Lutheran Church Herald*, April 20, 1920, 241; Wentz, *Lutherans in Concert*, 50–51; D. H. Steffens to Theodore Graebner, July 28, 1919, Graebner Papers, box 101.

64. "Die Konferenz für lutherische Heidenmission in Chicago"; Meyer, *Moving Frontiers*, chap. 7.

65. Hashinger, "The Contribution of Lutheranism to America"; "Preachers and the Treaty of Peace."

66. See the articles collected by Jacobsen and Trollinger, *Re-forming the Center*, especially Granquist, "Lutherans in the United States."

Chapter 5

1. See Norwood, *The Story of American Methodism*; Hatch and Wigger, *Methodism and the Shaping of American Culture*; and Richey, Rowe, and Schmidt, *Perspectives on American Methodism*.

2. See Chiles, *Theological Transition in American Methodism*.

3. Synan, *The Holiness-Pentecostal Tradition*, 34–50; Stanley, "Wesleyan/Holiness Churches"; Brock, *Freedom from War*, 303–4.

4. Sutton, "'To Extract Poison from the Blessings of Providence'"; Carwadine, "Methodists, Politics, and the Coming of the American Civil War."

5. Meyer, *The Protestant Search for Political Realism*, 38–40, 145–53, 186–88; Powers, *Not Without Honor*, 35, 161.

6. William B. Riley to J. D. Adams, April 5, 1919, Riley Papers, folder 14.

7. The Methodist Episcopal Church in the South did not have an official convention in 1919–21, so it never officially gave its endorsement to the League. However, its bishops and periodicals were consistently supportive of ratification. See Lancaster, "The Protestant Churches," 606–7; Miller, *American Protestantism*, 320.

8. "Problems and Forces of Christian Reconstruction," *Methodist Review*, January 1919, 134; Cooke, "The Church and International Leagues"; Mathews, "The League of Nations"; Lewis, "America the Light of the World."

9. Cooke, *The Church and World Peace*, 32–35, 76–78, 87–92, 97, 102–3, 139–43.

10. Ibid.

11. E. L. Shumaker to Frank B. Brandegee, December 12, 1919, copy in Albert J. Beveridge Papers, box 216, Library of Congress, Manuscripts Division, Washington; Albert J. Beveridge to S. W. Haynes, February 21, 1920, Beveridge Papers, box 220.

12. Henry Robbins to Albert J. Beveridge, November 16, 1919, Beveridge Papers, box 217; *Congressional Record*, 66th Cong., 1st sess., vol. 58, 2067–68 (hereafter 58 CR 1919).

13. Albert J. Beveridge to Meyer Lissner, November 18, 1919, Beveridge Papers, box 216; Albert J. Beveridge to Elmer T. Peterson, July 15, 1920, Beveridge Papers, box 223. For more on Beveridge's religiosity, see Braeman, *Albert J. Beveridge*, 9, 18.

14. The senator in question was Lawrence Y. Sherman. See 58 CR 1919, 66th Cong., 1st sess., 5762–64. For more on Sherman's use of religion in the League debates, see chapter 6.

15. Thwing, *The League of Nations*, 3–6.

16. "China and Japan," *Christian Advocate* (Nashville), July 25, 1919, 931; Meyer, "Justice First for China"; Lancaster, "The Protestant Churches," 610–11, 616–18.

17. Kirby, Richey, and Rowe, *The Methodists*, 331–32; *Who Was Who in America, Volume 1*, 889.

18. Neely, *Present Perils of Methodism*, esp. 89–90, 134–35.

19. Neely, *The League*, 28–29, 118, 128.

20. Ibid., 29, 64–77, 102, 117–26, 193–203.

21. Ibid., 28–29, 69–72, 114–25, 136, 154–57, 215.

22. Ibid., 218–19.

23. "Bishop Neely on the League of Nations," *Christian Workers Magazine*, September 1919, 13–14; Gaebelein, *The League of Nations*, 7–8, 46–48.

24. Lancaster, "The Protestant Churches," 611.

25. Ibid.; Oliver, *The Church and Social Order*, 30–32, 37–38.

26. "Prayer for the League of Nations," *Living Church*, January 11, 1919, 365; "Christians of England and the League of Nations," *Churchman*, January 18, 1919, 70; "The Bishops and the League of Nations: A Symposium," *Living Church*, July 5, 1919, 350–51; Lancaster, "The Protestant Churches," 609.

27. "The Debate in the Senate," *Living Church*, March 1, 1919, 573–74; "Stand Behind the President," *Living Church*, March 8, 1919, 611; "The Senate Does Not Perceive," *Living Church*, March 15, 1919, 643.

28. Addison, *The Episcopal Church*, 280–88, 322–28; May, *Protestant Churches and Industrial America*, 178–87, 239–47. For the British context, see Norman, *The Victorian Christian Socialists*, esp. chaps. 1–3, 10.

29. See Chorley, *Men and Movements in the American Episcopalian Church*; Katerberg, *Modernity and the Dilemma of North American Anglican Identities*.

30. Katerberg, *Modernity and the Dilemma of North American Anglican Identities*, 70–71, 89–91.

31. See Davies, *Worship and Theology in England, Volume V*, 124–30, 134–50.

32. Mullin, *Episcopal Visions / American Reality*, 42–66, 72–76, 87–91, 96, 120–34; Katerberg, *Modernity and the Dilemma of North American Anglican Identities*, 107–14, 123.

33. Pepper, *A Voice from the Crowd*, 134, 140, 147–71, 173; Pepper, *Philadelphia Lawyer*, 297–98, 305–6; Addison, *The Episcopal Church*, 368–76; Katerberg, *Modernity and the Dilemma of North American Anglican Identities*, 112–15, 122, 126–27. See also the further discussion in chapter 7.

34. See Reichley, *Religion in American Public Life*, 179–80, 200–201.

35. Pepper, *Men and Issues*, 27–31.

36. Addison, *The Episcopal Church*, 355–63; Lawrence, *Fifty Years*, 24–31, 54, 56–57, 66–73.

37. Lawrence, *Memories of a Happy Life*, 409, 413–14.

38. "The League of Nations: A Symposium," *Churchman*, April 5, 1919, 15.

39. Shipler, "Side Lights on the General Convention." The vote in favor of this ambiguous statement was fifty-nine to forty-four.

40. "Where We Stand," *Churchman*, March 15, 1919, 6; "The League Again," *Churchman*, April 5, 1919, 7; "Diocesan Conventions and the League," *Churchman*, June 14, 1919, 5–6; "The Treaty of Peace," *Churchman*, October 25, 1919, 9; "The Killing of the Treaty," *Churchman*, March 27, 1920, 8–9.

41. "The Peace Treaty and the Senate," *Living Church*, June 14, 1919, 227–28.

42. Lancaster, "The Protestant Churches," 613–19.

Chapter 6

1. See Stone, *The Irreconcilables*.

2. Stone, *The Irreconcilables*, 6–9, 178–82; Johnson, *The Peace Progressives*, 86–104.

3. See Margulies, *The Mild Reservationists*; Widenor, *Henry Cabot Lodge*.

4. This is covered by Kuehl and Dunn, *Keeping the Covenant*.

5. See Ambrosius, *Woodrow Wilson*; Cooper, *Breaking the Heart of the World*; and, for the anticollectivist track, Ruotsila, *British and American Anticommunism*, esp. 126–31, 146–52.

6. Marshall, *Recollections*, 288–90.

7. *The National Cyclopaedia*, vol. 15, 101; Stone, *The Irreconcilables*, 187–88.

8. 58 CR 1919, 66th Cong., 1st sess., 77683.

9. Thomas's unpublished and untitled autobiography, 353–54, Thomas Papers, box 8; Marshall, *Recollections*, 290.

10. Sherman's notes, n.d. [c. 1905?], Sherman Papers, box 161; Sherman's address, August 4, 1918, Sherman Papers, box 156; Sherman to Warren G. Harding, n.d. [c. 1922], Sherman Papers, box 157.

11. Ruotsila, *British and American Anticommunism*, 60, 78, 93, 97, 100, 117–18, 123–27.

12. Sherman's address, November 28, 1917, Sherman Papers, box 156; Stone, "Two Illinois Senators among the Irreconcilables," 446–50.

13. See Sherman Papers, boxes 74, 76, 132, 133, and 148; Stone, *The Irreconcilables*, 78–81, 104–5.

14. 58 CR 1919, 66th Cong., 1st sess., 7680–83. On the motion to table the Sherman Amendment, fifty-seven voted yes, twenty-seven voted nay, and twelve did not vote. 58 CR 1919, 66th Cong., 1st sess., 7683.

15. Sherman, "My Political Impressions of the War"; Sherman, "Political Psychology of the War," 211–12; 57 CR 1919, 65th Cong., 3rd sess., 58 CR 1919, 66th Cong., 1st sess., 1971, 164–71, 1435–38, 7000, 7680–83.

16. 57 CR 1919, 65th Cong., 1st sess., 1013–14; 58 CR 1919, 66th Cong., 1st sess., 2722–24.

17. 56 CR 1918, 65th Cong., 2nd sess., 8990–92; 57 CR 1919, 65th Cong., 3rd sess., 1969–72, 4867; 58 CR 1919–20, 66th Cong., 1st sess., 164–70, 1013–14, 2722–23.

18. Sherman to Lucy A. Hall, January 6, 1919, Sherman Papers, box 67.

19. 56 CR 1918, 65th Cong., 2nd sess., 5483–91, 8065; 57 CR 1919, 65th Cong., 3rd sess., 2260–62.

20. 58 CR 1919, 66th Cong., 1st sess., 7107.

21. Sherman to George F. Moore, c. June 1919, Sherman Papers, box 148; Sherman's address, July 4, 1920, Sherman Papers, box 157.

22. 58 CR 1919, 66th Cong., 1st sess., 1435–38, 2723; Sherman, "The Aims of the Republican Congress," 738–94.

23. "Catholics Deny a Catholic Peril," *Literary Digest*, July 19, 1919, 32; 58 CR 1919, 66th Cong., 1st sess., 1445–46.

24. 57 CR 1919, 65th Cong., 3rd sess., 4864–65; 58 CR 1919, 66th Cong., 1st sess., 7681–82; Sherman's address, March 9, 1921, Sherman Papers, box 157.

25. Gaebelein, *The League of Nations*, 28–29, 37–38; "The Roman Catholic Church and the League of Nations," *Lutheran Witness*, July 8, 1919, 214–15; Graebner, "The Vatican and Diplomatic Relationships," 231–32; Foster, *The Covenant Treaty*, 3.

26. Theodore Graebner to D. H. Steffens, August 8, 1919, Theodore Graebner Papers, Concordia Historical Institute, Saint Louis, box 101.

27. Livermore, *Woodrow Wilson and the War Congress*, 3.

28. See Phillips, "Asle J. Gronna: Self-Made Man of the Prairies."

29. 58 CR 1919, 66th Cong., 1st sess., 6427–28, 7418, 7427.

30. 58 CR 1919, 66th Cong., 1st sess., 7418–29.

31. 57 CR 1919, 65th Cong., 3rd sess., 2730, 2732–34.

32. 57 CR 1919, 65th Cong., 3rd sess., 4026–27.

33. 58 CR 1919, 66th Cong., 1st sess., 2067–68. See also Scholes, "Philander C. Knox."

34. Foster, *Moral Reconstruction*, 137, 181; Knox, *The Altar of Our Nationality*, 1, 4–6.

35. 58 CR 1919, 66th Cong., 1st sess., 4500–4501, 7681, 7689, 8742.

36. Notes for an address, n.d. [c. May 1919], Philander C. Knox Papers, box 22, Library of Congress, Manuscripts Division, Washington; notes for an address, n.d. [1920], Knox Papers, box 48.

37. 57 CR 1919, 65th Cong., 3rd sess., 603–6, 2420, 4687–94.

38. 58 CR 1919, 66th Cong., 1st sess., 3492–99.

39. See Hughes, *Reviving the Ancient Faith*, 98–116; also see the further discussion in chapter 7. For Fall's career, see Stratton, "New Mexico Machiavellian?" 2–14.

40. 52 CR 1915, 63rd Cong., 3rd sess., 4270.

41. 58 CR 1919, 66th Cong., 1st sess., 3693, 6067–68, 8774–76; 59 CR 1919–20, 66th Cong., 2nd sess., 542, 3619–22; Frank B. Brandegee to Albert J. Beveridge, March 18, 1919, Beveridge Papers, box 214; Stone, *The Irreconcilables*, 118.

42. Cooper, *Breaking the Heart of the World*, 103; Stone, *The Irreconcilables*, 184.

43. Pepper, *In the Senate*, 33; Longworth, *Crowded Hours*, 287.

44. 58 CR 1919, 66th Cong., 1st sess., 6480–81.

45. 58 CR 1919, 66th Cong., 1st sess., 6613–15; Steffens to Graebner, July 28, 1919, Graebner Papers, box 101.

46. 57 CR 1919, 65th Cong., 3rd sess., 2731–32.

47. Meriwether, *Jim Reed*, 15–16, 20–30, 158, 247–51.

48. Reed, *The League of Nations*, 5, 7–9.

49. 58 CR 1919, 66th Cong., 1st sess., 3492–99.

50. 57 CR 1919, 65th Cong., 3rd sess., 603–6, 2420, 4687–94.

51. 58 CR 1919, 66th Cong., 1st sess., 2697–2721 (McCormick); 58 CR 1919, 66th Cong., 1st sess., 2989 (Moses).

52. 58 CR 1919, 66th Cong., 1st sess., 2992–95.

53. 58 CR 1919, 66th Cong., 1st sess., 7888; Fernald, "Will Nationality Survive?" 460–63.

54. Marquis, *Who's Who in America*, vol. 10, 962; Stone, *The Irreconcilables*, 184; "Senator France Outlines Policies," *Baltimore Sun*, May 19, 1920, Joseph I. France Papers, box 8, McKeldin Library, University of Maryland at College Park.

55. 57 CR 1919, 65th Cong., 3rd sess., 1383; 58 CR 1919, 66th Cong., 1st sess., 6598–6615; 59 CR 1919, 66th Cong., 2nd sess., 4684–89.

56. D. H. Steffens to Theodore Graebner, July 28, 1919, Graebner Papers, box 101.

57. 58 CR 1919, 66th Cong., 1st sess., 6612–15.

58. France, "Nikolai Lenine Revolutionist from Boyhood," *Baltimore Sun*, September 19, 1921, France Papers, box 25; "Senator France," *New Republic*, April 7, 1920, 173–75.

59. France's address, April 26, 1918, France Papers, box 25; 58 CR 1919, 66th Cong., 1st sess., 6005; 60 CR 1919, 66th Cong., 2nd sess., 4689.

60. 58 CR 1919, 66th Cong., 1st sess., 7427 (Gronna); 58 CR 1919, 66th Cong., 1st sess., 2989 (Moses).

61. 58 CR 1919, 66th Cong., 1st sess., 2594–95, 4961, 6810, 6817–26. For biographical details, see Lowitt, *George W. Norris*.

62. McKenna, *Borah*, 9–17, 57–58, 91, 127.

63. 58 CR 1919, 66th Cong., 1st sess., 2067, 4350, 4354, 7681.

64. 57 CR 1919, 65th Cong., 3rd sess., 191–96.

65. Borah, "Militarism in a League of Nations?" 303–4.

66. Borah is quoted by McKenna, *Borah*, 153. For clerical comment, see James, "The Saviour or the Senator?" 577–78; "Fruits of Political Preaching," *Lutheran Witness*, January 6, 1920, 7.

67. 58 CR 1919, 66th Cong., 1st sess., 7680–81, 8270–71.

68. See Johnson, *The Peace Progressives*, esp. 3–9, 70–71, 87–97, 152–73, 198–99.

69. 57 CR 1918, 65th Cong., 3rd sess., 727.

70. 58 CR 1919, 66th Cong., 1st sess., 7682.

71. Cooper, *Breaking the Heart of the World*, 40–41; Schriftgiesser, *The Gentleman from Massachusetts*, 327–28.

72. 58 CR 1919, 66th Cong., 1st sess., 5844.

73. 58 CR 1919, 66th Cong., 1st sess., 5219–21.

74. Russell, *The Shadow of Blooming Grove*, 325, 408, 411.

75. 58 CR 1919, 65th Cong., 1st sess., 1265.

76. 58 CR 1919, 66th Cong., 1st sess., 3098, 3100.

77. Cooper, *Breaking the Heart of the World*, 301–14; Margulies, *The Mild Reservationists*, 191–211; Stone, *The Irreconcilables*, 152–60.

78. 58 CR 1919, 66th Cong., 1st sess., 3694.

79. 58 CR 1919, 66th Cong., 1st sess., 6331–32; 58 CR 1919, 66th Cong., 1st sess., 8706–17; 59 CR 1920, 66th Cong., 2nd sess., 3129.

80. 58 CR 1919, 66th Cong., 1st sess., 7957; 59 CR 1920, 66th Cong., 2nd sess., 3129, 6212.

81. 57 CR 1919, 65th Cong., 3rd sess., 3748–55 (Poindexter); 58 CR 1919, 66th Cong., 1st sess., 3318 (Thomas); 58 CR 1919, 66th Cong., 1st sess., 3693–94 (Brandegee); 58 CR 1919, 66th Cong., 1st sess., 4500–4501 (Knox); 58 CR 1919, 66th Cong., 1st sess., 3778–84 (Lodge); 58 CR 1919, 66th Cong., 1st sess., 5840–45 (Frelinghuysen); 58 CR 1919, 66th Cong., 1st sess., 6139 (Fall); 58 CR 1919, 66th Cong., 1st sess., 7889 (Fernald); 58 CR 1919, 66th Cong., 1st sess., 7920–36 (Sherman); 58 CR 1919, 66th Cong., 1st sess., 7938–49 (McCormick); 58 CR 1919, 66th Cong., 1st sess., 7957–61 (Myers and Reed); 58 CR 1919, 66th Cong., 1st sess., 8706–17 (Myers and King); 58 CR 1919, 66th Cong., 1st sess., 8719 (Sterling); 59 CR 1919, 66th Cong., 2nd sess., 3954 (Reed).

82. Cooper, *Breaking the Heart of the World*, 218–20, 232, 340–45.

83. See Merrill, *Reed Smoot*, 254–55.

84. Ibid.; Heath, *In the World*, 418, 449–50.

85. Cooper, *Breaking the Heart of the World*, 194; Margulies, *The Mild Reservationists*, 123–24; Merrill, *Reed Smoot*, 256–58, 261–62.

86. 59 CR 1920, 66th Cong., 2nd sess., 1219–22; "Senator King Would Amend League Plan," *Louisville Courier-Journal*, March 22, 1919; Heath, *In the World*, 410, 421–22.

87. Arrington and Bitton, *The Mormon Experience*, 39, 207–9, 312, 245–46, 290–91; Heath, *In the World*, 449–50, 451.

88. Merrill, *Reed Smoot*, 258; Heath, *In the World*, 418, 419, 423–24, 446.

89. See Freud and Bullitt, *Thomas Woodrow Wilson*.

90. The interpretation offered in Thomas W. Bailey's *Woodrow Wilson and the Great Betrayal* and *Woodrow Wilson and the Lost Peace*—which stressed nationalist, partisan, and personal animosity to Wilson—profoundly influenced later accounts. Cf. Stone, *The Irreconcilables*, 178–82; Adler, *The Isolationist Impulse*, 34–40, 80–90, 102–8; and Widenor, *Henry Cabot Lodge*, 52–71, 269–80, 296–99.

Chapter 7

1. Watterson, "*Marse Henry,*" vol. 2, 297.

2. Marquis, *Who's Who in America, 1918–1919*, 2130; James, *The Dictionary of American Biography*, vol. 3, 400, 402–3.

3. James, *The Dictionary of American Biography*, vol. 11, supplement 1, 733–34, and supplement 3, 330–31.

4. Parkman, "President Hill."

5. Cooper, *Breaking the Heart of the World*, 80–84; Stone, *The Irreconcilables*, 79–82; Pepper, *Philadelphia Lawyer*, 125–31.

6. Lee Meriwether to Henry Watterson, December 9, 1919, Henry Watterson Papers, box 9, Library of Congress, Manuscripts Division, Washington; Henry A. Wise Wood to James A. Reed, October 31, 1919, Beveridge Papers, box 223.

7. *Declaration of Principles of the League for the Preservation of American Independence* (n.p., 1919), 1, copy in the Watterson Papers, box 4. See also Cooper, *Breaking the Heart of the World*, 82–83; Stone, *The Irreconcilables*, 79.

8. Pepper, *League of Nations Primer*, 2–4, 6–7, 8; League for the Preservation of American Independence, *Freedom to Defend Right*, 1–4; Wood, *Address Opposing the Ratification of the Constitution of the League of Nations*, 3–6.

9. Hobbs, *The Conspiracy against the Independence of the American Republic,* 3–7, 10–14; Hobbs, *Would President Wilson's Covenant of the League of Nations Prevent War?* 3–4; *Declaration of Principles of the League for the Preservation of American Independence,* 1.

10. Cooper, *Breaking the Heart of the World,* 83 n. 48.

11. Pepper, *League of Nations Primer,* 2; Hobbs, *Would President Wilson's Covenant of the League of Nations Prevent War?* 4.

12. See Wall, *Henry Watterson.*

13. Krock, *The Editorials of Henry Watterson,* 176–77, 182–83; Watterson, "Marse Henry," vol. 2, 263–64; Watterson, "A Protest against Hypocrisy and Pessimism"; notes for a speech, n.d. [1919], Watterson Papers, reel 5.

14. Wall, *Henry Watterson,* 323–31; Watterson, "Marse Henry," vol. 2, 263–86; Krock, *The Editorials of Henry Watterson,* 427–30; notes for a speech, n.d. [1919], Henry Watterson Papers, Filson Historical Society, Louisville, reel 5.

15. Watterson, "Marse Henry," vol. 1, 20–23, and vol. 2, 297–99.

16. Edward L. Powell to Henry Watterson, December 31, 1910, Watterson Papers, Library of Congress, box 11; Powell to Watterson, October 29, 1918, Watterson Papers, Filson Historical Society, reel 2; "Church Not Losing Hold on Men," newspaper clipping of an address by Watterson, n.d. [1910], Watterson Papers, Filson Historical Society, reel 5.

17. See Brock, *Freedom from War,* 142–52.

18. McAlliser and Tucker, *Journey in Faith,* 68–80, 106–26, 140–46, 216–18; Hughes, *Reviving the Ancient Faith,* 98–116.

19. McAlliser and Tucker, *Journey in Faith,* 237–50, 251–54; Hughes, *Reviving the Ancient Faith,* 12–18, 137–50.

20. "The Dilemma of the Covenanter," *Christian Century,* September 25, 1919, 7–8. For details on Morison and Kirby, see Meyer, *The Protestant Search for Political Realism,* 48–52, 153–58, 204–16, 351–55; McAlliser and Tucker, *Journey in Faith,* 364–79, 397, 422–24. For a similar Churches of Christ comment, see Hughes, *Reviving the Ancient Faith,* 149–50.

21. Krock, *The Editorials of Henry Watterson,* 380–87, 392–96, 398–401, 418–21.

22. Watterson, "The Hope of the World"; "Bishop Candler and Henry Watterson," *Montgomery Advocate,* n.d. [1918], copy in Watterson Papers, Filson Historical Society, reel 5.

23. Watterson, "Marse Henry," vol. 2, 263–64, 280–81.

24. Ibid., vol. 2, 274–75; Watterson, "The League of Nations."

25. Pepper, *The Way,* 121.

26. Pearlman, *To Make Democracy Safe,* 61–62, 88–89, 214–15, 227, 234–37; Pepper, *Philadelphia Lawyer,* 24–25, 101–8, 298–310.

27. Pepper, *A Voice from the Crowd,* 19–20, 45–51, 55–57, 102–3, 145–48, 171, 192–93; Pepper, *Philadelphia Lawyer,* 313, 317; Pepper, *The Way,* 15, 22, 24–25.

28. Pearlman, *To Make Democracy Safe,* 48–49, 59–62, 82–89, 93–103, 122–23, 235–37.

29. Pepper, *Men and Issues,* 8–9, 13–16, 27–31, 57–63, 170–71; Pepper, *Philadelphia Lawyer,* 288–90; Pepper, "The Struggle for World Freedom."

30. Pepper, *Philadelphia Lawyer,* 297–98.

31. Pepper, *A Voice from the Crowd,* 68, 138–40.

32. Pepper, *Philadelphia Lawyer*, 300–310.

33. Pepper, *League of Nations Primer*, 2; Pepper, *Philadelphia Lawyer*, 125–27; Pepper, *In the Senate*, 83–84.

34. Pepper, *A Voice from the Crowd*, 57–59, 138–40.

35. Ibid.

36. *Addresses Delivered by the Rt. Rev. Dr. Charles Gore*, 6.

37. Pepper, *America and the League of Nations*, 3–13; Pepper, *League of Nations Primer*, 2, 4–5, 7–8; Pepper, *In the Senate*, 139.

38. Pepper, "What Is an Anarchist?"

39. Pepper, *In the Senate*, 108–20; Pepper, *Philadelphia Lawyer*, 175–83.

40. Pepper, *Philadelphia Lawyer*, 309–10; George Wharton Pepper to John Spargo, April 10, 1934, George Wharton Pepper Papers, box 9, University Archives and Records Center, University of Pennsylvania, Philadelphia.

41. Bebbington, *Evangelicalism in Modern Britain*, 235–42; Pearlman, *To Make Democracy Safe*, 235–37.

42. Buchman, *Remaking the World*, 4, 14, 20–26, 34, 64–65, 76–77, 108–11.

43. Parkman, *David Jayne Hill*, 67–80, 109–19, 183–84, 202–23.

44. Parkman, "President Hill."

45. See Hill, *Genetic Philosophy*; Hill's handwritten, undated manuscript "Religion and Science"; fragments of other handwritten, untitled notes, David Jayne Hill Papers, box 36, University of Rochester, Rochester.

46. Hill, "Taking Soundings," 678; Hill, *Impressions of the Kaiser*, 115.

47. Hill, *Principles and Fallacies of Socialism*, 8–10, 33–34, 64–66, 96; Hill, "Representative Government"; Hill, *The National Association for Constitutional Government*, 3, 5–7, 9–10.

48. Hill, "Relation of the Emperor and the Pope," n.d., Hill Papers, box 36.

49. See Hill, "Taking Soundings"; Hill, "In the Valley of the Decision"; Hill, *The Rebuilding of Europe*, 49–63.

50. See Hill, "The President's Challenge to the Senate," 738; Hill, "International Law and International Policy"; Hill, "Americanizing the Treaty"; Hill, *Our Great Inheritance*, 5–11; Hill, *Two Lectures on the Revised Covenant*, 5–6, 15–19.

51. Hill, *The Authority of International Law*, 1–12, 14–22, 23–26, 29.

52. Hill, "General Principles of American Foreign Policy," n.d. [1919], Hill Papers, box 28; Hill, "International Law and International Policy"; Hill, "The Obstruction of Peace," 470–71.

53. Hill, *Americanism*, 229–30; Hill, "The Entente of Free Nations"; Hill, "The President's Attack on the Senate."

Chapter 8

1. See Trollinger, *God's Empire*, 41–61; Kazin, *A Godly Hero*.

2. See Carpenter, *Revive Us Again*; Ribuffo, *The Old Christian Right*; Beale, *In Pursuit of Purity*.

3. Contrary to the popular impression, opinion polls of the mid-1930s showed that less than half of Protestant clergy actually hoped for U.S. membership in the League. Kuehl and Dunn, *Keeping the Covenant*, 61.

4. Marty, *Modern American Religion, Volume 2*, 230–33; Eighmy, *Churches in Cultural Captivity*, 98–99; Miller, *American Protestantism and Social Issues*, 323–25.

5. Riley, *Wanted: A World Leader!* 18–19; Grether, "Disarmament and the Signs of the Times"; "Current Events in the Light of the Bible," *Our Hope*, January 1922, 433–34.

6. "The Twelfth Convention of the World's Christian Fundamentals Association," *The Christian Fundamentalist*, July 1929, 248.

7. Dulles, *Peace or War*, 34–41, 198–204; Pruessen, *John Foster Dulles*, 187, 190–217.

8. Bachman, *The United Lutheran Church*, 234.

9. Norwood, *The Story of American Methodism*, 411–12.

10. For decades to come, evangelicals would return in righteous anger to this felt blasphemy; see Hagee, *Final Dawn over Jerusalem*, 196.

11. Hoopes and Brinkley, *FDR and the Creation of the U.N.*, 111–20, 184–204; Alcock, *History of the International Labor Office*, 176–85, 284–87.

12. Federal Council of Churches of Christ press statement, June 26, 1945, Walter A. Maier Papers, box 73, Concordia Historical Institute, Saint Louis.

13. See Lower, *A Bloc of One*, 335; Smith, *Thomas E. Dewey and His Times*, 382–95, 412–13.

14. "The San Francisco Conference," *King's Business*, June 1945, 207; "The Charter," *King's Business*, September 1945, 327; "Current Events in the Light of the Bible," *Our Hope*, October 1946, 244; "Current Events in the Light of the Bible," *Our Hope*, January 1947, 426.

15. Riley, *Righting a Wrecked World*, 3–7, 11–15.

16. Riley, *The Only Solution for the Sordid World Problems!* 5; Riley, "The Church and World Redemption"; Riley, *Righting a Wrecked World*, 13.

17. No evangelicals were consulted. See Nurser, *For All Peoples and All Nations*; Glendon, *A World Made New*.

18. "Current Events in the Light of the Bible," *Our Hope*, December 1948, 354; "Leave God Out," *King's Business*, December 1948, 5.

19. Smith, *The Increasing Peril*, 9–15, 39–40; Gordon, "'UNESCO.'"

20. "Human Rights in an Age of Tyranny," *Christianity Today*, February 4, 1957, 22.

21. Bauman, "The Nations Marshalling for Armageddon."

22. Matthews, "Christ and Communism."

23. McIntire, *The Modern Tower of Babel*; McIntire, *Servants of Apostasy*.

24. Lindsey, *The Late Great Planet Earth*, 137.

25. See Boyer, *When Time Shall Be No More*; Claburgh, *Thunder on the Right*.

26. See Lienesch, *Redeeming America*; Wilcox, *God's Warriors*; Martin, *With God on Our Side*.

27. McIntire, *Servants of Apostasy*, 198; McDowell, *Barry Goldwater*, 99–101.

28. Maier, *Broadcasts of His Grace*, 51–61, 163–64, 252–53; Walter A. Maier sermon notes, May 7 and 14, 1944, and November 20, 1945, Maier Papers, box 12.

29. See Van Til, *The Defense of the Faith*, 179–218; Roberts, "Cornelius Van Til."

30. See Barron, *Heaven on Earth?*

31. Rushdoony, *The Nature of the American System*, 113.

32. Ibid., 113–32.

33. Ibid.

34. Ibid., 52, 63, 86–90, 113–32, 140–56; North, *Conspiracy*.

35. Rushdoony, *The Nature of the American System*, 146.

36. See Buss and Herman, *Globalizing Family Values*; Butler, *Born Again*.

37. Kah, *The Demonic Roots of Globalism*, 53–56, 90–91, 131–37; LaHaye and Jenkins, *Are We Living in the End Times?* 167–87, 234, 326–34; Hunt, *A Woman Rides the Beast*, 38–99 (quotation).

38. Hagee, *Day of Deception*, 49–54, 62; Robertson, *The New World Order*, 31–32, 54–58, 131–43, 207–8; LaHaye and Jenkins, *Are We Living in the End Times?* 167–77, 195–205; Buss and Herman, *Globalizing Family Values*, 22, 60–64, 70–75.

39. Halper and Clarke, *America Alone*, 58–60, 86–91; Friedman, *The Neoconservative Revolution*, 207–22.

40. Buchanan, *The Great Betrayal*.

41. See Buss and Herman, *Globalizing Family Values*, 142–43; Butler, *Born Again*, 55, 78–81; Kaplan, *With God on Their Side*, 31–33, 224–42.

42. See Frykholm, *Rapture Culture*.

43. Diamond, *Not by Politics Alone*, 45, 198, 202–3.

44. Robertson, *The New World Order*, xi–xii, 4–14, 37–67, 92–96, 109, 158–63, 226–59.

45. See ibid., 6–14, 56–59, 252–68; Robertson, *The New Millennium*, 264–67, 284–318. See also Hagee, *Day of Deception*, 52–54.

46. Lind, "Rev. Robertson's Grand International Conspiracy Theory."

47. See Weber, *On the Road to Armageddon*, 175–86, 213–48.

48. See Lincoln, *Holy Terrors*, 30–32; Kaplan, *With God on Their Side*, 13–22; Kengor, *God and George W. Bush*, 128–32, 144–63, 217–18, 316–19; Northcott, *An Angel Directs the Storm*, 58–67, 73–93.

Conclusion

1. See Gamble, *The War for Righteousness*, 2–23, 25–67.

Bibliography

Manuscript Collections

Albert J. Beveridge Papers, Library of Congress, Manuscripts Division, Washington.
Randall T. Davidson Papers, Lambeth Palace Library, London.
Theodore Graebner Papers, Concordia Historical Institute, Saint Louis.
David Jayne Hill Papers, Department of Rare Books and Special Collections, University of Rochester Library, Rochester.
J. Gresham Machen Papers, Westminster Theological Seminary, Philadelphia.
Walter A. Maier Papers, Concordia Historical Institute, Saint Louis.
J. C. Massee Papers, American Baptist Historical Society, Atlanta.
George Wharton Pepper Papers, University of Pennsylvania, Philadelphia.
William B. Riley Papers, Northwestern College, Saint Paul.
Lawrence Y. Sherman Papers, Abraham Lincoln Presidential Library, Springfield, Illinois.
J. R. Straton Papers, American Baptist Historical Society, Atlanta.
William Howard Taft Papers (microfilm), Library of Congress, Washington.
Charles S. Thomas Papers, Colorado Historical Society, Denver.
Henry Watterson Papers (microfilm), Filson Historical Society, Louisville.
Henry Watterson Papers, Library of Congress, Manuscripts Division, Washington.

Contemporary Books, Pamphlets, and Signed Articles

Addams, Jane. "Feed the World and Save the League." *New Republic*, November 24, 1920, 326.
Addresses Delivered by the Rt. Rev. Dr. Charles Gore, Lord Bishop of Oxford, and Mr. George Wharton Pepper at a Luncheon Given in Honor of the Rt. Rev. Dr. Charles Gore at the Ritz-Carlton Hotel, Philadelphia, Mr. Joseph Widenor Presiding, Thursday, October Thirty-first, 1918. N.p., 1918.
Advent Testimony Messages, Delivered at the Meeting at Queen's Hall, London, December 13th, 1917. London: Chas. J. Thynne, 1918.
Ames, Allan P. "What Shall We Do with Victory?" *Watchman-Examiner*, October 17, 1918, 1310–11.

Baptist Fundamentals, Being Addresses Delivered at the Pre-Convention Conference at Buffalo, June 21 and 22, 1920. Philadelphia: Judson Press, 1920.

Bauman, Louis S. "The Nations Marshalling for Armageddon." *King's Business*, December 1950, 13–15, 30.

Baushlin, Daniel H. "The Collapse of a Bad Theory." *Lutheran Quarterly*, April 1919, 161–97.

Behnken, J. W. "Testimonials for Old-Fashioned Truths." *Theological Quarterly*, April 1920, 65–82.

Borah, William E. "Militarism in a League of Nations? An International Superstate Resting upon Prussian Force." *The Forum*, March 1919, 298–305.

Brandt, Walther I., ed. *Luther's Works, Volume 45: The Christian in Society, II.* Philadelphia: Fortress Press, 1962.

Bridgman, Raymond L. "A World-Unity Conference." *Biblioteca Sacra*, January 1918, 133–42.

Buchanan, Patrick J. *The Great Betrayal: How American Sovereignty and Social Justice Are Being Sacrificed to the Gods of the Global Economy.* Boston: Little, Brown, 1998.

Buchman, Frank D. *Remaking the World: The Speeches of Frank D. Buchman.* London: Blandford Press, 1947.

Burton, Ernest D. "Ought the United States to Be a Missionary Nation?" *Baptist*, February 21, 1920, 120–21.

Carver, William Owen. "'The Church and World Peace' by Bishop Richard J. Cooke," *Review and Expositor*, July 1920, 366–67.

———. "The Effect of the War on Foreign Missions." *Baptist World*, May 29, 1919, 3.

———. "'Some Aspects of International Christianity' by John Kelman." *Review and Expositor*, October 1920, 478–80.

Cooke, Richard J. "The Church and International Leagues." *Methodist Review*, March 1919, 203–18.

———. *The Church and World Peace.* New York: Abingdon Press, 1920.

Crane, Frank. "The Cement of the League of Nations." *World Outlook*, June 1919, 5.

Croly, Herbert. "The Obstacle to Peace." *New Republic*, April 26, 1919, 404–6.

Dixon, A. C. "The League of Nations." *King's Business*, May 1919, 402–5.

Dulles, John Foster. *Peace or War.* London: George D. Harrap, 1950.

Edmonds, Richard H. "Against the League of Nations." *Religious Herald*, July 17, 1919, 9.

Erdman, William J. "The Prophetic Mold of the Present Dispensation." *Our Hope*, February 1920, 476–78.

Faunce, William H. P. "The Church and Social Reconstruction." *Standard*, May 31, 1919, 991–92.

Fereday, W. W. "After the Great War." *Our Hope*, July 1919, 33–38.

———. "The Present Crisis." *Our Hope*, December 1914, 361.

Fernald, Bert M. "Will Nationality Survive? Influence of the League on Diplomatic and Social Conditions." *The Forum*, September 1919, 460–63.

Fischer, William E. "Christ's Return to Judgement." *Lutheran Quarterly*, July 1919, 330–53.

Foster, J. M. *The Covenant Treaty: Humanity's Despair.* N.p., 1919.

———. *Reformation Principles: Stated and Applied.* Chicago: Fleming H. Revell, 1890.

———. "Rome, the Antagonist of the Nation." In *The Fundamentals: A Testimony to the Times*, vol. 11. Chicago: Testimony Publishing Co, n.d.

Gaebelein, Arno C. "The Capture of Jerusalem and the Great Future of That City." In *Christ and Glory: Addresses Delivered at the New York Prophetic Conference, Carnegie Hall, November 25–28, 1918*, ed. A. C. Gaebelein. New York: Publication Office, Our Hope, 1918.

———. *The Conflict of the Ages: The Mystery of Lawlessness: Its Origin, Historic Development, and Coming Defeat*. New York: Publication Office, Our Hope, 1936.

———. *Current Events in the Light of the Bible*. New York: Publication Office, Our Hope, 1914.

———. *Half a Century: Autobiography of a Servant*. New York: Publication Office, Our Hope, 1930.

———. *The League of Nations in the Light of the Bible*. New York: Publication Office, Our Hope, 1919.

———. "The Pre-Eminence of the Lord Jesus Christ and His Coming Glory." In *Christ and Glory: Addresses Delivered at the New York Prophetic Conference, Carnegie Hall, November 25–28, 1918*, ed. A. C. Gaebelein. New York: Publication Office, Our Hope, 1918.

Gaffin, Richard B., ed. *Redemptive History and Biblical Interpretation: The Shorter Writings of Geerhardus Vos*. Phillipsburg, N.J.: P&R Publishing, 1980.

Gage, Daniel S. "Problems of Peace." *Princeton Theological Review* 18 (January 1920): 123–56.

Gannett, Lewis S. "The Third Internationale." *Survey*, February 8, 1919, 660–61.

Gimmell, Benjamin M. "The League of Nations." *Presbyterian*, February 20, 1919, 9–10.

God Hath Spoken: Twenty-five Addresses Delivered at the World Conference on Christian Fundamentals, May 25–June 1, 1919. New York: Garland Publishing, 1988.

Gordon, Ernest, "'UNESCO,' a Dangerous Movement." *Sunday School Times*, July 12, 1947, 673–74, 692.

Gordon, James L. "Predictions about the Peace Table." *Christian World Pulpit*, January 15, 1919, 32.

Gore, Charles. *The League of Nations: The Opportunity for the Church*. London: Hodder & Stoughton, 1918.

Graebner, Theodore. "Moral Issues and Religious Aspects of the Great War: III. Shall We Go to War 'for Humanity'?" *Lutheran Witness*, May 2, 1916, 126–28.

———. "Moral Issues and Religious Aspects of the War: IV. Will They Make the Pope King?" *Lutheran Witness*, December 12, 1916, 383–85.

———. "The Vatican and Diplomatic Relationships." *Theological Monthly*, August–September 1921, 225–34.

Gray, James M. "The Age and Its Apostasy." *Christian Herald*, May 1, 1918, 537.

———. "The English Manifesto on the Second Advent." *Christian Herald*, February 20, 1918, 208, 237.

———. "The League of Nations and the Danger of Federation." *Moody Bible Institute Monthly*, September 1920, 7–8.

———. *Prophecy and the Lord's Return: A Collection of Popular Articles and Addresses*. New York: Fleming H. Revell, 1917.

———. "Prophecy Changing the Map of Europe." *Christian Herald*, May 29, 1918, 667.

Grether, D. "Disarmament and the Signs of the Times." *Moody Bible Institute Monthly*, February 1922, 806.

Haas, John A. W. *Freedom and Christian Conduct: An Ethic*. New York: Macmillan, 1923.
———. "The Present Problems of Political Philosophy." *Lutheran Church Review*, April 1918, 179–94.
———. *The Problem of the Christian State*. Boston: Stratford, 1928.
Hagee, John. *Day of Deception: Separating Truth from Falsehood in These Last Days*. Nashville: Thomas Nelson, 1996.
———. *Final Dawn over Jerusalem*. Nashville: Thomas Nelson, 1998.
Hall, Arthur J. "Fundamental Factors in World Peace." *Lutheran Quarterly*, January 1919, 61–72.
Hashinger, W. Roy. "The Contribution of Lutheranism to America." *Lutheran Church Review*, January 1918, 45–46.
Heath, Harvard, ed. *In the World: The Diaries of Reed Smoot*. Salt Lake City: Signature Books, 1997.
Henderson, Arthur. *The League of Nations and Labor*. London: Oxford University Press, 1918.
Herron, George D. "Labor and the New Order." *The Appeal to Reason*, May 19, 1917, 1.
———. *The Menace of Peace*. London: George Allen and Unwin, 1917.
———. *Woodrow Wilson and the World's Peace*. New York: Mitchell Kennerly, 1917.
Hertzberger, F. W. "Perverted Democracy and Religious Education." *Theological Quarterly*, July 1919, 129–41.
Hill, David Jayne. *Americanism: What It Is*. New York: D. Appleton, 1918.
———. "Americanizing the Treaty." *North American Review*, August 1919, 158–70.
———. *American World Policies*. New York: George H. Doran, 1920.
———. *The Authority of International Law*. New York: N.p., 1919.
———. "The Entente of Free Nations." *North American Review*, January 1919, 16–27.
———. *Genetic Philosophy*. New York: Macmillan, 1893.
———. *Impressions of the Kaiser*. London: Chapman and Hall, 1919.
———. "International Law and International Policy." *North American Review*, March 1919, 320–29.
———. "In the Valley of Indecision." *North American Review*, July 1919, 18–23.
———. *The National Association for Constitutional Government: A Statement of Its Aims and Purposes*. Washington, D.C.: National Association for Constitutional Government, 1920.
———. "The Obstruction of Peace." *North American Review*, April 1919, 453–71.
———. *Our Great Inheritance: An Address Before the Daughters of the American Revolution and the Sons of the American Revolution on February 22nd, 1919*. Washington, D.C.: National Association for Constitutional Government, 1919.
———. "The President's Attack on the Senate." *North American Review*, November 1919, 592–603.
———. "The President's Challenge to the Senate." *North American Review*, June 1919, 738–44.
———. *Principles and Fallacies of Socialism*. New York: John W. Lowell, 1885.
———. *The Rebuilding of Europe: A Survey of Forces and Conditions*. New York: Century Company, 1917.
———. "Representative Government." *Constitutional Review*, April 1917, 3–10.
———. "Taking Soundings." *North American Review*, May 1914, 673–83.

———. *Two Lectures on the Revised Covenant of the League of Nations.* Washington, D.C.: George Washington University, 1919.

Hobbs, William H. *The Conspiracy against the Independence of the American Republic.* Ann Arbor, Mich.: League for the Preservation of American Independence, 1920.

———. *Would President Wilson's Covenant for the League of Nations Prevent War?* Ann Arbor, Mich.: League for the Preservation of American Independence, 1920.

Hunt, Dave. *A Woman Rides the Beast: The Roman Catholic Church and the Last Days.* Eugene, Ore.: Harvest House, 1994.

James, Fleming. "The Saviour or the Senator?" *The Living Church,* March 1, 1919, 577–78.

Janssen, Weert. "The Roman Catholic Ideal of a League of Nations." *Lutheran Witness,* May 13, 1919, 150–51.

Jefferson, Charles E. "The League of Nations and Religion." *Christian Century,* March 13, 1919, 7–8.

Johnston, Paul J., ed. *Anthology of the Sermons of J. Michael Reu.* 2 vols. Lewiston, N.Y.: Edwin Mellen Press, 1995.

Kah, Gary. *The Demonic Roots of Globalism.* Lafayette, La.: Huntington House, 1995.

Keyser, Leander S. *The Conflict of Fundamentalism and Modernism.* Burlington, Iowa: Lutheran Literary Board, 1926.

———. *Contending for the Faith: Essays in Constructive Criticism and Positive Apologetics.* New York: George H. Doran, 1920.

———. "Handling the Word of Truth Aright: Its Importance for the Lutheran Church." *Lutheran Quarterly,* January 1919, 94–111.

Kistler, Charles E. "No New World as Yet." *Lutheran Church Review,* January 1920, 19–24.

Knox, Philander C. *The Altar of Our Nationality: Address of Hon. Philander C. Knox Delivered at Independence Square, Philadelphia, July Fourth, 1921.* Washington, D.C.: U.S. Government Printing Office, 1921.

Krock, Arthur, ed. *The Editorials of Henry Watterson.* Louisville: Louisville Courier-Journal Publishing Company, 1923.

Kuyper, Abraham. *Calvinism.* London: Sovereign Grace Union, 1932.

LaHaye, Tim, and Jerry Jenkins. *Are We Living in the End Times?* Wheaton, Ill.: Tyndale House, 1999.

Lawrence, William. *Fifty Years.* Boston: Houghton Mifflin, 1923.

———. *Memories of a Happy Life.* Boston: Houghton Mifflin, 1926.

League for the Preservation of American Independence. *Declaration of Principles of the League for the Preservation of American Independence.* N.p., 1919.

———. *Freedom to Defend Right: Freedom to Refuse to Fight: Freedom to Mind Our Own Business.* N.p., 1919.

Lewis, John Tillery. "America the Light of the World." *Christian Advocate* (Nashville), May 9, 1919, 584.

Lillegard, George O. "What Should Be the Contribution of the Lutheran Church to the Religious Life of America? I." *Lutheran Witness,* April 29, 1919, 129–31.

Lindsey, Hal. *The Late Great Planet Earth.* In *The Greatest Works of Hal Lindsey.* New York: Inspirational Press, 1994.

Link, Arthur S., et al., eds. *The Papers of Woodrow Wilson.* 68 vols. Princeton, N.J.: Princeton University Press, 1966–93.

Longworth, Alice Roosevelt. *Crowded Hours: Reminiscences of Alice Roosevelt Longworth*. New York: Charles Scribner's Sons, 1933.

Luther, Martin. "Temporal Authority: To What Extent It Should Be Obeyed." In *Luther's Works, Volume 45: The Christian in Society*, ed. Walther I. Brandt. Philadelphia: Fortress Press, 1962.

Machen, J. Gresham. *Christianity and Liberalism*. Grand Rapids: William B. Eerdmans, 1999 (reprint of 1923 edition).

———. "The Church and the War." *Presbyterian*, May 29, 1919, 10–11.

———. "Does Fundamentalism Obstruct Social Progress? The Negative." *Survey Graphic*, July 1924, 392.

———. *God Transcendent*. Edinburgh: Banner of Truth Trust, 1982.

Maier, Walter A. *Global Broadcasts of His Grace: Radio Messages of the Second Part of The Fourteenth Lutheran Hour*. Saint Louis: Concordia Publishing House, 1949.

Marshall, Thomas R. *Recollections of Thomas R. Marshall, Vice President and Hoosier Philosopher: A Hoosier Salad*. Indianapolis: Bobbs-Merrill, 1925.

Massee, J. C. *The Second Coming*. Philadelphia: Philadelphia School of the Bible, 1919.

Mathews, J. B. "Christ and Communism." *Christian Beacon*, August 28, 1958, 7.

Mathews, Shailer. *The Gospel and the Modern Man*. New York: Macmillan, 1910.

Mathews, Thomas B. "The League of Nations." *Christian Advocate* (Nashville), October 31, 1919, 1401.

McIntire, Carl. *The Modern Tower of Babel*. Collingswood, N.J.: Christian Beacon Press, 1949.

———. *Servants of Apostasy*. Collingswood, N.J.: Christian Beacon Press, 1955.

Meyer, Henry H. "Justice First for China." *Sunday School Journal*, September 1919, 513–15.

Minutes of the First Convention of the United Lutheran Church in America, New York City, November 14–18, 1918. Philadelphia: Board of Publication of the United Lutheran Church in America, 1919.

Minutes of the Second Biennial Convention of the United Lutheran Church in America, Washington, DC, October 19–27, 1920. N.p., 1920.

Minutes of the Sixteenth Biennial Convention of the United Synod of the Evangelical Lutheran Church in the South. N.p., 1918.

Moore, John M. "The League of Nations." *Watchman-Examiner*, March 20, 1919, 355–56.

Mottern, R. W. "Blessings of the War." *Lutheran Church Work and Observer*, February 27, 1919, 6.

Mullins, Edgar Young. "Recent Phases of Democracy." *Review and Expositor*, April 1920, 158–66.

Myers, Cortland. *Christ Is Coming Back*. N.p., n.d.

———. "Things Not Shaken." In *Baptist Fundamentals, Delivered at the Pre-Convention Conference at Buffalo, June 21 and 22, 1920*. Philadelphia: Judson Press, 1920.

———. "War on German Theology." In *Light on Prophecy: A Coordinated, Constructive Teaching, Being the Proceedings and Addresses at the Philadelphia Prophetic Conference, May 28–30, 1918*. New York: Christian Herald, 1918.

Neely, Thomas Benjamin. *The League: The Nation's Danger: A Study of the So-Called "League of Nations."* Philadelphia: E. A. Yakel, 1919.

———. *Present Perils of Methodism*. Philadelphia: E. A. Yakel, 1920.

Nevins, W. M. "Unfair to Roosevelt." *Baptist World*, February 4, 1919, 4.

North, Gary. *Conspiracy: A Biblical View*. Tyler, Tex.: Dominion Press, 1996.

Panton, D. M. "The Latest Preparations of Antichrist." *Moody Bible Institute Monthly* 21 (September 1920): 14–15, 24.

Peercy, R. B. "The World's Unfinished Task." *Lutheran*, July 15, 1920, 179.

Pepper, George Wharton. *America and the League of Nations*. London: N.p., 1920.

———. *In the Senate*. Philadelphia: University of Pennsylvania Press, 1930.

———. *League of Nations Primer: An Analysis of the League Covenant through Questions and Answers*. New York: League for the Preservation of American Independence, 1919.

———. *Men and Issues: A Selection of Speeches and Articles*. New York: Duffield, 1924.

———. *Philadelphia Lawyer: An Autobiography*. Philadelphia: J. P. Lippincott, 1944.

———. "The Struggle for World Freedom." In *Win the War for Permanent Peace: Addresses Made at the National Convention of the League to Enforce Peace, in the City of Philadelphia, May 16th and 17th, 1918*. New York: League to Enforce Peace, 1918.

———. *A Voice from the Crowd*. New Haven, Conn.: Yale University Press, 1915.

———. *The Way: A Devotional Book for Boys*. London: Longmans, Green, 1909.

———. "What Is an Anarchist?" *North American Review*, October 1919, 470–74.

Pfatteicher, E. P. "'Christian Internationalism.'" *Lutheran Church Review*, October 1919, 356–61.

Pollard, Edward B. "Religious Liberty and World Peace." *Watchman-Examiner*, December 26, 1918, 1593.

Proceedings of the Forty-eighth Convention of the General Synod of the Evangelical Lutheran Church in the United States. N.p., 1918.

Rall, H. F. "Methodism and Premillennialism." *Methodist Review*, March 1920, 209–19.

Ranck, Henry H. "Christianizing International Relations." *Reformed Church Review*, October 1918, 425–52.

Rauschenbusch, Walter. *A Theology for the Social Gospel*. New York: Wipf and Stock, n.d. (reprint of 1917 edition).

Reed, James A. *The League of Nations, Speech of Senator James A. Reed of Missouri in the United States Senate, September 22, 1919*. Washington, D.C.: U.S. Government Printing Office, 1919.

Reu, J. Michael. "Homiletical Sketches on Old Testament Texts." *Kirchliche Zeitschrift*, November–December 1919, 570–71.

———. "Homiletical Sketches on the Gospels of the Church Year." *Kirchliche Zeitschrift*, July–August 1919, 388–89.

Riley, William B. "Challenge of Orthodoxy." *School and Church* 2, July–September 1920, 361–72.

———. "The Church and World Redemption." *King's Business*, January 1946, 4–5.

———. "The Eclipse of Faith." *School and Church* 2, April–June 1920, 313–20.

———. "The Fall of Mystical Babylon." *School and Church*, October 1918, 82–85.

———. *The Gospel for War Times*. Los Angeles: BIOLA, 1918.

———. "The Great Divide." In *God Hath Spoken: Twenty-five Addresses Delivered at the World Conference on Christian Fundamentals, May 25–June 1, 1919*. New York: Garland Publishing, 1988.

———. "Inter-Church World Movement." *School and Church* 2, April–June 1920, 320–25.

———. "The Last Day; the Last War and the Last King." In *Christ and Glory: Addresses Delivered at the New York Prophetic Conference, Carnegie Hall, November 25–28, 1918*, ed. A. C. Gaebelein. New York: Publication Office, Our Hope, 1918.

———. *The Only Solution for the Sordid World Problems!* Minneapolis: N.p., 1945.

———. *Reasons for the King's Delay*. Chicago: Star Printing Co. [1897?].

———. *Righting a Wrecked World*. Minneapolis: N.p., n.d.

———. "The Significant Signs of the Times." In *The Coming and the Kingdom of Christ: A Stenographic Report of the Prophetic Bible Conference Held at the Moody Bible Institute of Chicago, February 24–27, 1914*. Chicago: Bible Institute Colportage Association, 1914.

———. "A Study in Revelation. The Usurper's Short Reign." *School and Church* 2, April 1918, 74–76.

———. "Wanted: A World Leader!" N.p., 1940.

———. "When Will the Lord Come." In *Christ and Glory: Addresses Delivered at the New York Prophetic Conference, Carnegie Hall, November 25–28, 1918*, ed. A. C. Gaebelein. New York: Publication Office, Our Hope, 1918.

———. "The World Premillennial Conference v. The Coming Confederacy." *School and Church*, January–March 1919, 91–96.

Robertson, Pat. *The New Millennium*. Dallas: Word, 1990.

———. *The New World Order*. Dallas: Word, 1991.

Roehner, Henry C. "Let the Churches Speak Out." *Lutheran Church Work and Observer*, December 19, 1918, 5.

Root, Elihu. *Letters of the Hon. Elihu Root Relative to the League of Nations*. Washington, D.C.: U.S. Government Printing Office, 1919.

Ross, E. A. *Social Control: A Survey of the Foundations of Order*. Cleveland: Press of Case Western Reserve University, 1969 (reprint of 1901 edition).

Rushdoony, Rousas J. *The Nature of the American System*. Fairfax, Va.: Thoburn Press, 1978.

Russell, Robert McWatty. "The Earthly Destiny of Israel." *Christian Workers Magazine* 16 (January 1916): 362–66.

Schmauk, Theodore E. "National Will and World Tragedy." *Lutheran Church Review*, July 1918, 280–88.

———. "Politics and the Church." *Lutheran Church Review*, January 1920, 32–42.

Schoenfeld, William. "Old Truths for a New Age." *Theological Quarterly*, April 1919, 65–88.

Scott, Walter. "Signs of the Near Return of Our Lord." *Our Hope*, August 1921, 116–23.

Sherman, Lawrence Y. "The Aims of the Republican Congress: Some of the Problems That Our Legislators Must Grapple." *The Forum*, December 1918, 738–43.

———. "My Political Impressions of the War, Act I: Prologue to the Safety of Democracy." *The Forum*, July 1919, 1–10.

———. "The Political Morality of Democracy, Act III of the National Drama and Unpublished Epilogue." *The Forum*, September 1919, 292–97.

———. "Political Psychology of the War, II: Unfolding of the National Drama." *The Forum*, August 1919, 206–13.

Shipler, Guy Emory. "Side Lights on the General Convention." *Churchman*, October 25, 1919, 20–21.

Shotwell, James M., ed. *The Origins of the International Labor Organization*, vol. 2. New York: Columbia University Press, 1934.

Sinclair, Upton. "Explaining President Wilson." *Appeal to Reason*, August 23, 1919, 4.

Skevington, Samuel. "A Great War and Peace Meeting." *Standard*, October 5, 1918, 107.

Smith, Wilbur. *The Increasing Peril of Permitting the Dissemination of Atheistic Doctrines on the Part of Some Agencies of the United States Government*. Chicago: Van Kampen Press, 1947.

Snape, John. "'On Earth Peace.'" *Standard*, October 4, 1919, 103.

Spargo, John. "Christian Socialism in America." *American Journal of Sociology* 15 (1909–10): 16–20.

———. *Marxian Socialism and Religion*. New York: B. W. Huebsch, 1915.

———. "Socialism and Internationalism." *Atlantic Monthly*, September 1917, 300–301.

———. *The Spiritual Significance of Modern Socialism*. New York: B. W. Huebsch, 1908.

Sproul, R. C. *The Last Days According to Jesus*. Grand Rapids: Baker Books, 1998.

Stalker, James. "Kant on Perpetual Peace." *Review and Expositor*, July 1919, 273–77.

Strong, Augustus Hopkins. "My Views on the Universe in General." *Baptist*, May 29, 1920, 625–26.

Taft, William Howard. *The Obligations of Victory*. New York: League to Enforce Peace, 1918.

———. *Why Is a League of Nations Necessary?* New York: League to Enforce Peace, 1918.

Taylor, J. J. "Supplanting the Gospel." *Religious Herald*, July 31, 1919, 9.

Taylor, S. Earl. "The World Movement." *Lutheran Quarterly*, October 1919, 468–78.

Thomas, W. H. Griffith. "The German Attitude to the Bible." *Biblioteca Sacra*, April 1919, 165–75.

———. "German Moral Abnormality." *Biblioteca Sacra*, January 1919, 84–104.

Thwing, Eugene. *The League of Nations as a Moral Issue*. N.p., 1919.

Torrey, Reuben A. "The Blessed Hope." In *Christ and Glory: Addresses Delivered at the New York Prophetic Conference, Carnegie Hall, November 25–28, 1918*, ed. A. C. Gaebelein. New York: Publication Office, Our Hope, 1918.

———. *The Return of the Lord Jesus: The Key to the Scripture, and the Solution of All Our Political and Social Problems, or the Golden Age That Is Soon Coming to the Earth*. Los Angeles: BIOLA, 1913.

Triglot Concordia: The Symbolical Books of the Ev. Lutheran Church. Saint Louis: Concordia Publishing House, 1921.

Van Til, Cornelius. *The Defense of the Faith*. Phillipsburg, N.J.: Presbyterian and Reformed Publishing Company, 1967.

Vos, Geerhardus. *Biblical Theology: Old and New Testaments*. Edinburgh: Banner of Truth Trust, 1996 (reprint of 1948 edition).

———. "Eschatology of the New Testament." In *Redemptive History and Biblical Interpretation: The Shorter Writings of Geerhardus Vos*, ed. Richard B. Gaffin Jr. Phillipsburg, Pa.: P&R Publishing, 1980.

———. "The Eschatology of the Psalter." *Princeton Theological Review* 18 (January 1920): 1–43.

———. *Grace and Glory: Sermons Preached in the Chapel of Princeton Theological Seminary*. Edinburgh: Banner of Truth Trust, 1994.

———."Hebrews, the Epistle of the Diatheke." In *Redemptive History and Biblical Interpretation: The Shorter Writings of Geerhardus Vos*, ed. Richard B. Gaffin Jr. Phillipsburg, Pa.: P&R Publishing, 1980.

———. "The Kingdom of God." In *Redemptive History and Biblical Interpretation: The Shorter Writings of Geerhardus Vos*, ed. Richard B. Gaffin Jr. Phillipsburg, Pa.: P&R Publishing, 1980.

———. *Redemptive History and Biblical Interpretation: The Shorter Writings of Geerhardus Vos*, ed. Richard B. Gaffin Jr. Phillipsburg, Pa.: P&R Publishing, 1980.

———. "The Second Coming and the Millennium." In *Redemptive History and Biblical Interpretation: The Shorter Writings of Geerhardus Vos*, ed. Richard B. Gaffin Jr. Phillipsburg, Pa.: P&R Publishing, 1980.

Wadsworth, Charles, Jr. *Nebuchadnezzar's Image: A Modern View of an Ancient Autocrat.* N.p., 1920.

Walling, William E. "Comparison of Wilsonian Peace Terms and the Socialists of the Entente." *New Appeal*, September 21, 1918, 1, 4.

Warfield, Benjamin Breckinridge. *Biblical Doctrines*. New York: Oxford University Press, 1929.

Watterson, Henry. *The Editorials of Henry Watterson*, ed. Arthur Krock. Louisville: Louisville Courier-Journal Company, 1923.

———. "The Hope of the World." *Watchman-Examiner*, September 5, 1918, 1142.

———. "The League of Nations." *Louisville Courier-Journal*, March 5, 1919.

———. *"Marse Henry": An Autobiography.* 2 vols. New York: George H. Doran, 1919.

———. "A Protest against Hypocrisy and Pessimism." *Louisville Courier-Journal*, February 5, 1919.

Willey, J. H. "World Democracy and the Christian Sabbath." *Methodist Review*, March 1918, 191–95.

Wood, Henry A. Wise. *Address Opposing the Ratification of the Constitution of the League of Nations.* New York: League for the Preservation of American Independence, 1919.

Newspapers and Periodicals

American Federationist
Baptist
Baptist World
Biblioteca Sacra
Christian Advocate, Nashville
Christian Advocate, New York
Christian Century
Christian Fundamentalist
Christian Herald
Christianity Today
Christian Standard
Christian Workers Magazine
Christian World Pulpit
Churchman
Independent, New York

Intercollegiate Socialist
Journal and Messenger
King's Business
Kirchliche Zeitschrift
Lehre und Wehre
Literary Digest
Living Church
Lutheran
Lutheran Church Herald
Lutheran Church Review
Lutheran Church Work and Observer
Der Lutheraner
Lutheran Quarterly
Lutheran Witness
Methodist Review
Missions
Monthly Bulletin of the Advent Preparation Prayer Union
Moody Bible Institute Monthly
New Republic
New Statesman
North American Review
Our Hope
Presbyterian
Presbyterian of the South
Princeton Theological Review
Reformed Church Review
Religious Herald
Review and Expositor
School and Church
Standard
Sunday School Journal
Survey
Theological Monthly
Theological Quarterly
Union Seminary Review
Watchman-Examiner

Secondary Sources

Addison, James Thayer. *The Episcopal Church in the United States, 1789–1931*. New York: Charles Scribner's Sons, 1951.

Adler, Selig. *The Isolationist Impulse: Its Twentieth-Century Reaction*. New York: Abelard-Schuman, 1957.

Alcock, Anthony. *History of the International Labour Office*. London: Macmillan, 1971.

Ambrosius, Lloyd E. *Wilsonianism*. New York: Palgrave Macmillan, 2003.

————. *Woodrow Wilson and the American Diplomatic Tradition: The Treaty Fight in Perspective*. Cambridge: Cambridge University Press, 1990.

Anderson, John Mapes. *Vision of the Disinherited: The Making of American Pentecostalism*. New York: Oxford University Press, 1979.

Arden, G. Everett. *Augustana Heritage: The Story of the Augustana Lutheran Church*. Rock Island, Ill.: Augustana Press, 1963.

Arrington, Leonard J., and David Bitton. *The Mormon Experience: A History of the Latter-day Saints*. Urbana: University of Illinois Press, 1992.

Bachman, E. Theodore, with Mercia Breme Bachman. *The United Lutheran Church in America, 1918–1962*, ed. Paul Rorem. Minneapolis: Fortress Press, 1997.

Baepler, Walter. *A Century of Grace: A History of the Missouri Synod, 1847–1947*. Saint Louis: Concordia Publishing House, 1947.

Bailey, Thomas W. *Woodrow Wilson and the Great Betrayal*. New York: Macmillan, 1945.

————. *Woodrow Wilson and the Lost Peace*. New York: Macmillan, 1944.

Barron, Bruce. *Heaven on Earth? The Social and Political Agendas of Dominion Theology*. Grand Rapids: Zondervan, 1992.

Bartlett, Ruhl L. *The League to Enforce Peace*. Chapel Hill: University of North Carolina Press, 1944.

Beale, David O. *In Pursuit of Purity: American Fundamentalism since 1850*. Greenville, S.C.: Unusual Publications, 1986.

Bebbington, D. W. *Evangelicalism in Modern Britain: A History from the 1780s to the 1980s*. London: Routledge, 1993.

Bentley, Michael. *The Climax of Liberal Politics: British Liberalism in Theory and Practise 1868–1918*. London: Arnold, 1987.

Blumhofer, Edith L. *Restoring the Faith: The Assemblies of God, Pentecostalism, and American Culture*. Urbana: University of Illinois Press, 1993.

Boyer, Paul. *When Time Shall Be No More: Prophecy Belief in Modern American Culture*. Cambridge, Mass.: Belknap Press, 1992.

Braeman, John. *Albert J. Beveridge: American Nationalist*. Chicago: University of Chicago Press, 1971.

Bratt, James D. "The Dutch Schools." In *Reformed Theology in America: A History of Its Modern Development*, ed. David F. Wells. Grand Rapids: Baker Books, 2000.

Brock, Peter. *Freedom from War: Nonsectarian Pacifism, 1814–1914*. Toronto: University of Toronto Press, 1991.

Buss, Doris, and Didi Herman. *Globalizing Family Values: The Christian Right in International Politics*. Minneapolis: University of Minnesota Press, 2003.

Butler, Jennifer S. *Born Again: The Christian Right Globalized*. London: Pluto Press, 2006.

Carpenter, Joel A. *Revive Us Again: The Reawakening of American Fundamentalism*. New York: Oxford University Press, 1997.

————, ed. *Earthen Vessels: American Evangelicals and Foreign Missions, 1880–1980*. Grand Rapids: William B. Eerdmans, 1990.

Carter, Paul A. *The Decline and Revival of the Social Gospel: Social and Political Liberalism in American Protestant Churches, 1920–1940*. Hamden, Conn.: Archon Books, 1971.

Carwadine, Richard J. "Methodists, Politics, and the Coming of the American Civil War." In *Methodism and the Shaping of American Culture*, ed. Nathan O. Hatch and John H. Wigger. Nashville: Kingswood Books, 2001.

Chiles, Robert E. *Theological Transition in American Methodism, 1790–1935.* New York: Abingdon Press, 1965.

Chorley, E. Clowes. *Men and Movements in the American Episcopalian Church.* Hamden, Conn.: Archon Books, 1961.

Claburgh, Gary K. *Thunder on the Right: The Protestant Fundamentalists.* Chicago: Nelson-Hall, 1974.

Clouse, Robert G., ed. *The Meaning of Millennium: Four Views.* Downers Grove, Ill.: Inter-Varsity Press, 1977.

Cohn, Norman. *The Pursuit of the Millennium: Revolutionary Millenarians and Mystical Anarchists of the Middle Ages.* New York: Oxford University Press, 1970.

———. *Warrant for Genocide: The Myth of the Jewish World-Conspiracy and the Protocols of the Elders of Zion.* New York: Harper & Row, 1966.

Cooper, John Milton. *Breaking the Heart of the World: Woodrow Wilson and the Fight for the League of Nations.* Cambridge: Cambridge University Press, 2001.

Davies, Horton. *Worship and Theology in England, Volume V, The Ecumenical Century, 1900–1965.* Grand Rapids: William B. Eerdmans, 1996.

DeBenedetti, Charles. *Origins of the Modern American Peace Movement, 1915–1929.* Milwood, N.Y.: KTO Press, 1978.

Diamond, Sara. *Not by Politics Alone: The Enduring Influence of the Christian Right.* New York: Guilford Press, 1998.

Edwards, Mark U., Jr. *Luther's Last Battles: Politics and Polemics, 1531–46.* Ithaca, N.Y.: Cornell University Press, 1983.

Eighmy, John Lee. *Churches in Cultural Captivity: A History of the Social Attitudes of Southern Baptists.* Knoxville: University of Tennessee Press, 1987.

Fevold, Eugene L. "Coming of Age, 1875–1900." In *The Lutherans in North America*, ed. E. Clifford Nelson. Philadelphia: Fortress Press, 1980.

Flegg, Columba Graham. *"Gathered under the Apostles": A Study of the Catholic Apostolic Church.* Oxford: Clarendon Press, 1992.

Fleming, Denna Frank. *The United States and the League of Nations 1918–1920.* New York: G. P. Putnam's Sons, 1932.

Foster, Gaines M. *Moral Reconstruction: Christian Lobbyists and the Federal Legislation of Morality, 1865–1920.* Chapel Hill: University of North Carolina Press, 2002.

Freeden, Michael. *The New Liberalism: An Ideology of Social Reform.* Oxford: Clarendon Press, 1978.

Freud, Sigmund, and William C. Bullit. *Thomas Woodrow Wilson: A Psychological Study.* Boston: Houghton Mifflin, 1967.

Friedman, Murray. *The Neoconservative Revolution: Jewish Intellectuals and the Shaping of Public Policy.* Cambridge: Cambridge University Press, 2005.

Frykholm, Amy Johnson. *Rapture Culture: Left Behind in Evangelical America.* New York: Oxford University Press, 2004.

Gamble, Richard M. *The War for Righteousness: Progressive Christianity, the Great War, and the Rise of the Messianic Nation.* Wilmington, Del.: ISI Books, 2003.

George, Timothy. "The Future of Baptist Theology." In *Theologians of the Baptist Tradition*, ed. Timothy George and David S. Dockery. Nashville: Broadman Press, 2001.

———. "James Petigru Boyce." In *Theologians of the Baptist Tradition*, ed. Timothy George and David S. Dockery. Nashville: Broadman Press, 2001.

Glass, William R. *Strangers in Zion: Fundamentalists in the South, 1900–1950*. Macon, Ga.: Mercer University Press, 2001.

Glendon, Mary Ann. *A World Made New: Eleanor Roosevelt and the Universal Declaration of Human Rights*. New York: Random House, 2001.

Graebner, Norman A. "Lutherans and Politics." In *The Lutheran Church in North American Life, 1776–1976, 1580–1980*, ed. John E. Groh and Robert H. Smith. Saint Louis: Clayton Publishing House, 1979.

Granquist, Mark. "Lutherans in the United States, 1930–1960: Searching for the 'Center.'" In *Re-forming the Center: American Protestantism, 1900 to the Present*, ed. Douglas Jacobsen and William Vance Trollinger Jr. Grand Rapids: William B. Eerdmans, 1998.

Gritsch, Eric W., and Jenson, Robert N. *Lutheranism: The Theological Movement and Its Confessional Writings*. Philadelphia: Fortress Press, 1976.

Halper, Stefan, and Jonathan Clarke. *America Alone: The Neo-Conservatives and the Global Order*. Cambridge: Cambridge University Press, 2004.

Hamstra, Sam, Jr. "Geerhardus Vos." In *Twentieth-Century Dictionary of Christian Biography*, ed. J. D. Douglas. Grand Rapids: Baker Books, 1995.

Hankins, Barry. *God's Rascal: J. Frank Norris and the Beginnings of Southern Fundamentalism*. Lexington: University Press of Kentucky, 1997.

Hart, D. G. *Defending the Faith: J. Gresham Machen and the Crisis of Conservative Protestantism in Modern America*. Grand Rapids: Baker Books, 1994.

Harvey, Paul. *Redeeming the South: Religious Cultures and Racial Identities among Southern Baptists, 1865–1925*. Chapel Hill: University of North Carolina Press, 1997.

Hatch, Nathan O., and John H. Wigger, eds. *Methodism and the Shaping of American Culture*. Nashville: Kingswood Books, 2001.

Helbich, Wolfgang J. "American Liberals in the League of Nations Controversy." *Public Opinion Quarterly* 31 (Winter 1967–68): 568–96.

Hennesey, James. *American Catholics: A History of the Roman Catholic Community in the United States*. Oxford: Oxford University Press, 1981.

Higham, John. "Ethnicity and American Protestants: Collective Identity in the Mainstream." In *New Directions in American Religious History*, ed. Harry S. Stout and D. G. Hart. New York: Oxford University Press, 1997.

Hoopes, Townsend, and Alan D. Brinkley. *FDR and the Creation of the U.N.* New Haven, Conn.: Yale University Press, 1997.

Hughes, Richard T. *Reviving the Ancient Faith: The Story of the Churches of Christ in America*. Grand Rapids: William B. Eerdmans, 1996.

Hunt, Michael. *Ideology and U.S. Foreign Policy*. New Haven, Conn.: Yale University Press, 1987.

———. *The Making of a Special Relationship: The United States and China to 1914*. New York: Columbia University Press, 1983.

Hutchison, William R. *Errand to the World: American Protestant Thought and Foreign Missions*. Chicago: University of Chicago Press, 1987.

———. *The Modernist Impulse in American Protestantism*. Cambridge, Mass.: Harvard University Press, 1976.

Jacobsen, Douglas, and William Vance Trollinger Jr., eds. *Re-forming the Center: American Protestantism, 1900 to the Present*. Grand Rapids: William B. Eerdmans, 1998.

James, Edward T., ed. *The Dictionary of American Biography*. New York: Charles Scribner's Sons, 1933.

Johnson, Robert David. *The Peace Progressives and American Foreign Relations.* Cambridge, Mass.: Harvard University Press, 1995.

Jordahl, Leigh D., ed. *The History of the Wisconsin Synod.* Saint Cloud, Minn.: Sentinel, 1970.

Kaplan, Esther. *With God on Their Side: George W. Bush and the Christian Right.* New York: New Press, 2005.

Katerberg, William. *Modernity and the Dilemma of North American Anglican Identities 1880–1950.* Kingston and Montreal: McGill–Queen's University Press, 2001.

Kazin, Michael. *Godly Hero: The Life of William Jennings Bryan.* New York: Alfred A. Knopf, 2006.

Kelsey, George D. *Social Ethics among Southern Baptists, 1917–1969.* Metuchen, N.J.: Scarecrow Press, 1973.

Kengor, Paul. *God and George W. Bush.* New York: Regan Books, 2004.

Kirby, Dianne. "Religion and the Cold War: An Introduction." In *Religion and the Cold War,* ed. Dianne Kirby. London: Palgrave Macmillan, 2003.

Kirby, James E., Russell E. Richey, and Kenneth E. Rowe. *The Methodists.* Westport, Conn.: Greenwood Press, 1996.

Kloppenberg, James T. *Uncertain Victory: Social Democracy and Progressivism in European and American Thought, 1870–1920.* New York: Oxford University Press, 1986.

Knock, Thomas J. *To End All Wars: Woodrow Wilson and the Quest for a New World Order.* New York: Oxford University Press, 1992.

Kristof, Nicholas. "Following God Abroad." *New York Times,* May 21, 2002.

———. "Hope Is on the Right." *Kansas City Star,* December 23, 2004.

Kuehl, Warren F., and Lynne K. Dunn. *Keeping the Covenant: American Internationalists and the League of Nations, 1920–1939.* Kent, Ohio: Kent State University Press, 1997.

Lancaster, James L. "The Protestant Churches and the Fight for the Ratification of the Versailles Treaty." *Public Opinion Quarterly* 31 (Winter 1967–68): 597–619.

Leith, Keith H., ed. *Creeds of the Churches: A Reader in Christian Doctrine from the Bible to the Present.* Oxford: Basil Blackwell, 1973.

Lienesch, Michael. *Redeeming America: Piety and Politics in the New Christian Right.* Chapel Hill: University of North Carolina Press, 1993.

Lincoln, Bruce. *Holy Terrors: Thinking about Religion after September 11.* Chicago: University of Chicago Press, 2003.

Lind, Michael. "Rev. Robertson's Grand International Conspiracy Theory." *New York Review of Books,* February 2, 1995, 22–25.

Livermore, Seward. *Woodrow Wilson and the War Congress, 1917–1918.* Seattle: University of Washington Press, 1968.

Lower, Richard Coke. *A Bloc of One: The Political Career of Hiram W. Johnson.* Stanford, Calif.: Stanford University Press, 1993.

Lowitt, Richard. *George W. Norris: The Making of a Progressive.* Syracuse: Syracuse University Press, 1963.

Luebke, Frederick C. *Bonds of Loyalty: German-Americans and World War I.* DeKalb: Northern Illinois University Press, 1974.

Lueker, Edwin L., ed. *Lutheran Cyclopedia.* Saint Louis: Concordia Publishing House, 1954.

Margulies, Herbert F. *The Mild Reservationists and the League of Nations Controversy in the Senate.* Columbia: University of Missouri Press, 1989.

Marquis, Albert N., ed. *Who's Who in America, 1918–1919*. Chicago: A. N. Marquis, 1919.

Marsden, George M. *Fundamentalism and American Culture: The Shaping of Twentieth-Century Evangelicalism, 1870–1925*. New York: Oxford University Press, 1980.

———. *Understanding Fundamentalism and Evangelicalism*. Grand Rapids: William B. Eerdmans, 1991.

Martin, William. *With God on Our Side: The Rise of the Religious Right in America*. New York: Broadway Books, 1996.

Marty, Martin E. *Modern American Religion, Volume 1: The Irony of It All, 1893–1919*. Chicago: University of Chicago Press, 1997.

———. *Modern American Religion, Volume II: The Noise of Conflict, 1919–1941*. Chicago: University of Chicago Press, 1997.

Matthew, H. G. C. *Gladstone 1809–1898*. Oxford: Oxford University Press, 1999.

May, Henry F. *Protestant Churches and Industrial America*. New York: Harper & Brothers, 1949.

Mayer, Arno J. *Political Origins of the New Diplomacy, 1917–1918*. New Haven, Conn.: Yale University Press, 1959.

McAlliser, Lester G., and William E. Tucker. *Journey in Faith: A History of the Christian Church, Disciples of Christ*. Saint Louis: Chalice Press, 1975.

McBeth, H. Leon. *The Baptist Heritage*. Nashville: Broadman Press, 1987.

McCloskey, Robert G. *American Conservatism in the Age of Enterprise, 1865–1910*. New York: Harper Torchbooks, 1951.

McDougall, Walter A. *Promised Land, Crusader State*. Boston: Houghton Mifflin, 1997.

McDowell, Edwin. *Barry Goldwater: Portrait of an Arizonan*. Chicago: Henry Regnery, 1964.

McKenna, Marian C. *Borah*. Ann Arbor: University of Michigan Press, 1961.

McShane, Joseph M. *"Sufficiently Radical": Catholicism, Progressivism and the Bishops' Program of 1919*. Washington, D.C.: Catholic University of America Press, 1986.

Meriwether, Lee. *Jim Reed: "Senatorial Immortal," A Biography*. Webster Groves, Mo.: International Mark Twain Society, 1948.

Merrill, Milton D. *Reed Smoot: Apostle in Politics*. Logan: Utah State University Press, 1990.

Meuser, Fred W. "Facing the Twentieth Century, 1900–1930." In *The Lutherans in North America*, ed. E. Clifford Nelson. Philadelphia: Fortress Press, 1980.

Meyer, Carl S., ed. *Moving Frontiers: Readings in the History of the Lutheran Church–Missouri Synod*. Saint Louis: Concordia Historical Institute, 1964.

Meyer, Donald B. *The Protestant Search for Political Realism, 1919–1941*. Berkeley: University of California Press, 1960.

Miller, Robert Moats. *American Protestantism and Social Issues, 1919–1939*. Chapel Hill: University of North Carolina Press, 1958.

Moellering, Ralph L. "Some Lutheran Reactions to War and Pacifism, 1917 to 1941." *Concordia Historical Institute Quarterly*, August 1968, 122–31.

Mullin, Robert Bruce. *Episcopal Visions / American Reality: High Church Theology and Social Thought in Evangelical America*. New Haven, Conn.: Yale University Press, 1986.

The National Cyclopedia of American Biography. New York: James T. White, 1935.

Nelson, E. Clifford, ed. *The Lutherans in North America*. Philadelphia: Fortress Press, 1980.

Nelson, E. Clifford, and Eugene Fevold. *The Lutheran Church among the Norwegian-Americans*. 2 vols. Minneapolis: Augsburg Publishing House, 1960.

Ninkovich, Frank. *The Wilsonian Century: U.S. Foreign Policy since 1900*. Chicago: University of Chicago Press, 1999.

Noll, Mark A. "American Lutherans Yesterday and Today." In *Lutherans Today: American Lutheran Identity in the 21st Century*, ed. Richard Cimino. Grand Rapids: William B. Eerdmans, 2003.

Noll, Mark A., ed. *The Princeton Theology, 1812–1921: Scripture, Science and Theological Method from Archibald Alexander to Benjamin Warfield*. Grand Rapids: Baker Books, 1983.

Norman, E. *The Victorian Christian Socialists*. Cambridge: Cambridge University Press, 1987.

Northcott, Michael. *An Angel Directs the Storm: Apocalyptic Religion and American Empire*. London: I. B. Tauris, 2004.

Norwood, Frederick A. *The Story of American Methodism: A History of the United Methodists and Their Relations*. Nashville: Abingdon Press, 1974.

Nurser, John S. *For All Peoples and All Nations: The Ecumenical Church and Human Rights*. Washington, D.C.: Georgetown University Press, 2005.

Olinger, Danny. "The Writings of Geerhardus Vos." *Kerux* 15 (September 2000): 3–30.

Oliver, John. *The Church and Social Order: Social Thought in the Church of England, 1918–1939*. London: A. R. Mowbray, 1968.

Ottersberg, Gerhard S. "The Evangelical Lutheran Synod of Iowa and Other States, 1854–1904." PhD diss., University of Nebraska, 1949.

Parkman, Aubrey. *David Jayne Hill and the Problem of World Peace*. Lewisburg, N.Y.: Bucknell University Press, 1975.

———. "President Hill and the Sectarian Challenge at the University of Rochester." *Rochester History* 33 (October 1971): 1–24.

Pearlman, Michael. *To Make Democracy Safe for America: Patricians and Preparedness in the Progressive Era*. Urbana: University of Illinois Press, 1984.

Phillips, William. "Asle J. Gronna: Self-Made Man of the Prairies." PhD diss., University of Missouri, 1960.

Piper, John F., Jr. *The American Churches in World War I*. Athens: Ohio University Press, 1985.

Powers, Richard Gid. *Not Without Honor: The History of American Anticommunism*. New Haven, Conn.: Yale University Press, 1995.

Pruessen, Ronald W. *John Foster Dulles: The Road to Power*. New York: Free Press, 1982.

Rausch, David. *Fundamentalist-Evangelicals and Anti-Semitism*. Valley Forge, Pa.: Trinity Press International, 1993.

Reichley, A. James. *Religion in American Public Life*. Washington, D.C.: Brookings Institution Press, 1985.

Ribuffo, Leo R. *The Old Christian Right: The Protestant Far Right from the Depression*. Philadelphia: Temple University Press, 1983.

Richey, Russell E., Kenneth E. Rowe, and Jean Miller Schmidt, eds. *Perspectives on American Methodism*. Nashville: Kingswood Books, 1993.

Roberts, Wesley A. "Cornelius Van Til." In *Reformed Theology in America: A History of Its Modern Development*, ed. David F. Wells. Grand Rapids: Baker Books, 2000.

Rossiter, Clinton. *Conservatism in America*. Cambridge, Mass.: Harvard University Press, 1982.

Rudnick, Milton L. *Fundamentalism and the Missouri Synod: A Historical Study of Their Interaction and Mutual Influence*. Saint Louis: Concordia Publishing House, 1966.

Ruotsila, Markku. "American Baptists and the League of Nations." *American Baptist Quarterly* 25 (Spring 2006): 49–62.

———. *British and American Anticommunism before the Cold War*. London: Frank Cass, 2001.

———. " 'The Great Charter for the Liberty of the Workingman': Labour, Liberals and the Creation of the ILO." *Labour History Review* 67 (April 2002): 29–47.

———. *John Spargo and American Socialism*. New York: Palgrave Macmillan, 2006.

Russell, Francis. *The Shadow of Blooming Grove: Warren G. Harding in His Times*. Norwalk, Conn.: Easton Press, 1988.

Sandeen, Ernest R. *The Roots of Fundamentalism: British and American Millenniarism, 1800–1930*. Chicago: University of Chicago Press, 1970.

Scholes, Walter. "Philander C. Knox." In *An Uncertain Tradition: American Secretaries of State in the Twentieth Century*, ed. Norman A. Graebner. New York: McGraw-Hill, 1961.

Schriftgiesser, Karl. *The Gentleman from Massachusetts: Henry Cabot Lodge*. Boston: Little, Brown, 1944.

Shannon, David A. *The Socialist Party of America: A History*. New York: Macmillan, 1955.

Smith, Gary Scott. *The Seeds of Secularization: Calvinism, Culture and Pluralism in America, 1870–1915*. Saint Paul: Christian University Press, 1985.

Smith, Morton. "The Southern Tradition." In *Reformed Theology in America: A History of Its Modern Development*, ed. David F. Wells. Grand Rapids: Baker Books, 2000.

Smith, Richard Norton. *Thomas E. Dewey and His Times*. New York: Simon & Schuster, 1982.

Sotirovich, William V. *Grotius' Universe: Divine Law and a Quest for Harmony*. New York: Vantage Press, 1978.

Stanley, Susie C. "Wesleyan/Holiness Churches: Innocent Bystanders in the Fundamentalist/Modernist Controversy." In *Re-forming the Center: American Protestantism, 1900 to the Present*, ed. Douglas Jacobsen and William Vance Trollinger Jr. Grand Rapids: William B. Eerdmans, 1998.

Stone, Ralph. *The Irreconcilables: The Fight against the League of Nations*. Lexington: University Press of Kentucky, 1970.

———. "Two Illinois Senators among the Irreconcilables." *Mississippi Valley Historical Review* 50 (December 1963): 443–65.

Stonehouse, Ned B. *J. Gresham Machen: A Biographical Memoir*. Carlisle, Pa.: Banner of Truth Trust, 1954.

Straton, David. "New Mexico Machiavellian? The Story of Albert B. Fall." *Montana: Magazine of Western History* 7 (October 1957): 2–14.

Sutton, William R. " 'To Extract Poison from the Blessings of Providence': Producerist Respectability and Methodist Suspicions of Capitalist Change in the Early Republic." In *Methodism and the Shaping of American Culture*, ed. Nathan O. Hatch and John H. Wigger. Nashville: Kingswood Books, 2001.

Sykes, Alan. *The Rise and Fall of British Liberalism, 1776–1988*. London: Longman, 1997.

Synan, Vinson. *The Holiness-Pentecostal Tradition: Charismatic Movements in the Twentieth Century*. Grand Rapids: William B. Eerdmans, 1997.

Thompson, Ernest T. *The Spirituality of the Church: A Distinctive Doctrine of the Presbyterian Church in the United States*. Richmond: John Knox Press, 1961.

Thompson, John A. *Woodrow Wilson: Profiles in Power*. London: Longman, 2002.

Trollinger, William F., Jr. *God's Empire: William Bell Riley and Midwestern Fundamentalism*. Madison: University of Wisconsin Press, 1990.

Tuveson, Ernest Lee. *Redeemer Nation: The Idea of America's Millennial Role*. Chicago: University of Chicago Press, 1968.

Vintz, Warren L. *Pulpit Politics: Faces of American Protestantism in the Twentieth Century*. Albany: State University of New York Press, 1997.

Wacker, Grant. *Heaven Below: Early Pentecostals and American Culture*. Cambridge, Mass.: Harvard University Press, 2001.

Wall, Joseph Frazier. *Henry Watterson: Reconstructed Rebel*. New York: Oxford University Press, 1956.

Waltz, Jeff, Steve Montreal, and Dan Hoffering. "Pastors in the Two Kingdoms: The Social Theology of Lutheran Clergy." In *Lutherans Today: American Lutheran Identity in the 21st Century*, ed. Richard Cimino. Grand Rapids: William B. Eerdmans, 2003.

Weber, Timothy P. *Living in the Shadow of the Second Coming: American Premillennialism 1875–1925*. New York: Oxford University Press, 1979.

———. *On the Road to Armageddon: How Evangelicals Became Israel's Best Friend*. Grand Rapids: Baker Academic, 2004.

Welch, Richard E., Jr. *Response to Imperialism: The United States and the Philippine-American War, 1899–1902*. Chapel Hill: University of North Carolina Press, 1979.

Wentz, Abdel Ross. *A Basic History of Lutheranism in America*. Philadelphia: Fortress Press, 1964.

Wentz, Frederick K. *Lutherans in Concert: The Story of the National Lutheran Council, 1918–1966*. Minneapolis: Augsburg Publishing House, 1968.

Who Was Who in America, Volume I, 1897–1942. Chicago: A. N. Marquis, 1943.

Widenor, William C. *Henry Cabot Lodge and the Search for an American Foreign Policy*. Berkeley: University of California Press, 1980.

Wilcox, Clyde. *God's Warriors: The Christian Right in Twentieth Century America*. Baltimore: Johns Hopkins University Press, 1992.

Winkler, Henry R. *Paths Not Taken: British Labour and International Policy in the 1920s*. Chapel Hill: University of North Carolina Press, 1994.

Zwaanstra, Henry. *Reformed Thought and Experience in the New World: A Study of the Christian Reformed Church and Its American Environment, 1890–1918*. Kampen: J. H. Kok, 1973.

Index

Abbott, Lyman, 12
ACLU (American Civil Liberties Union),
    106
adiaphora, 82
Advent Testimony and Preparation Move-
    ment, 32–33
African American Churches, 5
Ambrosius, Lloyd, 6, 20
American Civil Liberties Union (ACLU),
    106
American Defense Society, 163
American exceptionalism
    Christian anti-internationalist belief in,
        2–3, 190–92
    modern liberalism and, 15–16, 24
    Mormon belief in, 143
    Senatorial anti-internationalism and,
        136, 143
    Social Gospeler belief in, 190–91
American Federation of Labor, 22
American Peace Society, 10, 17, 31
American Society for International Law,
    163
American unilateralism and nationalism
    among Senate Irreconcilables, 123, 124
    Calvinist support for, 64
    Christian anti-internationalist belief in,
        2, 190–92
    dispensationalist support for, 47–49, 51
    Episcopal anti-League sentiments and,
        117–19, 120
    Independence League on, 150, 152–53
    Methodist nationalism, 104, 110–12,
        120
    post-cold war, 184–85, 190–91
    of Social Gospelers, 190–91
    United Nations and, 178

amillennialism, 73, 82
Anglican communion worldwide, 113, 116
Anglicans in America. See Episcopalians
Anglo-Catholic or High Church Episcopa-
    lians, 113–15, 157, 162
Anglophilia, 135, 151, 161
Anglophobia, 72, 123, 134, 145, 151
anti-Christ and anti-Christian empire
    Calvinist opposition to League and, 67,
        77, 78
    in dispensationalist belief, 27, 29–33,
        41–42, 51, 189
    interwar period fears of, 173
    Left Behind, 3, 182
    Lutheran anti-Catholicism, 97–99
    post-cold war fears of, 181–83
    United Nations as, 175–78, 180, 181
anti-internationalism, Christian. See
    Christian anti-internationalism
anti-Semitism. See Jews and Judaism
apocalyptic. See eschatological beliefs
apostasy
    Christian participation in secular inter-
        national movement viewed as, 2, 29–
        31, 33. See also secular millennialism
    Jewish, 40–41
arbitration movement, 18
Arminianism, 54, 56, 104–5
Augsburg Confession, 90–91
Augustana (Swedish American) Synod of
    Lutherans, 85, 88

Baptists
    cogent conservative position, difficulty
        of working out, 62–65
    dispensationalist influence on, 28, 49
    endorsement of League, Southern Bap-
        tist rejection of, 25, 76, 79

235

Baptists (*continued*)
  Hill, David Jayne, modernist anti-
    internationalism of, 163, 164, 167
  mild Reservationist position, 63
  motivations for and results of anti-
    internationalism for, 189
  Northern Baptist Convention, 54, 63,
    65
  Southern Baptist Convention, 25, 54,
    56, 57, 75–76, 79, 182
  theological beliefs leading to anti-
    internationalism, 54, 56, 57
Bauman, Louis A., 177
Behnken, J. W., 95
Benedict XV (pope), 96
Berne Conference, 21, 75, 175
Beveridge, Albert J., 108, 148
biblical criticism, modernist, 30, 56, 72,
  83, 109
Bilderbergs, 181
Bishops' Program of Reconstruction, 96
Bolshevism, Russian, 26, 89, 98, 106, 110,
  128, 136, 141, 173
Book of Concord, 80
Borah, William E., 137–38, 149
Brandegee, Frank B., 132–34
Brent, Charles H., 115
Brethren, Church of the, 177
Bricker Amendment, 178
Britain, Anglophobia and Anglophilia
  regarding, 72, 123, 134, 135, 145,
  151, 161
British Society for the Promotion of Per-
  manent and Universal Peace, 10
Bryan, William Jennings, 18, 95, 172
Buchanan, Pat, 182
Buchman, Frank N. D., 162
Bush, George W., 182, 184

Calvinists, 4, 53–78
  Baptist. *See* Baptists
  Christian Reformed Church, 25, 53, 57,
    66
  cogent conservative position, difficulty
    of working out, 60–66
  common grace, doctrine of, 55–56
  culturalist mission, League of Nations as
    usurpation of, 57–60, 77–78
  eschatological beliefs of, 54–56, 69
  Kingdom Theology of, 55–56, 66–67
  Kuyperian or Dutch School, 53, 57–59,
    66–71, 74–75
  Lutheran critique of worldview, 91–92,
    95, 96, 102

  motivations for and results of anti-inter-
    nationalism for, 189
  on non-Christian/Catholic and Chris-
    tian nations working together, 69,
    70–71, 75, 77–78
  postmillennialism of, 54–55, 73
  Presbyterian. *See* Presbyterians
  public means of grace for, 56, 68, 69, 78,
    91
  Social Gospelers, opposition to, 55–59,
    67–68, 71, 76–78
  socialism as viewed by, 71, 75–76
  theological beliefs leading to anti-inter-
    nationalism, 54–60
Campbell, Alexander, 154–55
Carnegie, Andrew, 133
Carnegie Endowment for International
  Peace, 134, 163
Carver, William O., 76
Catholic Apostolic Church (Irvingites),
  28, 30
Catholics. *See* Roman Catholics
Cecil, Lord Robert, 38
Chiliasts, 29, 132
China, Japanese expansion into, 109, 123,
  137
Christian Anti-Communism Crusade, 178
Christian anti-internationalism, 1–7
  American nationalism/exceptionalism,
    belief in, 2–3, 190–92
  of Calvinists. *See* Calvinists
  continued existence of, 3
  defined, 3
  of dispensationalists. *See* dispensational
    premillennialists
  of Episcopalians. *See* Episcopalians
  foreign policy formation, relevance of
    religious conviction to study of, 5–7
  isolationism/parochialism, differentiated
    from, 3
  key positions of, 2–3
  League for the Preservation of American
    Independence and. *See* League for the
    Preservation of American
    Independence
  of Lutherans. *See* Lutherans
  of Methodists. *See* Methodists
  modernist theology, as subtheme of
    opposition to, 188
  motivations for and results of anti-
    League activism, 187–92
  persistence of, 171–85
    in interwar years, 171–75